Mass Trauma and Emotional Healing around the World

MASS TRAUMA AND EMOTIONAL HEALING AROUND THE WORLD

Rituals and Practices for Resilience and Meaning-Making

VOLUME 2: HUMAN-MADE DISASTERS

Ani Kalayjian and
Dominique Eugene,
EDITORS

PRAEGER
An Imprint of ABC-CLIO, LLC

Santa Barbara, California • Denver, Colorado • Oxford, England

Copyright 2010 by Ani Kalayjian and Dominique Eugene

Library of Congress Cataloging-in-Publication Data

Mass trauma and emotional healing around the world : rituals and practices
for resilience and meaning-making / Ani Kalayjian, Dominique Eugene, editors
    p. cm.
  Includes bibliographical references and index.
  ISBN 978-0-313-37540-8 (set hbk. : alk. paper) — ISBN 978-0-313-37541-5
(set ebook) — ISBN 978-0-313-37542-2 (v. 1 hbk. : alk. paper) —
ISBN 978-0-313-37543-9 (v. 1 ebook) — ISBN 978-0-313-37544-6
(v. 2 hbk. : alk. paper) — ISBN 978-0-313-37545-3 (v. 2 ebook)
1. Disasters—Psychological aspects—Cross-cultural studies. 2. Psychic
trauma—Cross-cultural studies. 3. Post-traumatic stress disorder—Cross-cultural
studies. I. Kalayjian, Ani. II. Eugene, Dominique.
  BF789.D5M38 2010
  155.9'35—dc22   2009031607

14 13 12 11 10   1 2 3 4 5

This book is also available on the World Wide Web as an eBook.
Visit www.abc-clio.com for details.

Praeger
An Imprint of ABC-CLIO, LLC

ABC-CLIO, LLC
130 Cremona Drive, P.O. Box 1911
Santa Barbara, California 93116-1911

This book is printed on acid-free paper (∞)

Manufactured in the United States of America

CONTENTS

Volume 2

HUMAN-MADE DISASTERS

Chapter 12

THE ONGOING IMPACT OF COLONIZATION

Man-made Trauma and Native Americans

Hilary Weaver and
Elaine Congress

Where in your history books is the tale of the genocide basic to this country's birth? Of the preachers who lied? How the Bill of Rights failed? . . . And where will it tell of the Liberty Bell as it rang with a thud over Kinzua mud? . . . My country 'tis of thy people you're dying.

—Saint Marie

INTRODUCTION

Trauma can originate from many different sources that are experienced as threatening and overwhelming. Trauma can result from a large scale force of nature, such as an earthquake, or an event with human origins, such as a terrorist attack. The way that trauma is experienced may be qualitatively different when it originates from the actions of other humans (rather than being an act of nature). The fact that other people deliberately threatened or injured a person or group can significantly undermine the ability to trust others. Likewise, trauma that results from large scale actions (such as ethnic cleansings) can be qualitatively different than that experienced solely by an individual (from an event such as a car accident). When large numbers of people are impacted by a traumatic event or events it may undermine community or group resources that would typically be available to assist in the healing process. Examining the societal context of the traumatic event is helpful in understanding how an individual responds to trauma and can help prevent labeling the traumatized person and his/her behaviors in a stigmatizing way.

This chapter gives an overview of large-scale, man-made trauma as it has impacted Native Americans in the United States. The chapter begins with an overview of the colonization process, including trauma and the resulting sequelae. This is followed by a discussion of theories of trauma and two case examples that illustrate historical and more recent man-made trauma and efforts to promote healing and resilience. The chapter concludes with a discussion of clinical and macro-level implications.

THE COLONIZATION PROCESS

Native Americans are the original indigenous people of the countries that have become North America. While there are similarities in colonization processes that took place in different countries, for purposes of this chapter we will focus on the United States and its original peoples. There are still more than 4 million self-identified Native Americans in the United States from more than 500 Native nations (Ogunwole 2002) but many more Native nations existed prior to colonization. While population estimates are controversial and politically charged, it is estimated that there were between 5–15 million indigenous people in what is now the United States (excluding Alaska) in 1492. By 1900 only 250,000 remained (Venables 2004). Likewise, colonization resulted in the loss of 98 percent of indigenous territories (Venables 2004).

Colonization was facilitated through many different processes, beginning with warfare, disease, and massacres. Clearing the land of savages was a central tenet of Manifest Destiny. In order for European settlers to expand across the continent it was necessary to clear the land of the original inhabitants. When outright killing was not practical, dispossession or removal was a common practice, resulting in millions of people being disposed of their traditional territories and confined to reservations. These areas were often small and lacking in resources to support daily life, such as abundant game or fertile soil for farming. Ironically, vast mineral wealth was later found on some reservations originally considered virtually uninhabitable.

Assimilation was also a major component of the colonization process. It was believed that those who remained alive could/should be transformed into mainstream Americans, thus shedding the values, beliefs, spirituality, and world views that distinguished them as indigenous peoples. Assimilation processes included the federal policy of removing Native children from their homes and communities for training in residential schools, often far from their homelands. Christian missionaries were deployed to convert reservation residents as a way of eradicating indigenous cultures and spiritual traditions. By the 1950s, relocating Native people to urban areas and terminating tribes as distinct legal entities had become federal policy (Venables 2004). Attempts at physical and cultural genocide continued with large scale removal of Native children into foster care and sterilization of Native women of childbearing age. These practices became the subject of public outrage by the 1960s and 1970s (Lawrence 2000; Mannes 1995; Torpy 2000).

Centuries of ongoing traumatic events have had a significant impact on Native Americans. Native people were subjected to many removals and massacres, when they were left to rebuild their lives with few resources. Removal was part of U.S. policy for many years (Venables 2004). The proliferation of traumatic events and experiences has led to historical trauma symptoms that include survivor guilt, trauma, anger, depression, and sadness. It also includes self-destructive behaviors such as alcohol and drug use, suicidal ideology, low self-esteem, difficulty recognizing and expressing emotions, and somatic symptoms (Deschenie 2006; Yellow Horse Brave Heart 1999). While Native peoples have survived the aftereffects of many traumatic experiences, they continue to experience cumulative psychological and emotional wounding across generations.

Colonization, including U.S. policies designed to disrupt indigenous cultures and lifeways, are a source of intergenerational stress and historical trauma (Struthers and Lowe 2003). Policies of taking land, assimilation, and termination "have resulted in a trauma of catastrophic proportions with accordingly destructive outcomes" (Struthers and Lowe 2003, 259). The cataclysmic history of genocide has resulted in cumulative and collective emotional and psychological injury over lifespans and across generations. Indeed, historical trauma and its resulting sequelae such as self-destructive behavior are major contributors to perpetuating health disparities (Struthers and Lowe 2003).

Loss of traditional territory and environmental devastation has reduced opportunities for resilience. When Native people can no longer access their traditional foods and medicines they suffer loss of control over the way of life that they knew and the things needed to sustain themselves (Struthers and Lowe 2003). The loss of traditional resources compounds trauma as well as reduced coping abilities.

While many historical events have led to trauma for Native people it is important to note that traumatic events are not just a thing of the past. High levels of violence continue to pervade the lives of Native people, thus compounding trauma (Balsam et al. 2004). For an excellent review of violence in the lives of Native Americans see *Death and Violence on the Reservation* (Bachman 1992). Indeed, Native people experience higher rates of personal victimization (i.e., rape and other violent attacks) and trauma than whites (Balsam et al. 2004). Likewise, the United States still exercises its power of eminent domain at will, thus leaving feelings of vulnerability and insecurity for many Native people.

THEORIES OF TRAUMA

There are a growing number of theories about the causes and interventions for people who have endured traumatic events. As Garland (1998) indicates, originally the word trauma referred to inflicting a physical wound. In recent years trauma has been extended to include psychological wounding as well as physical injury; recurring attacks as well as one critical incident. A traumatic event affects individuals differently: two people can experience an identical physical/psychological event and demonstrate very different psychological outcomes. It is impossible to predict how the same event or series of events will affect different individuals.

Included in the American Psychiatric Association Diagnostic and Statistical Manual IV (APA DSM-IV), post-traumatic stress disorder (PTSD) is described as "the development of characteristic symptoms following exposure to an extreme traumatic stressor involving direct personal experience of an event that involves actual or threatened death or serious injury, or other threat to one's physical integrity; or witnessing an event that involves death, injury, or a threat to the physical integrity of another person; or learning about unexpected or violent death, serious harm, or threat of death or injury experienced by a family member or other close associate (Criterion A1). The person's response to the event must involve intense fear, helplessness, or horror (or in children, the response must involve disorganized or agitated behavior) (Criterion A2). The characteristic symptoms resulting from exposure to extreme trauma include persistent re-experiencing of the traumatic event (Criterion B), persistent avoidance of stimuli associated with the trauma and numbing of general responsiveness (Criterion C), and persistent symptoms of increased arousal (Criterion D). The full symptom picture must be present for more than 1 month (Criterion E), and the disturbance must cause clinically significant distress or impairment in social, occupational, or other important areas of functioning (Criterion F)" (Mental Health Today 2009). This diagnosis has been used to describe diverse types of physical, social, and political traumas. Waldram (2004) has noted that the trauma does not have to be experienced firsthand by the person in order to produce PTSD symptomatology.

Post-traumatic stress reactions do not always occur only to individuals, but may refer to the experience of certain social or ethnic groups, as for example, survivors of the Holocaust. At times, the trauma was so excessive that its consequences have been passed on to future generations.

Historical trauma has been defined as the "cumulative emotional and psychological wounding over the lifespan and across generations, emanating from massive group trauma experiences" (Yellow Horse Brave Heart 2003, 7). Other terms that have been used to describe historical trauma include collective trauma, historic grief, intergenerational trauma, intergenerational PTSD, and multigenerational trauma. As individuals react differently to trauma, it is most important to distinguish between historical trauma and the historical trauma response. Some observed psychological reactions to trauma include depression, suicide, anxiety, poor interpersonal relationships, insomnia, nightmares, and social isolation. Often, those who have experienced trauma are continually retraumatized by social and economic deprivation, poor access to health care, oppressive government policies, and racism.

Historical trauma experienced by Native Americans includes governmental policies that removed American Indians from their homelands, residential schools for children that separated families, adoption programs, and forced loss of traditional ways and culture.

Kellerman (2001) cites four major ways in which trauma may be transmitted from generation to generation: psychodynamic, sociocultural, family systems, and biological. Psychodynamic refers primarily to unconscious ways trauma is transmitted, sociocultural relates to the effect that the parents and community have on the child, while family systems applies to communication patterns, and biological to genetic and biological risk factors. A consideration of all theories may be helpful in understanding intergenerational trauma among Native American people. There is concern that too much focus has been put on the psychological, focusing on the pathology of the individual family without looking at the larger social, cultural and historical context (Gottschalk 2003).

Untreated or unspoken survivor trauma may be particularly virulent in passing on traumatic responses to a new generation. While some trauma theorists have spoken about avoiding "the conspiracy of silence," that it is healing for a traumatized individual to talk about these feelings, it has been suggested that talking about trauma might not be therapeutic for many Native Americans (Denham 2008).

CASE EXAMPLES

The following case examples illustrate historical and more recent examples of man-made trauma and Native Americans. These examples begin with a description of the event. followed by a discussion of the impact of the event and the resulting trauma. The examples review how Native people have mourned their losses and moved to promote healing. While the first case example describes a well known historical event, the second example discusses a more recent one that, while highly controversial in the 1950s and 1960s, is all but forgotten to those outside its immediate region. Although there is a span of some 70 years between the two events it is clear that there still remained little regard for the human rights of Native Americans even in the 1950s and 1960s.

Case 1: The Wounded Knee Massacre (1890)

The Wounded Knee Massacre of December 29, 1890, is often cited as the last major confrontation between the U.S. military and Native Americans. Big Foot's band of Lakota, seeking to join other Lakota bands for Ghost Dance ceremonies, were stopped by the 7th Cavalry and brought to a campsite near Wounded Knee Creek on December 28th. Hotchkiss guns (rapid-fire artillery with exploding shells) were set up on a hill overlooking the camp. In the Lakota encampment the men were separated from the women and children. On the morning of the 29th, while soldiers were disarming the Native men, shots rang out. The Hotchkiss guns opened fire on all in the men's encampment, killing many Native men and some soldiers. The military also fired the Hotchkiss guns at the camp of the women and children. They continued to shoot women in the back as they fled as much as three miles away from the camp. More than 200 Lakota people were killed during the Wounded Knee Massacre, more than half of them women and children (Venables 2004).

Even today, this massacre is remembered as a pivotal event that continues to take a devastating toll on the Lakota people. Unresolved grief from the event has been linked to contemporary substance abuse and violence (Yellow Horse Brave Heart 1999). This assertion of U.S. military power became a turning point in Native American and American relations. As Native Americans lost any hopes of military resistance their opportunity to control their own destinies waned.

Healing from the devastation of the massacre was nearly impossible. At the time of the massacre, federal law made traditional ceremonies and mourning practices illegal (Forbes-Boyte 1999), thus hindering healing processes. Additionally, the ongoing federal military occupation made traditional burial practices impossible. Victims of the massacre were dumped in a mass grave after lying exposed for two days during a blizzard. The powerlessness of the Lakota to mourn in accordance with any of their cultural practices and their captivity compounded the trauma of the event.

The fact that many Americans cheered the massacre and saw it as a positive event denied the Lakota their own understanding of what had happened. The massacre was typically portrayed as a glorious battle where the forces of good had triumphed over evil savages, thus supporting the interests of the United States and the American people. Only in recent years have Native people been able to claim/reclaim their own perspectives.

Recalling and retelling history from an indigenous perspective to bear witness to the events is a powerful component of healing. "The imposition of colonial ideas, knowledge, and historical accounts and censorship of indigenous knowledge has resulted in not only doubting one's own . . . historical accounts, but has also delegitimized one's own . . . Historical experiences" (Faimon 2004, 241). Those who perpetuate and support the myths of conquest (i.e., those who fail to recognize or deny the extent of the killing and removal of indigenous people for land and economic expansion) become modern-day colonizers and perpetrators. It is important to recognize that Americans still reap the rewards of governmental policies and actions that exterminated and removed Native peoples (Faimon 2004).

Healing from historical trauma requires culturally appropriate strategies based on traditional knowledge, philosophies, and world views of indigenous peoples (Struthers and Lowe 2003). A respect for culture and a strong belief in and affirmation of resiliency can be integrated with helping methods such as cognitive behavioral therapy (Engel 2007). This can be a tool in moving toward survivor's pride. Reclaiming traditional ways, healing the spirit, and reclaiming the self are part of recovering from historical trauma (Struthers and Lowe 2003). Traditional healing can also be a viable option for returning to wellness, particularly given that many western psychological interventions are incongruent with traditional indigenous practices and beliefs (McCabe 2007). Indeed, western ways of helping may be viewed as forms of social control and extensions of colonialism, and therefore as part of the problem rather than part of the solution.

The Takini Network, an indigenous organization led by a Lakota social worker, was founded in 1992. *Takini* is a Lakota word that means survivor or to come back to life. They have conducted more than 100 workshops on historical trauma as well as healing events and parent training, designed to restore communities and move beyond survival to empowering communities (Deschenie 2006). The Takini intervention consists of a four-day training event that is tribally-specific and includes an orientation, overview, and a community presentation. One of the founders of the Takini Network, Maria Yellow Horse Brave Heart, stated, "The healing is like a wound that leaves a scar—it hurts less and shrinks over time, but it remains. Like grief literature says, we cannot grieve alone. Mourning is a communal experience. So, I think that our historical trauma intervention is the most effective thing we have at this time—it is a beginning, it gets us started down the healing path and can be followed up by some individual work" (Deschenie 2006, 9).

One of the most visible and tangible ways in which the Lakota community has moved toward healing is through the annual Big Foot Memorial Ride. In this event, people retrace Big Foot's journey of almost 300 miles in the harsh South Dakota winter. Many youths are involved and this has become an empowering way of remembering and reclaiming Lakota history and identity.

Case 2: Kinzua Dam and the Flooding of Allegany Reservation (Late 1950s–Mid-1960s)

Reservations have typically been considered sacrifice areas, parts of which could be easily taken in the name of progress. Indeed, the state of New York has often dealt with its Native inhabitants by using the power of eminent domain, thus bypassing federal authority (Haupman 1988).

In the 25 years after World War II, the Haudenosaunee people (aka Iroquis Confederacy) lost significant land in five different communities, beginning with a dam project at Onondaga in the late 1940s followed by the St. Lawrence Seaway project in 1950s, which led to the expropriation of 1,300 acres from Kahnawake and 130 acres from Akwesasne (both Mohawk reservations). In addition to the loss of living space, these land takings weakened economic self sufficiency by destroying fishing and cattle industries and increasing industrialization and pollution of air and water (Haupton 1988). The Kinzua Dam project pushed by interests in Pennsylvania led to flooding the entire Cornplanter Tract (the last Native American lands in Pennsylvania) and over 9,000 acres of land of the Seneca Nation in western New York State. Additionally, the New York State Power Authority's Niagara Power Project, completed in 1961, condemned 560 acres or one-eighth of the Tuscarora reservation (Haupton, 1988). While this case example focuses on Kinzua specifically, it is important to recognize that it is one in a series of land losses for the Haudenosaunee that came in rapid succession.

The Kizua Dam project was designed to promote flood control and enhance recreational activities by creating a reservoir (Haupton 1988). It resulted in the loss of substantial prime farming land and the removal of 160 families from the take area (Bilharz 1998). This project undermined traditional Seneca life. When the land adjoining the river was flooded it destroyed access to a significant source of medicine plants and spiritual sustenance. The threat of the dam existed decades before it was built and the removal process took place over four years, thus leading to a long drawn out period of stress for the Senecas (Bilharz 1998).

The Kinzua dam project was a violation of the Canandaigua Treaty of 1794 that guaranteed that no land would ever be taken or disturbed that belonged to the Seneca Nation or any of the Haudensaunee Confederacy. Federal courts justified the breaking of the Treaty because financing for the project was included in the 1958 federal budget, thus assuming the Congressional action needed to abrogate a treaty (Haupton 1986).

Alternative flood control plans were proposed by Arthur E. Morgan, former head of the TVA, that should have prevented flooding Seneca lands (Haupton 1986). The Senecas mounted an active lobbying campaign and court battles. They had a broad coalition of support, including the American Civil Liberties Union, the American Friends Service Committee, and the National Congress of American Indians. Ultimately, the Seneca and their allies were no match for the Army Corp of Engineers and their allies in Congress and the White House (Haupton 1986). Ironically, George Heron, President of the Seneca Nation of Indians during 1959–60, had three citations for battle valor in World War II and had fought valiantly for the United States, only to have his land taken by the United States in spite of viable alternatives (Haupton 1986).

Years later, one woman recalls taking her doll to each corner of the house to say goodbye before the family home was destroyed. Neither schools nor families were offered any supportive mechanisms for dealing with their grief (Bilharz 1998). The bulldozing of houses often came with little notice and several were razed and burned before families had a chance to remove their contents. Those who lost their homes often still speak tearfully of their experiences (Bilharz 1998).

Kinzua Dam was formally dedicated September 16, 1966. Losses in the Kinzua controversy may have laid the foundation for the awakening of the Red Power movement and activism of the 1970s. There was a growing awareness that policy makers had to be stopped if they continued to operate in such a high-handed, insensitive manner toward Native people (Haupton 1986).

The Kinzua project resulted in reducing the Allegany Reservation from 33,000 acres to 20,000 acres. Many of the settlements on the reservation were rendered uninhabitable. The relocation areas provided for those removed from the settlements amounted to only 750 acres (Williams 2007), only a small fraction of the land taken. Loss of land represented not only a loss of space but since land is intimately tied to identity, culture, and spirituality these damages could not be mitigated. The community-specific identities of Allegany residents became fractured for those from communities that were flooded (Williams 2007).

In addition to relocating the living, the project necessitated the removal or abandonment of many graves, including that of Cornplanter, a significant Seneca chief who negotiated with George Washington. Although they were supposed to be removed from the area to be flooded and reinterred elsewhere there is considerable suspicion that his remains were mishandled by the Army Corp of Engineers and may not have been removed at all (Williams 2007).

In the process of condemnation, expropriation, and removal, the Iroquois Indians' psyche was also affected. Destroying the old Cold Spring Longhouse and taking the Cornplanter Heirs from a source of their medicine and spirituality, the Allegheny River, and placing them in more crowded communities in two ranch-style housing developments with far different spatial relationships, produced nightmares and lifelong tragic memories. These travesties occurred at a time when Indian land needs were becoming acute on reservations (Haupton 1988, 20).

As part of the removal, some Seneca assisted in moving graves as well as the Longhouse. One woman expressed her grief at seeing the exposed bones of her brothers as well as the devastation of the land where houses had been bulldozed (Williams 2007). That the project was supposedly conducted in the name of progress reinforced the psychological trauma of being expendable and undesirable in the eyes of the United States. Indeed, the relocation bill for the Kinzua project included a rider requiring the Seneca to draft a termination plan for putting an end to the tribe as a legal entity under federal trust responsibility (Williams 2007).

The fact that the United States could break one of the oldest treaties signed with a Native nation left the Seneca and other Native people feeling completely vulnerable and unsupported. The dam became a symbol that the United States could and would act with total impunity and disregard for those living within its territories. While this tragedy was lamented in songs of the era by such notables as Johnny Cash and Buffy Saint Marie, the federal government, including Presidents Eisenhower and Kennedy, remained largely oblivious. In her book on the Kinzua dam and relocation Bilharz (1998) refers to the broken treaties associated with building the dam and the broken hearts associated with the relocation.

The Allegany Seneca struggled to both mourn and mitigate their losses. Since the Cold Springs Longhouse, the spiritual center of the reservation, was to be lost, the community and other Haudesaunee communities throughout the region worked to maintain spiritual protocols and move to a new location, concluding with a nine-hour ceremony. While the community of Cold Springs is gone, the new Longhouse is a vibrant source of spiritual sustenance.

Decades after the removal the events are still remembered in an annual commemoration ceremony held the last Saturday of September. At this event, community members from the affected generations as well as those born later gather to "Remember the Removal." At these gatherings the story is told from a Seneca perspective so that future generations will know what happened and that something similar will never be allowed to happen again. This is a significant way of continuing to promote community healing.

CLINICAL IMPLICATIONS

Four major issues are important to consider in providing direct service to those who have experienced historic trauma (Evans-Campbell 2008). First, it is most important to consider what a dysfunctional response actually is. Symptoms such as guilt and denial should not always be considered pathological, but rather adaptive and protective responses to historic trauma (Danieli 1998). The clinician needs to avoid interpreting all behaviors of those who have experienced historic trauma diagnosable as symptoms of PTSD. Some symptoms can be expected and may help strengthen resilience, while others may signal dysfunction. Secondly, the clinician needs to be sensitive to the impact of current life stressors and traumatic events. While trauma literature traditionally considers the negative effect of cumulative trauma, those who work with Native Americans who have experienced historical trauma need to consider whether they have some immunity to current assaults or whether current traumatic events will serve to retrigger the effect of past traumatic events. A third major consideration in working clinically with Native Americans is to think of family and community approaches, rather than individual treatment. Healing interventions on a community level are often much more effective in helping those who have experienced group historical trauma than individual treatment. The creation and development of narratives that depict historical traumatic events has been used effectively to help Native Americans cope with historical trauma (Denham 2008). A final issue in clinical work with Native Americans involves a focus on resilience and healing. Although much trauma literature has focused on treating negative symptoms, identifying and reinforcing strengths and resilience may be more effective in providing clinical help to Native Americans (Evans-Campbell 2008).

MACRO-LEVEL IMPLICATIONS

Since much of the ongoing trauma experienced by Native Americans has happened on a macro-, or community-level, interventions can be particularly meaningful. Ultimately, decolonization and healing go hand in hand. While the ongoing occupation of traditional indigenous territories is not likely to end with the descendents of European colonists leaving the continent (as the British withdrew from their former colony India), it is still necessary to implement a form of decolonization in which the disastrous effects of colonization are recognized and accounted for in order to ameliorate their on-going effects. It is important to recognize that "the policies that govern and regulate reservation life are still under the control of the colonizer/perpetrator" (Faimon 2004, 245). Clearly, decolonization is easier said than done but denial and minimization of the impact of colonization hinders any possibility of healing.

Truth telling and remembering are the central tenets of an ability to move forward with healing on a community level. These typically take the form of remembrance events such as marches, but can also involve seeking reparations, apologies, or changes in curricula to address past wrong doings.

Dakota scholar Waziyatawin points out that a compensation fund was established for victims of 9/11 less than two weeks after the terrorist attacks. "The victims of 9/11 will never recover their losses, but they will begin to heal from their wounds, not so much because of the financial support, but because of the recognition by the rest of the country that they have suffered. On the contrary, the pain suffered by Indigenous Peoples in the United States has been forgotten, considered a thing of the past, and become normalized. Rather than acknowledging that there has been a terrible wrong committed, colonization has imposed on us the responsibility for our own pain" (Waziyatawin 2005, 190).

Waziyatawin recommends creation of a Truth and Reconciliation Commission. There is a need to prepare a formal body of evidence to submit to a U.S. committee to hear grievances. This differs from government initiated and sanctioned truth commissions in other parts of the world in that it is not organized and supported by the colonizing government. "The commission is a worthwhile venture, however, since the purpose of such work is to seek truth about the injustices perpetrated against us, to contribute to a state of well-being among our people, and to promote justice in our lands" (Waziyatawin 2005, 190).

The transformative power of telling the truth is apparent for participants in commemorative marches (Waziyatawin 2005). The opportunity to tell our stories in an environment that is validating and empowering is central to healing transformations. Ceremonies facilitated by spiritual leaders and prayers of many people on behalf of the marchers and ancestors also facilitate healing. Events that remember massacres and other traumatic events allow the participants an opportunity to grieve and they can gain a sense of empowerment from taking long overdue action (Waziyatawin 2005).

Having perpetrators acknowledge their wrong doings is important but survivors and their descendents can also facilitate their own healing independently (Waziyatawin 2005).

It is important to strive for reparation of the spirit. A white American social work educator reflecting on her experiences on the Dakota Commemorative March reflects on "thinking about the psychological consequences of colonialism, the desecration of those who were murdered on the march, and those who died along the march. How are they to be treated when the oppressors have desecrated them? What ceremonies and rituals are needed? How does one adequately mourn so massive a catastrophe as the genocide of a people?" (Faimon 2004, 249).

The Dakota Commemorative March is one of many remembrances that have been organized to commemorate different traumatic events. This event is a grassroots effort organized by Dakota women descendents of the 1862 forced march. In this annual event, people walk a route that replicates the original march to remember and honor those who were forcibly removed. Each mile marker bears the name of an ancestor on the original march. Every day begins and ends with a ceremony. The marchers carry an eagle staff and offer tobacco and prayers (Faimon 2004). This and other marches create community and strong voices for justice. They are healing rituals embodied with spiritual values, beliefs, and meaning (Faimon 2004). Likewise, a sacred relay run from Fort Snelling to Mankato is held annually to commemorate the hanging of 38 Dakota warrior patriots in the largest mass execution in U.S. history on December 26, 1862 (Faimon 2004).

In another example, the 130th Fort Robinson Outbreak Spiritual Run took place January 2009. This 400 mile run is done to commemorate the anniversary of the Cheyenne imprisoned at Ft. Robinson, Nebraska, attempting to return home to Montana. Most were slaughtered immediately upon breaking out of their barracks and some 40 miles later by the Cavalry at the Last Hole. Only a small group found sanctuary with Red Cloud's Lakota people (Whiteman and Two Bulls 2009).

In some cases the perpetrators of trauma have taken steps to facilitate healing of those they harmed. In 2001, the Truth Commission into Genocide in Canada released their report, "Hidden from History: The Canadian Holocaust" (Waziyatawin 2005). Reparations (i.e., the returning of land or other settlements) are separate issues from truth telling, but are also a necessary part of healing and achieving justice (Waziyatawin 2005).

The educational arena also provides an appropriate venue for sharing stories of atrocities and ultimately for promoting healing. A prime example of this are recent efforts by the Native American Program of the Syracuse, New York, school district to develop a curriculum about Kinzua so youths can learn not only what happened, but also what can be done to prevent similar tragedies in the future (Wulff and Blancke 2003). Similar programs would fit well in other regions to promote understanding of the trauma experienced by other Native populations.

CONCLUSION

Clearly, Native Americans have experienced extensive trauma as part of the colonization process, and their colonization experiences continue under their current status as domestic dependent nations subject to federal oversight. The legacy of terror initiated by massacres, forced removals, and other byproducts of colonization leaves many Native people with psychological symptoms, struggles with alcohol, and doubt in their selves and their cultures (Faimon 2004).

It is important to recognize that the traumatic affects of colonization are ongoing and not just a historical artifact. Native people are still subject to removal from their territories, as, for example, the removal of Navajo and Hopi people from Big Mountain from the 1970s into the early 1990s (Venables 2004). Ongoing conflicts with the federal government and lack of success in the U.S. legal system leave Native people little reason to believe that their rights will be respected. It is also important to note that Americans cannot get away with believing that injustice and oppression happen only in other places. Indeed, the Kinzua example illustrates that disenfranchisement and oppression happen within U.S. borders in contemporary times. The traumatic impact of such events cannot be denied or ignored. The fact that much of the trauma experienced by Native Americans is manmade, large-scale, and ongoing poses substantial challenges for healing.

In spite of these challenges, many Native American communities have developed effective mechanisms for addressing trauma. Most notably, it is important for the truth about traumatic events, both historical and contemporary, to be acknowledged. Many annual community events of remembrance serve the function of both retelling events from a Native perspective and validating their significance. Many of these efforts are grassroots programs developed by community members themselves rather than by professionals. The power of these movements is a significant factor in healing. These events contain many lessons for all of us about resilience, healing, reclaiming our voices, and moving forward as healthy indigenous people.

REFERENCES

Bachman, R. 1992. *Death and Violence on the Reservation.* New York: Auburn House.

Balsam, K. F., Huang, B., Fieland, K. C., Simoni, J., and K. F. Walters. 2004. "Culture, Trauma, and Wellness: A Comparison of Heterosexual and Lesbian, Gay, Bisexual, and Two-Spirit Native Americans." *Cultural Diversity and Ethnic Minority Psychology* 10 (3): 287–301.

Bilharz, J. A. 1998. *The Allegany Senecas and the Kinzua Dam: Forced Relocation through Two Decades.* Lincoln: University of Nebraska Press.

Danieli, Y. 1998. *International Handbook of Multicultural Legacies of Trauma.* New York: Plenum.

Denham, A. 2008. "Rethinking Historic Trauma: Narratives of Resilience." *Transcultural Psychiatry* 45 (3): 391–414.

Deschenie, T. 2006. "Historical Trauma." *Tribal College Journal* 17 (3): 8–11.

Engel, B. 2007. "Eagle Soaring: The Power of the Resilient Self." *Journal of Psychosocial Nursing* 45 (2): 44–49.

Evans-Campbell, T. 2008. "Historical Trauma in American Indian/Native Alaskan Communities: A Multilevel Framework for Exploring Impacts on Individuals, Families and Communities." *Journal of Interpersonal Violence* 23 (3): 316–38.

Faimon, M. B. 2004. "Ties that Bind: Remembering, Mourning, and Healing Historical Trauma." *American Indian Quarterly* 28: 238–51.

Forbes-Boyte, K. 1999. "Fools Crow versus Gullett: A Critical Analysis of the American Indian Religious Freedom Act." *Antipode* 31 (3): 304–23.

Garland, C. 1998. "Thinking about Trauma." In *Understanding Trauma: A Psychoanalytic Approach,* ed. C. Garland, 9–31. London: Karnac.

Gottschalk, S. 2003. "Reli(e)ving the Past: Emotion Work in the Holocaust's Second Generation." *Symbolic Interaction* 26 (3): 355–80.

Hauptman, L. M. 1986. *The Iroquois Struggle for Survival: World War II to Red Power.* Syracuse, NY: Syracuse University Press.

Hauptman, L. M. 1988. *Formulating American Indian Policy in New York State, 1970–1986.* Albany: State University of New York Press.

Kellerman, N. 2001. "Transmission of Holocaust Trauma: An Integrative View." *Psychiatry* 64 (3): 256–67.

Lawrence, J. 2000. "The Indian Health Service and the Sterilization of Native American Women." *American Indian Quarterly* 24 (3): 400–23.

Mannes, M. 1995. "Factors and Events Leading to the Passage of the Indian Child Welfare Act." *Child Welfare* 74 (1): 264–82.

McCabe, G. 2007. The Healing Path: A Culture and Community-Derived Indigenous Therapy Model." *Psychotherapy Theory: Research, Practice, Training* 44 (2): 148–60.

Mental Health Today 2009. *Post-traumatic Stress Disorder DSM-IV Diagnosis & Criteria.* Available at: http://www.mental-health-today.com/ptsd/dsm.htm.

Ogunwole, S. U. 2002. *The American Indian and Alaska Native Population: 2000.* U.S. Bureau of the Census.

Saint Marie, B. 1966. "My Country 'tis of thy People You're Dying" [song]. *Little Wheel Sit and Spin.* Gypsy Music.

Struthers, R., and Lowe, J. 2003. "Nursing in the Native American Culture and Historical Trauma." *Issues in Mental Health Nursing* 24: 257–72.

Torpy, S.J. 2000. "Native American Women and Coerced Sterilization: On the Trail of Tears in the 1970s." *American Indian Culture and Research Journal* 24 (2): 1–22.

Venables, R.W. 2004. *American Indian History: Five Centuries of Conflict and Co-existence.* Santa Fe, NM: Clear Light Publishers.

Waldram, J. 2004. *Revenge of the Windigo: The Construction of the Mind and Mental Health of North American Aboriginal Peoples.* Toronto, ON: University of Toronto Press.

Waziyatawin. 2005. "Relieving our Suffering: Indigenous Decolonization and a United States Truth Commission." In *For Indigenous Eyes Only,* ed. W.A. Wilson and M. Yellow Bird, 189–205. Santa Fe, NM: School of American Research.

Whiteman, P. Jr., and Two Bulls, L. 2009. *Fort Robinson Outbreak Spiritual Run.* Available at: www.yellowbirdinc.org.

Williams, V. 2007. *The Kinzua Dam Controversy.* Unpublished dissertation, State University of New York at Buffalo.

Wulff, B., and Blancke, B. 2003. "Remembering Kinzu!: Developing a History and Conflict Resolution Curriculum." *Research in Social Movements, Conflicts, and Change* 24: 363–407.

Yellow Horse Brave Heart, M. 1999. "Gender Differences in the Historical Trauma Response among the Lakota." *Journal of Health and Social Policy* 10 (4): 1–21.

Yellow Horse Brave Heart, M. 2003. "The Historical Trauma Response among Natives and its Relationship with Substance Abuse: A Lakota Illustration." *Journal of Psychoactive Drugs* 35 (1): 7–13.

Chapter 13

POST-SLAVERY SYNDROME

A Multigenerational Look at African American Injury, Healing, and Resilience

Joy Angela DeGruy

People of African descent continue to suffer from "grievous and slow-healing wounds" yet despite such injuries have been compared to the black pupil of the eye surrounded by the white. In this black pupil you see the reflection of that which is before it, and through it the light of the Spirit shines forth.

—Abdu'l-Bahá

INTRODUCTION

The first enslaved Africans arrived in the Americas in the early 1500s. The slave trade was made illegal in 1808, with slavery itself being dismantled with the ratification of the Thirteenth Amendment in 1865. For nearly 350 years people of African descent were held in bondage under the most brutal and oppressive conditions. The conservative numbers of those Africans who survived the capture and transport from Africa to the Americas has been estimated to be from 8 to 15 million (Curtain 1969; Thomas 1997). As to the numbers who died en route from the interior of western Africa, those who did not survive the conditions of the slave castles and those who actually died during the middle passage voyage, the estimates equal or surpass the 15 million who survived.

Slavery as an institution has existed in numerous societies throughout the world; however American chattel slavery differed greatly from most prior forms of enslavement. The manner in which it differed has a great bearing on the nature of the traumatic injury to Africans and their descendants and how they coped with their trauma. American chattel slavery differed in several distinct ways. First, it differed in how a person became a slave; secondly, it differed in how the enslaved were treated; and lastly, it differed in how slave owners perceived and viewed those whom they enslaved. In most societies where slavery existed, people became enslaved as a direct result of losing a war. Sometimes people were enslaved as a result of conquest, when a more powerful society would invade and attack a weaker one and then capture and enslave the inhabitants. In the above cases the enslaved were frequently granted a legal status and over time many were able to regain their own freedom and secure the freedom of their offspring. Europeans, unlike other societies, built an entire economy on the slave trade, and this involved centuries of capturing, shipping, and selling of millions of people, African people. Africans were then relegated by laws and pseudoscience to a permanent subhuman classification, and consequently they and their descendents were sentenced to entire lifetimes of enslavement.

During the middle passage, millions of enslaved Africans were crammed together on cargo ships with sometimes less than 18 inches of space between them. They would remain confined in this manner for weeks to months, depending upon the destination. This space was where they slept, wept, ate, defecated, urinated, menstruated, vomited, sometimes gave birth and died. Given the horrific nature of this voyage, it is now being referred to as the Black Holocaust.

This was just the beginning of a lifetime of brutal existence; they were beaten with whips which tore into the flesh, worked to the limits of human endurance, denied the minimal survival needs of food and water, raped and preparing their own children to be raped, used in painful medical experiments without anesthesia. They were treated like animals or worse. However, these were only the physical aspects of the assaults. The daily attack on their human dignity, their spirits, and humanity was no less severe.

How did Europeans reconcile their consciences, given the extent and intensity of violence against African Americans during and following slavery? The answer to this question leads to clarity about how and why Europeans dehumanized Africans and the long-term effects of this systematic dehumanization.

Over two centuries ago James Madison, a founding father and the primary author of the United States Constitution, for reasons of political power and control proposed that Africans should be considered equivalent to three-fifths of a human being. Others joined Jefferson, who asserted that blacks *"smelled bad, were physically unattractive, required less sleep, were dumb, cowardly and incapable of feeling grief,"* while 18th century scientists like Carl Von Linnaeus classified Africans as *"black, phlegmatic, cunning, lazy, lustful, careless and governed by caprice."* Phrenologists Orson and Lorenzo Fowler, claiming that intelligence could be determined by the size and shape of the human skull, concluded that Africans were inferior to all other races (Fowler and Fowler 1859; Haller 1971; Madison 1788).

Although clearly without any scientific merit, the above theories served to justify discriminatory, degrading, and brutal behavior by Europeans against Africans and other people of color by declaring them inferior and thus deserving of the treatment that was meted out to them. These statements at first glance may be seen as misguided scientific exploration. However, this dangerously underestimates the long-term influence on societal perceptions and, more importantly, the psychological costs of such injudicious, self-serving and fallacious assessments on generations of African Americans. The injury of slavery to enslaved Africans and their descendants is deeply rooted and observable in African Americans today but has remained a marginalized and greatly ignored area of clinical and sociocultural research.

The purpose of this chapter is to identify and better understand the strengths and resiliency that has allowed survival in the past as well as the present and to determine the needs vital for the future sustained well being of African Americans as a group.

POST-TRAUMATIC SLAVE SYNDROME: THE INJURY TO AFRICAN AMERICANS

Much of the research regarding mass trauma looks at events that have occurred with a limited duration. Rarely has trauma been explored over centuries. Catastrophic events like hurricane Katrina and the 9/11 World Trade Center disaster are examples of massive trauma where the actual trauma was brief in duration, although with devastating and lasting effects. Now imagine if the trauma was centuries in duration with no healing for the survivors for generations. Consider that the survivors (enslaved Africans) were not experiencing a single traumatic event but rather a lifetime of multiple and repeated trauma. Now you have the foundation for what is termed post-traumatic slave syndrome (PTSS). PTSS is a condition that exists when a population has been the victim of multigenerational oppression resulting from centuries of slavery and institutionalized racism (Leary 2005).

Post-traumatic Stress Disorder (PTSD): A Clinical View

The Diagnostic Statistical Manual of Mental Disorders IV Revised (DSM IV) describes features of PTSD and the conditions which usually cause the psychological injury that validate the diagnosis of PTSD:

- A serious threat or harm to one's life or physical integrity
- A threat or harm to one's children, spouse or close relative
- Sudden destruction of one's home or community
- Seeing another person injured, killed as result of accident or physical violence
- Learning about a serious threat to a relative or a close friend kidnapped, tortured or killed
- Stressor is experienced with intense fear, terror and helplessness
- Stressor and disorder is considered to be more serious and will last longer when the stressor is of human design (APA 1994)

Considering the diagnostic criteria listed above and what we now know from slave narrative accounts as well as forensic evidence, significant numbers of enslaved Africans experienced many and sometimes all of these stressors. Not surprisingly, they exhibited some or all of the following symptoms of the disorder:

- Intense psychological distress at exposure to internal or external cues that symbolize or resemble an aspect of the traumatic event
- Physiological reactivity on exposure to internal or external cues
- Marked diminished interest or participation in significant activities
- Feelings of detachment or estrangement form others
- Restricted range of affect
- Sense of foreshortened future, in other words does not expect to have a career, marriage, children or normal life span
- Difficulty falling or staying asleep
- Irritability or outbursts of anger
- Difficulty concentrating (APA 1994)

With what is known about trauma, it is all but certain that significant numbers of enslaved Africans experienced an ample amount of trauma to warrant multiple diagnoses of PTSD. This is especially true given the fact that they experienced these traumas throughout their lives and with no formal clinical assistance to deal with their injuries, which included being captured, removed from their country, branded with hot irons, worked nearly to death, being sold or having loved ones sold away, and being beaten, tortured, and raped.

Hundreds of years of American chattel slavery left an ineradicable mark on American culture in general and African Americans in particular. More importantly, the end of slavery did not end the traumas or oppression for African Americans. The dismantling of slavery with the 1863 Emancipation Proclamation suggested that African Americans were legally free, yet what followed was a virtual reenslavement through legislation reflected in Peonage (1865–1945), Black Codes (1866–1867), Convict lease (1880–1928) and Jim Crow (1896–1964). This legislation perpetuated the continual oppression and subjugation of African Americans, and contributed to lasting physical, emotional, and psychological injuries. The Civil Rights Act of 1964, which attempted to address the injustices, ended the legalized separation and isolation imposed upon African Americans. However, the attack on human rights and dignity went on.

Recurring racist incidents like the thousands of lynchings involving the Ku Klux Klan, and the 1955 brutal killing of 14-year-old Emmett Till, the 1989 beating death of Ethiopian-born Mulugeta Seraw by skinheads, the 1991 police assault on Rodney King, the dragging death of James Byrd in Jasper, Texas, in 1998, the 1999 killing of unarmed Amadou Diallo by New York police officers, the 2005 negligent treatment of the victims of the Katrina disaster and the 2008 killing of unarmed Sean Bell by a hail of 50 bullets on the day of his wedding serve as fresh reminders that the trauma continues.

MULTIGENERATIONAL TRANSMISSION OF THE TRAUMA

We know from research conducted on other groups that have experienced terrorism, oppression, and trauma that survivor syndromes exist and are persistent in the human development of second and third generation progeny. The characteristics of the survivor syndrome have been identified and include: stress, a lack of self confidence, difficulties with anger, hostility and aggression, and other psychological and interpersonal relationship problems (Danieli 1998). These survivor syndrome characteristics are evident in African Americans today.

> The intergenerational perspective reveals the impact of trauma, its contagion, and repeated patterns within the family. It may help explain certain behavior patterns, symptoms, roles, and values adopted by family members, family sources of vulnerability as well as resilience and strength, and job

choices (following in the footsteps of a relative, a namesake) through the generations. Viewed from a family systems perspective, what happened in one generation will affect what happens in the older or younger generation, though the actual behavior may take a variety of forms. Within an intergenerational context, the trauma and its impact may be passed down as the family legacy even to children born after the trauma (Danieli 1998, 9).

Unlike PTSD, PTSS is not a disorder but rather a pattern of behaviors that has been brought on by the specific circumstances of slavery. The resulting pattern of behavior falls into three categories: vacant esteem, ever-present anger, and racist socialization. Vacant esteem is characterized by feeling or believing oneself to be inferior or having minimal or even no self worth. This state comes about as a result of the three most significant areas of influence on the individual—the family, the community, and the society. When these three agencies of influence take on the distorted and demeaning perceptions that have been deliberately manufactured over time, the result can be disastrous. For African Americans this meant self-depreciation and compromised identity to which they felt confined. This is called the state of vacant esteem.

Racist socialization is perhaps the most dangerous and persistent of the symptoms of PTSS. This symptom is reflected in blacks who accept the devaluation of African and African American culture by Europeans and adopt the belief of white superiority. Carter G. Woodson says it best:

> The same educational process which inspires and stimulates the oppressor with the thought that he is everything and has accomplished everything worth while, depresses and crushes at the same time the spark of genius in the Negro by making him feel that his race does not amount to much and never will measure up to the standards of other peoples. The Negro thus educated is a hopeless liability of the race. The difficulty is that the "educated Negro" is compelled to live and move among his own people whom he has been taught to despise. As a rule therefore, the "educated Negro" prefers to buy his food from a white grocer because he has been taught that the Negro is not clean. It does not matter how often a Negro washes his hands, then, he cannot clean them, and no matter how often a white man uses his hands he cannot soil them (xiii).

Ever-present anger is the net result of cumulative oppression. African Americans often hear, "Slavery's over, you all have been free for over a hundred years and are all blessed to live in a nation where all you have to do is pull yourself up by your own bootstraps and work hard. So why are you still angry?"

In their 1968 book titled *Black Rage,* William H. Grier and Price M. Cobbs, two African American psychiatrists, provide a compelling answer to this question. In it they describe the ongoing traumas associated with slavery, discrimination and the failure of America in correcting this wrong. Fred R. Harris writes:

> The authors as psychiatrists are admirably equipped to see that white percep-
> tions of Negroes, and the historical inculcation of these perceptions in the
> minds of the Negroes themselves, are at the root of our present troubles. They
> demonstrate beyond challenge the crippling effects of white American culture
> on the attempts of Negro Americans to do here what all people everywhere
> must do if they are to develop fully—to find an identity, a sense of worth, to
> relate to others, to love, to work, and to create. Black rage is the result of our
> failure, after 300 years, to make these human values possible (viii).

This rage is neither surprising nor complex once we understand what causes anger. Dr. James R. Samuels explains:

> In its simplest form anger is the normal emotional response to a blocked
> goal. Often, if a person's goal remains blocked over time, they will begin to
> consider the possibility of failure and so experience fear and when we are
> fearful we also lash out in anger.

Violence was intrinsic to the enslavement process and the oppressive structures put into place after slavery ended. Europeans have consistently modeled both anger and violence in their behavior towards Africans and their descendants. *From capture and enslavement to the tyrannical vigilantism that still persists, the anger and violence committed against African Americans, together with the lies about freedom and justice which have spanned several centuries, have unsurprisingly led to its eventual use, however untenable, by African Americans in response to their plight.*

African Americans have managed to emerge, though not fully recovered, from the vestiges of PTSS as identified by vacant esteem, racist socialization, and ever-present anger. The impact of these three areas of injury has required the introduction of efficient ways to lessen or buffer their effect (Leary 2005).

HEALING AND RESILIENCE: MITIGATING THE DAMAGE CAUSED BY VACANT ESTEEM

Ancestral Connections and Familial Association

Starting from the early 1600s the majority of captured and enslaved indigenous Africans came from West Africa, from Senegal down to Angola.

West African culture was a unique blend of small tribal villages to major empires with sophisticated and complex organization. Land was of particular importance to West Africans because it served to bind them magically to their ancestral roots. They believed as long as they remained on the land they stayed spiritually connected to their departed relatives, something that they held sacred. Separation from the land was viewed as a grave violation of this connection and could produce dangerous consequences. *"To remove Africans by force from their land is an act of such great injustice that no foreigner can fathom it"* (Mbiti 1969, 35). Thus, one of the first blows to the African social and cultural structure was forced removal from their ancestral land.

One consistent characteristic of the entire West African region which survived the middle passage and enslavement was the collective belief about the importance of family, elders, and the connection to a common ancestry. West African culture was full of rich and diverse customs and rituals replete with ritual objects such as charms, masks, and statues made of wood, ivory, and bronze. Their rituals involved magic reflected in art, dance, and music for functional purposes like ensuring good crops or to strengthen kinship ties or to honor the death of an elder. There was also a clear and strong monotheistic belief in one High God who could also be called upon for assistance or guidance (Agbo 2006, 22; Fisher and Quarels 1967, 1–3; Thomas 1997, 16). One such ritual was the ash circle which was practiced in group and in private settings. A circle of special burnt herbs and plants was first spread around the individual or group. The circle of ash provided protection and spiritual powers for those inside of it. While within the circle, rituals were sometimes performed or discussions were held to solve a particular problem or to determine a specific action (Somé 1997).

It was these strong established rituals and beliefs which the enslaved Africans drew upon for power and courage when captured and imprisoned, or when forced to endure being beaten, tortured, and raped.

The Dagara are an ethnic group from Ghana and Burkina Faso that typify this concept of the sanctity of relationships. In the village of Dano, elders are held in very high esteem and are relied upon for the major decisions in the village. They are called upon to settle disputes and to address any emergency situations happening within the village and there are always rituals performed before any decisions are made (Somé 1997). This is consistent with African societies throughout the continent that are arranged based upon kinships. The family is extended beyond what westerners are accustomed to. Somé explains:

> The family in Africa is always extended. You would never refer to your cousin as "cousin," because that would be an insult. So your cousins are

your sister and brothers. Your nieces are your children. Your uncles are your fathers. Your aunts are your mothers . . . Children are also encouraged to call other people outside the family mothers and fathers, sisters and brothers (10–11).

It is important to note that this concept of extended family structure is not an arbitrary arrangement; rather, it is a strategy for survival. This form of social organization ensures that everyone within the village or clan is cared for, from children to elders. This required cooperation and accountability for all actions and dealings between individuals.

Asante and Asante (1995) explain:

There was an organic view that the whole order was related in a dynamic sense. Tampering with one part was believed to affect the whole. All parts had to be in rhythm and harmony with one another leading to a sense of connection for the cosmos. Time, in traditional African culture, has been viewed as a central phenomenon. The worldview has had a religious base and has emphasized an external locus of control and the need for humans to temporarily harmonize themselves with the forces of control and the forces around them. Time has been used in establishing a complexity of balanced relationships; one, time as used to establish a relationship with the Supreme Being; two, to establish a relationship of continuity between the present and past generations; three, to establish a relationship with nature and the forces of one's environment (nature); and four, to create group harmony and participation among the living (31).

It is crucial to understand the level of disruption to relationships and family that American chattel slavery wreaked upon Africans and their descendants to understand better how they managed to piece together the fragmented remains of their culture and people. When Africans were first forced upon the shores of the American continent, their families were ripped apart and they were alienated from their clans and tribes. Many were unable even to communicate with one another because they didn't speak the same language, and sometimes were from opposing or warring tribes. The relationship which was the foundation of their society and thus, their survival, was now endangered. Survival of this violent disruption of family and home required them to recreate what they could of their cultural practices and values. Additionally, they had to contend with the forced assimilation of a European ideology in all that pertained to culture, language, religion, and values.

African Americans responded to these traumas by utilizing what they remembered and what they developed in the way of cultural customs, spiritual and social practices. Many have suggested that enslaved Africans were completely stripped of their African cultural customs; however, it is evident that African Americans continued many of their traditions. In discussing the retention of African-centered orientation, Allen and Bagozzi (2001) suggest that the European subjugation of Africans during American chattel slavery did not destroy African cultural ways of life. Along with other notable black scholars, they assert that the oppression and subjugation of Africans by Europeans served to bolster the retention of African-oriented constructs and philosophy. An example of this was the rituals performed by enslaved Africans during this tumultuous period. Ani (1980) writes:

> The ultimate expression of the African world-view is the experience or phenomenon of ritual. It is only through ritual that death can be understood as rebirth. It is through ritual that new life was given to the African Spirit. We performed and experienced ritual drama in North America. The modality of ritual drama was foreign to the Euro-American ethos, and therefore, could not have come from that source (24).

Many of these rituals were performed at night where songs were sung and prayers were shouted and passed along from person to person. These meetings gave strength and made enduring the miseries of day to day life bearable.

> Away from white surveillance, when we could, we would come together. We would gather slowly, a few at a time, at night—a special time for us. Night was special not only because the day's work was over and because it could hide us, but also because that is when spiritual energies and powers are more potent. We gathered and enjoyed the warmth of our commonness, of our togetherness. We would form a circle, each touching those next to us as to physically express our spiritual closeness. We "testified," speaking on the day's or the week's experiences. We shared the pain of those experiences and received from the group affirmations of our existence as suffering beings (24).

Another way that African Americans mitigated the effects of slavery's assault on personal and familial relations was the continued practice of extended family with the added element of fictive kinship. After slavery, African Americans often sought to return to their southern homes and rejoin family and care for those who had been mistreated or abandoned by whites. The ties which white southerners thought to be severed during slavery had withstood the time and distance that had divided them. Herbert Gutman (1976) describes how important maintaining family ties were to freed Africans in 1865. He recounts the words of a northern missionary named W. T. Richardson:

To them, that is holy ground; for it has been watered by their tears and blood. Strange as it may seem to us, the freedmen exhibit strong desires to go back to their former homes if possible, and enjoy the blessing of freedom with their families. I know of no other class of persons who manifest stronger local ties (211).

Today African American families continue to honor the importance of strong kinship networks. Several generations can still be seen to live in close proximity to one another throughout the United States. Celebrations of family through planned annual gatherings and reunions are a common practice among African Americans. Even individuals that are not related by blood are often included in such gatherings. Many African Americans have shared personal stories about their family organization and kinship ties which extend beyond the traditional American boundaries. One African American family whom I interviewed in New York described their personal family structure: "*We were adults before we realized that many of the people whom we had addressed as 'aunt' or' uncle' throughout our lives were actually distant cousins adopted by immediate family members and many of those we had accepted as relatives since childhood had no blood ties to our family at all.*" These non-blood relationships fall under the category of fictive kinship. This kinship is readily observable in many contemporary African American families, regardless of class or geographical location. These individuals often enjoy many of the rights and privileges of those that are related by blood. These extended kinship relationships with individuals, whether blood related or fictive, have provided assistance and support where needed in the family and also receive this same support in return.

Another part of this tradition involves the remembering of ancestors. There is often a time set aside during gatherings to honor those who have passed away. This honoring is demonstrated in unique ways. The family lineage or tree is frequently displayed on shirts and banners bearing the family name. Elders are often called upon to tell stories about the family history, the struggles and triumphs during oppressive times even as far back as slavery. Prayers and songs are offered in remembrance and appreciation of the sacrifices and suffering of the ancestors who made it possible for the family to continue. By maintaining these relationships, each member of the family has an identified place where they belong, where they feel and experience a sense of connectedness and value, thereby building individual and group resilience while diminishing vacant esteem.

In 2006 and 2008, the Public Broadcasting Service (PBS) launched a series titled *African American Lives,* which traced the family histories of a number of famous contemporary African Americans back to their

African roots. These individuals included: Henry Louis Gates, Oprah Winfrey, neurosurgeon Ben Carson, NASA astronaut Mae Jemison, and Maya Angelou, among others. The overwhelming response of elation and pride by the participants and the millions of African American viewers exemplifies the lingering sentiments held by African Americans about the importance, the vital need, for African Americans to know and pass along to their heirs, their family legacy and history.

Naming Practices: Reconstructing the Identity

The practice of child naming in African and African American culture is also a very important way of building and sustaining a strong sense of identity and self-worth. In Africa, one's name could reveal a lot about who a person was, "who they were born after, how they were born (feet first for example), if they came after twins, if their mother died at birth, what people they belonged too" (Diouf 2007, 90). Enslaved Africans arriving in Alabama sought to hide their real African names for fear they would endanger their families. In places such as Ghana, everyone is named according to the day of the week that they were born to create continuity and community closeness.

African Americans from the mid 1700s through the mid to late 1800s started a pattern and practice of naming children after immediate family members. This occurred in an effort to draw connections between individual families and their larger kinship group. This showed a clear connection to their African roots and traditions regarding the belief in a common ancestry. Herbert Gutman (1976) writes:

> The naming of children for the fathers was a particular slave-naming practice sufficiently powerful to affect behavior in the immediate post-emancipation decades. It strongly disputes frequent assertions that assign a negligible role to slave fathers and insist that "patriarchal" status came only after black men "acquired property" or assimilated "American attitudes and patterns of behavior" following emancipation and the breakdown of social isolation . . . . By so dramatically affirming the important cultural role of the slave father, the slaves, once more, showed how their beliefs and practices differed from those of their owners (190–91).

Names that had come from white slave owners were not viewed with any fondness by African Americans. One of the reasons that African Americans in Mobile, Alabama, had chosen to keep them instead of their traditional African names was most likely to avoid becoming a target of xenophobic paranoia. The names were also a way of establishing continuity of the family line. Diouf (2007) explains:

The value of the title rested in the fact that it established a link to a place, the cradle of the family. By the time it had been transmitted to grandchildren the name had been imbued with a historical and personal identity. With it there was continuity, people knew who their family was, where to go back to if they could after having been sold away. Those names, known within the enslaved community, were fundamental in every sense of the term and were one of the only ways people had to keep track of one another as sales dispersed relatives throughout the South (133).

The significance of being able to chose one's own name cannot be over-emphasized as a practice which bolstered resilience, especially considering the powerlessness a people feels having their names taken away or changed for generations. During enslavement, African Americans were shown no deference and were never addressed by titles of respect by whites. They were never addressed as Sir or Mister, or Miss or Mrs., or Ma'am, and most certainly they were never referred to as ladies or gentlemen. However, having come from a strong culture and tradition of showing respect to elders and others they developed their own ways to bestow respect. They began to address their elder women as Big Mama, Ma-dea, or Nana, they addressed their elder men as Big Daddy, and they referred to each other as Sister or Brother as a way to convey honor. After emancipation, many freed slaves changed their names, and eventually African Americans took on more honorable names, often taking on religious titles and in many more instances even created their own names.

Individuals like Isabella Baumfree changed her name to Sojourner Truth, Malcolm Little changed his name to Malcolm X, and later to El Hajj Malik; Leroy Jones changed his name to Amiri Baraka, Cassius Clay changed his name to Muhammad Ali, and Erica Wright changed what she termed her slave name to Erykah Badu. The list goes on. African Americans continue to choose names for themselves and their children that are distinct and hold important cultural and spiritual meaning. Baby-naming books can now be purchased which contain African as well as African American names.

HEALING AND RESILIENCE: MITIGATING THE DAMAGE CAUSED BY EVER-PRESENT ANGER

Symbols and Language as Meaning-Making Tools

The use of symbols to convey meanings and as ritual objects is a common practice among Africans. The Adinkra are among the most well known West African symbols. The exact date of the origins of Adinkra symbols is not known; however, they date back to prehistoric drawings on cave walls. The cultural significance of the Adinkra symbols is that they convey values and meaning. Adinkra is an Akan word which means *saying good-bye when parting* and this parting could be temporary or permanent (Owoahene 1998, 43).

One of the most popular Adinkra symbols is the Gye Nyame (supremacy) symbol. Gye means except and Nyame means God. The proverb for this symbol states that God is the one creator of all, that God alone should be worshiped; thus Ghanaians say, "I will fear nothing except God." Sankofa (positive reversion) is another well known symbol; *San* means return, *ko* means go and *fa* means take, thus return and take. The proverb associated with this symbol is for the individual to seek the collective knowledge and wisdom of past ancestors for assistance in the future (Agbo 2006, 3–22).

African Americans continued to use the Adinkra symbols after arriving in the United States and throughout the enslavement period. Michael Blakey, scientific director for the African Burial Ground project in New York, the largest burial ground of its kind in the United States, identified Adinkra symbols carved into the coffins of enslaved African Americans, one of which was the Sankofa symbol.

Blakey (2003) writes about carvings found on the coffin of the remains of an individual identified as Number 101:

> But the most important thing to many people about 101 is that heart-shaped symbol on his coffin lid. That symbol nagged me for a while. I was sure that I had seen it somewhere before, but it was vague to me. One day, early on in the project, I was sitting in an African American cultural event and the program had several symbols on the cover. And there it was. The symbol that I thought I had seen. I had the lab in New York send me the drawing of the symbol. Then I took it to an art historian at Howard who specializes in this area. I tried my best not to appear excited. He too saw that it was some version of a symbol called the *sankofa*. And the *sankofa* symbol is so perfect. It resonates so completely with the African Burial Ground. It has to do with the idea that you need to go back and search in the past, to let the past be a guide. It has to do with the connection with past and present. That you have to look backwards in order to look forwards. It means to revere ancestors and to respect elders—all these kinds of ideas about the relationship between past and present are wrapped up in that symbol. I think the African Burial Ground has helped disseminate knowledge of that symbol and its message. This is a real reversal of the ahistorical thinking that Americans have been bombarded with.

The work of anthropologist Christopher Fennel (1913) sheds light on the significance of understanding various symbols of those Africans who were displaced in America. He suggested that investigating the symbols that survived the capture and enslavement period helps to understand the cultural traditions of African Americans. Core symbols, he emphasizes, help express a culture's identity and cosmology. He ties this idea to the concept of ethnogenic bricolage, a creative process in which individuals from cultural backgrounds interact in new settings. While people are suppressed, emblematic expressions and core symbols are brought underground and continue to be part of private and individual spaces. These symbols are employed in healing, protection, prayer, and love. These are important concepts for knowing how symbolism works within a culture while also understanding the impact of the diaspora (Fennel, xiv).

African American Freedom Symbols

Meaningful symbols of cultural significance for African Americans have emerged as emblems of freedom. One is the Pan African red, black and green flag which was originally created in 1920. It has been referred to as the flag of the Universal Negro Improvement Association and African Communities League (UNIA) flag, and the African American or Black liberation flag. The flag is an important symbol for Africans and African Americans of black unity, liberation, and power. The three colors of red, black and green represent respectively the red blood of Africa's people that has been shed in the fight for freedom, the black for all people of African ancestry, and the green for the richness of the land of Africa. This flag continues to be used in Africa, America, and around the world as it continues to carry the potent meaning of prior generations.

The clenched black fist is another noteworthy symbol for Africans and African Americans. In the 1960s, it appeared on posters, buttons and even as sculptures. The black fist symbolizes black power and resistance. It was a symbol associated with Black Nationalism and perhaps the most famous usage was at the 1968 Summer Olympics in Mexico City, where two African American medal winners, John Carlos and Tommie Smith, were barred from the Olympics after they raised their fists in salute as a sign of protest and solidarity. African Americans have continued this practice of the raised fists, which can be readily observed at special gatherings of African Americans and particularly at the summation of singing the Negro National Anthem. These and other symbols represent intangible ways that African Americans showed self-determination, a silent way of fighting against oppression while diminishing the anger and frustration that lingered.

Language

Prior to their forced migration to America, enslaved Africans who spoke different languages were held captive for long periods of time. They learned to communicate by developing an auxiliary or broken language which was usually a more simplified version of one of the languages that were spoken. Similarly, throughout the southern colonies Africans from differing backgrounds speaking different languages were placed on large plantations and suddenly brought into close proximity. They continued to speak and develop pidgin languages that were a combination of African languages and English. This eventually resulted in at least one entirely new language called Gullah, still in use in the Carolinas (Stewart 1996, 232).

According to Ogbu (1990), African Americans developed coping skills inclusive of a group phenomenon of bilingualism. They developed a transitional language (Ebonics) which symbolized that they belonged to the group and aided in establishing an identity. This language has remained a major way that African Americans connect with each other and they have learned to navigate in and out of the language according to whom they are interacting with and the nature of the interaction. This form of communication is now commonly referred to as code switching.

HEALING AND RESILIENCE: MITIGATING THE DAMAGE CAUSED BY RACIAL SOCIALIZATION

Racial Socialization as a Source of Resiliency: Rituals and Ceremonies

Racial socialization is the method through which we are able to communicate our strengths and pass along the knowledge needed to understand and function positively as an African American in the society and world. While socialization is a process enjoyed by all people regardless of their race or ethnicity, for African Americans this was especially difficult given the centuries of anti-black sentiment which characterized every major institution in America that African American men, women and children came in contact with. The process called for a deconstruction of the negative attributions while simultaneously reconstructing a positive one. Today, African Americans constantly have to be concerned about the images that are portrayed of black people by others in visual and print media. Racial socialization necessarily involves providing protection against negative stereotypes.

Up until the 19th century, rites of passage rituals had been an essential part of human societies throughout the world, these ceremonies often marking an initiation into a different status within the clan or society. This initiation frequently signals the start of menarche for females and a movement from puberty into manhood for males. The advancement from adolescence into adulthood symbolized the individual's acceptance of his/her responsibility to contribute to the welfare and progress of the society itself. While this practice has continued to decline in most industrialized nations, there has been an upsurge within African American culture. Many of these African-centered ceremonies have been instituted by community-based organizations, in predominately black primary and secondary schools as well as historically black colleges and by faith-based organizations. Additionally, African-centered models have been shown to aid in coping with the traumas and stressors experienced by Africans.

Traditional theories about coping propose that individuals when faced with stressors will either attempt to solve the identified problem which is producing the stressor or try to survive the ordeal by lessening the stressor. By using an *Africentric* lens, one can better understand the relevance of culture in establishing coping behaviors in African Americans. The model incorporates the religious and spiritual practices and rituals including prayer, and suggests a collective shared interdependence among persons necessary for establishing harmony and peace. Additionally, this model helps to build up the individual's sense of self worth and ego integrity that comes under attack during times of trouble, and allows the restoration of balance (Greer 2007).

In 1999 a study was conducted in Portland, Oregon, with 200 African American male youth ranging from age 14 to 18. All of the youth shared similar socioeconomic status and lived in proximity to one another. The only major difference between them was the fact that 100 of the youth were incarcerated and the remaining 100 were involved in local Africentric programs.

The Gentlemen's Rites of Passage programs enroll black male youth beginning at age 14 and require them to provide service to their religious organizations, their community and schools while maintaining good grades. The young men are monitored by program coordinators as well as parents and volunteers. They remain in the program until they have completed their first years of college, trade school, Job Corps, and so on. Participants are allowed to go through passage only if they have met all of the requirements of manhood as stipulated by the program. Once they have successfully completed their personal and collective responsibilities, they are part of a passage ceremony where they are presented to their families and community in a grand celebration which hundreds of community members attend.

The purpose of the study was to try to determine the predictors of violence among this population. Those young men involved in the Africentric programs showed a statistically significant reduction in their use of violence compared to their counterparts who had not experienced such programs (Leary 2001).

MUSIC AND THE ARTS AS TOOLS
FOR COPING AND HEALING

The first significant category of music developed during slavery was spirituals, which is consistent with the highly sacred traditional African tribal customs of West and Central Africa. The spirituals were reflective of African religion as well as a way of coping with the traumas associated with slavery (Jones and Jones 2001). This was followed by the creation of the blues.

> If you want to talk blues as an element of culture, you have to recognize that the blues is, first and foremost, an oral art and a performance ritual; then proceed to talk about its role as an oral tradition; the beliefs, values, and world view it presents; the impact and effects of its rituals; and its importance as a cultural repository and an adaptive mechanism (Jones and Jones 2001, 36).

Music has played a significant role for African Americans in alleviating their suffering and facilitating creative expression. Through music and other art forms they experienced a catharsis, allowing them to purge the daily mental and emotional burdens they carried. The music gave black people a way to testify to their plight, to bemoan their agony, to rebuff enemies without their knowing it, and all the while the music soothed and intoxicated with its unique melodies and rhythms.

> Whatever the music form, be it rhythm and blues, jazz rap, gospel, spirituals, or blues, black music is consistently "soulful." The "soul" is reflected in the feelings of Jubilation, well-being, and centeredness one experiences in making, listening to, or dancing to the music. These experiences signal the presence of a transpersonal spirit, even when the spirit is not named. Such experiences contribute to a sense of personal integrity that is difficult to put in words, but indisputably real (6).

The early 1900s was the start of an African American cultural epoch marked by the emergence of black arts. Black writers, painters, sculptors, and musicians began celebrating African American life through poetry and prose, visual arts, and musical composition and performance. This period reflected a renewed pride and optimism about the black experience, referred to as the Harlem Renaissance. Powerful writers of the era included Langston Hughes, Zora Neale Hurston, and Claude McKay, among others. They wrote about the hardships they faced as black intellectuals in racist urban ghettos and those of the thousands of blacks migrating from the South to Northern cities like New York, Chicago, and Washington, DC. Once again, the arts provided a way for African Americans to assert themselves as people with a distinct culture, worthy of respect and demanding to be acknowledged.

SPIRITUALITY, RITUALS, CEREMONIES, AND RELIGION

The African concept of spirit is all embracing and synchronized to flow between and within all of the elements in the universe. It is the life-sustaining force which emanates from the mineral, plant, animal, and human. This spirit is not confined to the living; it traverses the physical realm and moves smoothly between the living and the dead, through the past and into the future (Somé 1997, 12–15).

This indigenous African scheme suggests an ontological universe of interconnected spiritual and sequential networks, with which man ideally strives to harmonize himself. Mbiti (1970) describes this universe:

> There are five divisions of the ontology, ranked in order of descending importance: (1) God, (2) spirits, (3) man, (4) animals and plants, (5) inanimate objects. The ontology is anthropocentric in that attention is focused upon man (humans) as the center. Humans are acutely aware of their position in relation to other forms of existence since a balance must be maintained at all times and since all modes must keep their proper place and distance from each other. Unity and interdependence are crucial since an upset in one of the categories upsets the whole order. God is believed to be the creator, the sustainer, and the ultimate controller of life; Africans thus have little difficulty reconciling His intervention into the affairs of humans, even though the spirits are believed to be His emissaries (Mbiti 1970, 20).

As previously noted, traditional African religious cosmology places a great deal of emphasis on the spirits that are in and around them at any and all times with a particular focus by some groups like the Akan on the worship of their ancestors. It is important to note that the religious beliefs of Africans are varied and cannot be generalized to one set system of beliefs and practices. However, Mbiti sheds light on the consistent elements of indigenous African religions. He states:

> African people are aware of all these elements of religion: God, spirits and divinities are part of the traditional body of beliefs. Christianity and Islam acknowledge the same type of spiritual beings (Mbiti 1969, 10).

The spirit realm for most West African traditional societies consists of God, the creator of the earth and the sun, moon stars and sea. From the creator spirit several forces emanate. These forces include: positive, negative and neutral spirits; from the neutral spirits come witchcraft, sorcery and magic. The earth contains the mountain, rocks, animals, trees and man; from the earth come the anthropomorphic entities; from man comes the living, the dead and the unborn. The dead consist of bad and good ghosts; and from the good ghosts come the clan ancestors, lineage ancestors, family ancestors and personal guardian spirits (Assimeng 1989, 53–54).

The spirit realm described above is perhaps not so foreign a concept when westerners take into consideration the traditional western theology of saints, angels, demons, the concept of Satan, also referred to as Lucifer, Iblis and the evil whisperer, the belief in the exorcism of evil spirits as a result of possessions, and finally the belief in a heaven for the good, and hell for the bad or evil souls.

Religion has always played a protective role in the lives of African Americans. Approximately 20 percent of enslaved Africans who arrived in America were Muslim; some followed the Vodun, the Orisa, and the remainder practiced traditional religions (Diouf 2007). The Vodun, which means spirit, commonly referred to as Voodoo, is a traditional monotheistic religion from coastal West Africa, Benin, Nigeria, and Haiti. Enslaved Africans brought the religion with them from Africa and often practiced it secretly. The practice was often used to predict future events, to protect a person or group from harm or to cast spells on others. The priests, or conjurers as they came to be called, used sacred objects, created potions, and employed different forms of magic during the rituals. During slavery the white ruling class tried to prohibit the practice because they feared its power and influence over the slaves (Stewart 1996).

The Orisa is part of the Yuroba religious system that centers on the belief in the various manifestations of the Olodumare or God. A young enslaved man in Mobile, Alabama, by the name of Kupollee bore the distinctive filed teeth and wore the earrings which indicated that he practiced the spiritual teachings of the Orisa and had been formally initiated into the religion. The practice allows calling upon ancestors for help in times of peril or hardship (Diouf 2007). This practice of interdependence even between those that have passed away and the living would be particularly important to enslaved Africans as a means of coping with enslavement (44).

Invoking God and the ancestors was used as a way to maintain equilibrium and reestablish control, balance, and harmony during stressful periods or events. In their 2003 study, Constantine, Gainor, Ahuluwalia, and Berkel describe this method of control as a way that African Americans combine spiritual, social and related agencies to establish harmony during volatile conditions. The study of 240 African American students revealed that cooperative and shared approaches and interdependence were positively correlated with harmony control. Those who engaged interpersonally in the activities of others were also able to intuitively anticipate others' needs and tended to rely more on a Higher Power as a means of coping.

THE BLACK CHURCH

The enslaved Africans' religion was viewed by white slave owners as primitive and uncivilized, including those enslaved Africans who were Muslims. African Americans eventually merged their African religious and spiritual practices with those of their enforced Christian ideology and created what can truly be considered a unique African American theology. The black church became the centerpiece of spiritual, social, and political reform.

According to Jackson, Rhone, and Sanders (1973), free Negroes created the black church as a strategic social institution. The church created a sense of unity and refuge from the challenges and stresses of slavery by creating a place for social interaction. Religion provided comfort and hope and suspended the rage of blacks towards whites. The church was a hub of activity, from protest to recreation; it provided a safe shelter from political and physical storms.

Between 1780 and 1830 the first recognized independent churches emerged. The African Methodist Episcopal Church (AME), formed by Bishop Richard Allen, became the first black interstate organization. The black Baptist church was later organized on the east coast.

Islam, which had been practiced by many Africans prior to enslavement, conflicted with Christian orthodoxy, so enslaved Africans were forbidden to practice it. A growing number of African Americans have embraced orthodox Islam and many others have joined the Nation of Islam founded in 1930 by Wallace Fard Muhammad, the central tenets of which promote the end of white supremacy. In whatever manner or form that African Americans have and continue to carry on their religious practices, it has and does serve as a major source of resiliency and healing.

SUMMARY

Many African Americans have continued to thrive despite past and present injuries and have been able to build upon the strengths of individuals, family, and community through strong spiritual beliefs, cultural practices, and wisdom passed down through the generations. It were these cultural and religious rituals that African Americans used to cope with the traumas that they experienced and which established a sense of meaning and worth. Much can be learned from understanding how these practices continue to assist African Americans manage their mental and physical distress due to the continued assaults to their humanity, and thus, provide their children with positive and effective cultural and spiritual stratagems to protect and prepare them for the future.

REFERENCES

Agbo, A. H. 2006. *Values of Adinkra and Agama Symbols.* Kumasi, Ghana: Bigshy Designs.

Allen, R. L., and Bagozzi, R. P. 2001. "Consequences of the Black Sense of Self." *Journal of Black Psychology* 27 (3): 3–28.

American Psychiatric Association. 1994. *Diagnostic and Statistical Manual of Mental Disorders.* 4th ed. Washington, DC: Author.

Ani, M. 1980. *Let the Circle Be Unbroken: The Implications of African Spirituality in the Diaspora.* New York: Nkonimfo Publications.

Asante, M. K., and Asante, K. W. 1985. *African Culture: The Rhythms of Unity.* Westport, CT: Greenwood Press.

Assimeng, J. M. 1989. *Religion and Social Change in West Africa: An Introduction to the Sociology of Religion.* Accra: Ghana University Press.

Bandura, A. 1969. *Principles of Behavior Modification.* New York: Holt, Rinehart and Winston.

Blakey, M. L. 2003. *Return to the African Burial Ground.* Available at: www.archaeology.org/online/interviews/blakey/.

Comer, J. P. 1980. "The Black Family: An Adaptive Perspective" [unpublished manuscript]. Yale University Study Center.

Constantine, M. G., Gainor, K. A., Ahluwalia, M. K., and Berkel, L. A. 2003. "Independent and Interdependent Self-Construals, Individualism, Collectivism, and Harmony Control in African Americans." *Journal of Black Psychology* 29 (1): 81–101.

Curtain, P. 1969. *The Atlantic Slave Trade: A Census.* Madison: University of Wisconsin Press.

Danieli, Y. 1998. *International Handbook of Multigenerational Legacies of Trauma.* New York: Plenum Press.

Diouf, A. S. 2007. *Dreams of Africa in Alabama: The Slave Ship* Clotilda *and the Story of the Last Africans Brought to America.* New York: Oxford University Press,.

Ellwood, C. A. 1913. *Sociology and Modern Social Problems.* New York: American Book Company.

Fennell, C. 2007. *Crossroads and Cosmologies: Diasporas and Ethnogenesis in the New World.* Gainesville, FL: University Press.

Fishel, L. J., and Quarles, B. 1967. *The Negro American: A Documentary History.* Glenview, IL: Scott, Foresman and Company.

Fowler, O. S., and Fowler, L. N. 1859. *The Self-Instructor in Phrenology and Physiology: With over One Hundred New Illustrations, Including a Chart for the Use of Practical Phrenologists.* Rev. by Nelson Sizer. New York: Fowler and Wells.

Galton, F. 1883. *Inquiries into Human Faculty and its Development.* London: Macmillan.

Greer, T.M. 2007. "Measuring Coping Strategies among African Americans: An Exploration of the Latent Structure of the Cope Inventory." *Journal of Black Psychology* 33 (3): 260–76.

Grier, W.H., and Cobbs, P.M. 1968. *Black Rage.* New York: Basic Books.

Gutman, H.G. 1976. *The Black Family in Slavery and Freedom.* New York: Random House.

Haller, J.S. 1971. *Outcasts from Evolution.* Chicago, IL: Illinois Press.

Jackson, W.S., Rhone, J.V., and Sanders, C.L. 1973. *The Social Service Delivery System in the Black Community during the Ante-Bellum Period (1619–1860).* Alton M. Childs Series. Atlanta, GA: Atlanta University School of Social Work.

Jones, F., and Jones, A.C. 2001. *The Triumph of the Soul: Cultural and Psychological Aspects of African American Music.* Westport, CT: Praeger Publishers.

Leary, J.D. 2001. *Trying to Kill the Part of You That Isn't Loved* [doctoral dissertation]. Portland State University.

Leary, J.D. 2005. *Post-Traumatic Slave Syndrome: America's Legacy of Enduring Injury and Healing.* Portland, OR: Uptone Press.

Longres, J.F. 1995. *Human Behavior in the Social Environment.* 2nd. ed. Itasca, Illinois: F.E. Peacock.

Madison, J. 1788. "The Apportionment of Members among the States." *Federalist Papers,* 54.

Mbiti, J.S. 1970. *African Religions and Philosophy.* New York: Praeger Publishers.

Nichols, E.J. 1976. *Introduction to the Axiological Model.* Paper presented to the World Psychiatric Association and the Nigerian Association of Psychiatrists. University of Ibadan, Nigeria.

Ogbu, J.U. 1990. "Racial Stratification and Education." In *U.S. Race Relations in the 1980s and 1990s: Challenges and Alternatives,* ed. G.E. Thomas, 3–29. New York: Hemisphere Publishing Company.

Owoahene, A.S. 1998. *Inculturation and African Religion: Indigenous and Western Approaches to Medical Practice.* New York: Peter Lang.

Public Broadcasting Service. 2006. Rebroadcast in 2008. "Africans in America" series. Available at: http://www.pbs.org/wgbh/aia/home.html.

Samuels, J.R. 1980. *The M.O. Scale.* Lecture presented at the Mentat School, Inc., Portland, Oregon.

Somé, S. 1997. *The Spirit of Intimacy: Ancient African Teachings in the Ways of Relationships.* New York: Harper Collins Publishers.

Stewart, C.J. 1996. *1001 Things Everyone Should Know about African American History.* New York: Doubleday.

Thomas, H. 1997. *The Slave Trade: The Story of the Atlantic Slave Trade, 1440–1870.* New York: Touchstone.

Wiggins, R. C. 1996. *Captain Paul Cuffe's Logs and Letters 1808–1817: A Black Quaker's "Voice from within the Veil."* Washington, DC: Howard University Press.

Woodson, C. G. 1990 *The Mis-Education of the Negro.* Trenton, NJ: African World Press. (Originally published, 1933).

Chapter 14

STRIVING FOR PEACE THROUGH FORGIVENESS IN SIERRA LEONE

Effectiveness of a Psychoeducational Forgiveness Intervention

Loren L. Toussaint,
Nancy Peddle,
Alyssa Cheadle,
Anthony Sellu, and
Frederic Luskin

Learning to forgive those who have wronged us is the first step
we can take towards healing our traumatised nation.
—Bishop Joseph Christian Humper

ABSTRACT

The purpose of this chapter is twofold. First, forgiveness is discussed as a culturally relevant response for coping and meaning-making in the wake of a decade-long civil war in Sierra Leone. Cultural aspects of coping which include rituals and traditions are discussed. A case is made for forgiveness as a culturally appropriate means of coping with the trauma of civil war. Second, an adaptation of a university-based forgiveness education curriculum is discussed. Development of this curriculum for Sierra Leoneans is described and its scientific evaluation is presented. The results of our evaluation suggest that adapting a research-driven psychoeducational forgiveness curriculum was effective in eliciting individual-level change that ultimately can provide the foundation for group and cultural forgiveness.

FORGIVENESS, TRAUMA, AND HEALING

Geopolitical Census

Sierra Leone is located on the west coast of Africa on the Atlantic Ocean, with Guinea situated to the north, Liberia on the southeast, and the

Atlantic Ocean on the southwest. The country is small, covering a total area of only 73,000 square kilometers, and is divided into four regions: Northern, Southern, Eastern, and Western Area (where the capital, Freetown, is situated). There are 12 districts and 149 chiefdoms that use both modern and traditional governance styles.

Sierra Leone's latest census figures (Statistics Sierra Leone 2006) demonstrate that the population is approximately 5 million, with 13 different ethnic tribes and 23 different languages. The two main religions are Islam and Christianity. Also, the majority of citizens identify themselves as being Muslim (60%), while almost one-third continue to hold traditional beliefs. Religious tolerance is a unique feature of Sierra Leone and is not a contributing factor to the friction between groups.

Civil War

In 1991, rebel forces initiated the first power grab in eastern Sierra Leone. The country had a moment of hope in 1996 when popular former UN diplomat Ahmad Tejan Kabbah was elected president. In the following year, the rebels consolidated power in the villages and countryside and threatened the stability of Freetown, the capital. In 1997, the rebels overthrew the president and violently ruled the country for a period of 10 months. The ensuing three years were plagued with power struggles between the rebels and the former government of President Kabbah. During this time the people of Sierra Leone experienced significant carnage, disruption, and pain. Many civilians and soldiers joined the rebel forces while others were recruited against their will. An appalling number of children were recruited and forced to serve as child soldiers. In May 2000, British troops were deployed to Sierra Leone to stabilize the country and on January 18, 2002, President Kabbah declared that the civil war was officially over.

Seven-Year Aftermath

The decade-long war resulted in tens of thousands of deaths, hundreds of thousands maimed, mutilated and disabled, and more than 2 million people displaced from their homes. Some still remain refugees in neighboring countries. Rural-to-urban migration was accelerated during the war, as camps for displaced people were set up in and around the capital city of Freetown, thus contributing to massive overcrowding. People were slow to move back to their places of origin, which taxed Freetown's infrastructure and resulted in food shortages and an exorbitant cost of living.

The devastating effects of Sierra Leone's civil war on all aspects of life cannot be overestimated. In 2005, Sierra Leone scored lowest on the United

Nations Development Program's Human Development Index, which measures health, education, and economic indicators (2007/2008 Human Development Reports). The average life expectancy in Sierra Leone is 42 years, which is one of the lowest in the world. In addition, one in four children dies before the age of five. Sierra Leone has the highest infant and maternal mortality rate in the world, no doubt due to an underfinanced and overburdened health care system. More recently, Sierra Leone received the dubious distinction of being rated the worst place to be a woman in Sub-Saharan Africa. One in eight women die during pregnancy or childbirth and girls can expect to receive only six years of schooling. More than 80 percent of girls are subject to female genital mutilation (FGM) and an estimated one-third of the country's women and girls have suffered from sexual violence. Widows struggle to get by, survivors of wartime rape face stigma and discrimination, and men continue to assault women with impunity. In 2007 the Parliament finally enacted laws that criminalize wife-beating and allow women to inherit property. How well these laws will be enforced by the government and traditional leaders remains to be seen.

Many of the Sierra Leonean cultural traditions were strained and/or altered because of the war and resulted in poverty and migration. For example, in 2007 it was estimated that countless girls had not gone through the traditional rite of passage into womanhood because of the war (Female Genital Mutilation 2009). This ceremony traditionally involved female genital mutilation. It usually can last from six months to two years and is done with great secrecy. In addition, the Truth and Reconciliation Commission's (TRC) report on Sierra Leone demonstrated that many other long-held traditions and cultural rituals were discarded as more and more people joined the war (TRC Sierra Leone).

Cultural, Religious, and Ritualistic Forms of Coping

A variety of cultural traditions and rituals have been used in Sierra Leone by communities and aid workers to help those through the process of healing. The task is a daunting one, to help people deal with the atrocities they experienced, while aiding in the everyday concerns that make development problematic. Traditional cultural practices were extensively used by those attempting to heal during the war, even as people were still engaged in the fighting (Peddle 1998). These same practices were again called upon to assist with the reintegration of survivors, as well as the perpetrators of the war after the fighting ceased. Commonly used cultural traditions and rituals include: (1) storytelling, (2) singing, (3) drumming and dancing, (4) pouring of libations, (5) cleansing ceremonies, (6) proper burials, (7) respect for the dead, and (8) forgiveness. Traditional cultural practices are also currently used in variety of health and human welfare initiatives such as fighting HIV/AIDS, ending harmful traditional practices like female genital mutilation, understanding human rights, and other such initiatives. It is believed that using culturally appropriate interventions drawn from a community's experiences and knowledge can increase the long-term self-reliance of communities, families, and children (Peddle et al. 2005). Interventions encourage all community members, including children, to take active roles in identifying the problems and formulating workable solutions.

Forgiveness as a Culturally Relevant Way of Coping with Trauma

The TRC in Sierra Leone promoted the idea that healing practices should be based on the culture and traditions of the people when possible. Hence, the TRC sought assistance from traditional and religious leaders to facilitate public discussions and help with resolving conflicts arising from past violence to promote healing and if possible, reconciliation. Based on the South African TRC model, forgiveness was an important intervention in Sierra Leone. The president of the country provided strong leadership to promote forgiveness at every level throughout the country and pleaded with the population to forgive one another. Religious and traditional leaders were also instrumental in promoting and conducting ceremonies of forgiveness and reconciliation. Forgiveness, combined with other healing strategies, such as telling the trauma story, has been used as a therapeutic approach in a number of countries with some success (Dubrow and Peddle 1997; Schumm 1995; Staub and Perlman 2000). In addition, forgiveness has also been used to promote healing (Johnson et al. 1995; Truth & Reconciliation Commission, Sierra Leone 2004) with refugees (Peddle 2007), and with generational transmission of genocide (Kalayjian 1999).

In Sierra Leone, ceremonies were held in which chiefs acted on behalf of the community to symbolically acknowledge the wrongdoings and pave the way for victims and perpetrators to live together. The ceremonies were held in the villages and a former rebel member would kneel or lie in the dirt begging for forgiveness for himself and other former fighters in the village. Next, the chief would touch his head and accept him back into the community. While the chief can extend forgiveness on behalf of the community, and was encouraged to do so by the TRC, the chief cannot offer forgiveness on the *individual* level. Instead, this can only be done when the victim and perpetrator meet face to face.

Other interventions are needed to help facilitate forgiveness on the individual level. One of the difficulties with individual forgiveness involves the complications of intrapersonal and interpersonal dynamics. While a community may have extended a symbolic from of forgiveness, certain individual members of the community may still harbor resentment and a desire for revenge. These intrapersonal and interpersonal issues are important for victims to work through so that they can experience genuine forgiveness and remain integrated in the forgiving community.

Approaches to Forgiveness Education

Understanding the role of intergroup forgiveness as a mechanism of bringing peace to communities that have experienced violence is an important area of study. Recently an entire issue of the journal *Peace and Conflict: Journal of Peace Psychology* (Wagner 2007) was devoted to this topic. Authors discussed the important, though sometimes controversial, role of intergroup forgiveness in paving the way to lasting peace in such diverse settings as Australia, Congo, South Africa, Chile, and Northern Ireland (Chapman 2007; Ferguson et al. 2007; Kadiangandu and Mullet 2007; Manzi and Gonzalez 2007; Mellor, Bretherton, and Firth 2007). While journal discussions provide confirmation that scholars recognize the importance of intergroup forgiveness in the peace process, little attention has been paid to the role of *intrapersonal* and *interpersonal* forgiveness as the cornerstone of intergroup forgiveness. The reality is that individual-level forgiveness research and intervention work in violent and distressed areas of the world has only just begun.

Although limited, the research that does exist suggests that individual-level forgiveness plays an important role in reconciliation and peace. Some examples come from the work of Friedberg et al. (2005), Kaminer et al. (2001), Stein et al. (2008), and Peddle (2007). Friedberg et al. measured individual-level forgiveness of others, stress, and rumination on the one-year anniversary of the 9/11 terrorist attacks. What they found was that forgiveness of others predicted less rumination and stress. Furthermore, there was some evidence that forgiveness was associated with lower levels of rumination that appeared to have a positive association with stress.

Stein et al. (2008) measured participation and perceptions of the South African TRC and its relationship to forgiveness of others. They found that mere participation in the TRC was predictive of *less* rather than more forgiveness of others. Rather, positive perceptions of both victims' and perpetrators' experiences with the TRC were important factors associated with increased levels of forgiveness. Kaminer et al. (2001) evaluated the experience of forgiveness and psychiatric status among South Africans living in the Western Cape region. Their results demonstrated that lower levels of forgiveness were associated with higher risk of psychiatric morbidity. Peddle (2007) examined the role of forgiveness in healing following trauma in refugees affected by the war. She used both quantitative and qualitative measures and in both assessments it was revealed that those who scored higher in forgiveness also tended to score higher in positive well-being.

In sum, these studies suggest that with respect to populations that have experienced traumatic social violence, forgiveness may serve as an individual-level mechanism that reduces stress and promotes psychiatric health. Furthermore, forgiveness appears to be associated with one's perceptions of reconciliation efforts. To the extent that forgiveness is considered a necessary component of reconciliation (Worthington 2006), it is critical for peace workers to find and develop methods of fostering forgiveness which may then in turn promote reconciliation.

While effective approaches to fostering forgiveness in areas of the world with histories of violence and conflict are few and far between, there are a few examples that offer some optimism. The first example is Enright's work with children in Belfast, Northern Ireland (Enright et al. 2007; 2007; Holter, Martin, and Enright 2006). Enright and his colleagues used a process model of forgiveness similar to the one that has been successful in helping individuals that have experienced painful events (e.g., Freedman and Enright 1996). This process model consists of four major content units subdivided into 20 individual steps (Enright and Fitzgibbons 2000). In Belfast, Enright et al. chose to work with young children in first through third grades. As a result, they needed an appropriate curriculum for these children. Therefore they developed a three part curriculum that focused on five core themes including: (1) inherent worth, (2) moral love, (3) kindness, (4) respect, and (5) generosity. The results of Enright et al.'s work (2007) showed that children who received the forgiveness education exhibited less anger and depression and more prosocial behaviors.

The second example of an effective approach to fostering forgiveness and reconciliation is Staub, Pearlman, Gubin, and Hagengimana's intervention in Rwanda (2005). Staub et al. worked with group facilitators who conducted a nine-day seminar that focused on psychoeducational and experiential aspects of reconciliation and healing. The group facilitators then offered the curriculum to 194 rural Rwandese. Pre- and postevaluations of trauma symptoms and readiness to reconcile revealed that the intervention was successful in reducing trauma symptoms and facilitating a readiness to reconcile. However, it should be noted that Staub et al.'s work was comprehensive and multidimensional, and therefore the benefit of this training is due only in part, to the promotion of forgiveness.

The final example of an effective approach to forgiveness education in victims of conflict, violence, and trauma is the work of Luskin and Bland

(2000, 2001). Luskin and Bland worked with victims of violence from Northern Ireland in two studies. In the first study (2000), five women were brought to Stanford University for several days to complete the first Stanford-Northern Ireland HOPE Project. In the second study (2001), 17 men and women attended the second HOPE Project. In both cases, forgiveness training focused on nine key components: (1) telling one's story, (2) committing to forgiveness, (3) understanding what forgiveness is, (4) changing perspective, (5) stress relaxation, (6) adjusting unreasonable expectations, (7) refocusing on the positive, (8) empowerment, and (9) positively reframing one's story of hurt.

Participants in the HOPE projects showed measurable improvements in hurt, anger, depression, stress, optimism, and forgiveness. It is important to note that Luskin's approach to forgiveness focuses solely on the individual and not the group. While symbolic gestures of group forgiveness may be important in the quest for group reconciliation and peace, Luskin's (2002) approach is based on the belief that group forgiveness emerges through forgiving individuals. Hence, his attempt in Northern Ireland was to provide evidence for effective forgiveness education that could be used with victims of violence who were impeding progress toward peace. Luskin's model can easily be adapted and transferred to new individuals and new situations, due in large part to the accessibility of his training to the lay public. For this reason we chose to apply Luskin's forgiveness education in our work in Sierra Leone.

A PSYCHOEDUCATIONAL FORGIVENESS INTERVENTION IN SIERRA LEONE

In order to prepare to work in the Sierra Leone culture, one dramatically different from where Luskin's curriculum had been developed, we considered the critical areas described by Peddle et al (2005) and Nader, Dubrow, and Stamm (1999): place; time; religion, spirituality, and ceremonies; literature; primacy of the family-social status; death and dying; and coming in from the "outside." This provided us with a framework from which to design our education and research in a culturally sensitive way. Our main purpose and hope was to develop a culturally relevant version of Luskin's curriculum that could provide a positive stimulus for reconciliation and peace through forgiveness education.

Design and Methodology

Our project was both service and science-oriented. We wanted to provide useful training in forgiveness, but we also wanted to understand the effectiveness of this work. Hence, the design of our study included two parts: (1) curriculum development and implementation, and (2) intervention evaluation.

Curriculum

Development. To develop our forgiveness education curriculum we started with Luskin's established and validated *Forgive for Good* curriculum. We modified it to reflect the needs of the Sierra Leone culture by using Peddle et al.'s (2005) and Nader, Dubrow, and Stamm's (1999) work as a guide to cultural sensitivity. The leaders of the forgiveness training in Sierra Leone (Toussaint, Cheadle and Sellu) started by enrolling in a forgiveness course offered by Luskin. This course was offered via the internet, was fully interactive, and offered streaming video as well as private and public chat options. The course consisted of five 90-minute sessions spread over five weeks. During this time our team was in frequent conversation about the nature of forgiveness training and its essential elements. Our next step was to develop culturally relevant *Forgive for Good* materials for Sierra Leone. During this phase of the curriculum development Toussaint, Peddle, Luskin and team members Cheadle and Sellu worked collaboratively to adapt the original *Forgive for Good* materials.

First, we adapted them to the Sierra Leone culture, relying heavily on team members Anthony Sellu and Dr. Peddle to provide insight, suggestions, and modifications to ensure cultural appropriateness of the curriculum. Second, we developed two versions of the curriculum. The first is suitable for adults while the other is suitable for children. In developing the children's version we relied heavily on the input of our teaching consultants (Jan Krinsley and Meagan Cox) from the Palo Alto, California, school district. Our consultants provided age-appropriate activities and guidance for delivering the *Forgive for Good* curriculum. These activities made the children's curriculum more experiential than the adult version.

Materials. The curricular materials consisted of several items. First, Luskin found a donor to provide 100 copies of his book *Forgive for Good*. These books were transported to Sierra Leone and distributed to all adult participants. Several other copies were provided to school administrators, staff, and teachers. In addition, the remaining copies were donated to local schools and libraries. Second, 50 bound copies of a culturally-appropriate adult workbook based on Luskin's original workbook was developed and taken to Sierra Leone. Third, donors provided age appropriate supplies for use in delivering the children's curriculum. These supplies ranged from incentives and treats (e.g., toothbrushes, teddy bears, pencils and pens) to materials used for visualization and imagery tasks (i.e., Polaroid camera).

Implementation. To implement the curriculum, Toussaint, Cheadle and Sellu traveled to Sierra Leone in July of 2007. We were hosted at the Dele-Peddle International School in Freetown, a preparatory school sponsored by the LemonAid fund (www.lemonaidfund.org). We spent five days at this school working with teachers and students. Our first day was spent only with teachers and consisted of providing an orientation and completing the baseline assessment. Over the next four days, we met with the teachers for approximately one-and-a-half to two hours each day. During this time we discussed reading assignments, workbook exercises, and instructional strategies, answered questions, and discussed issues such as civil war, societal forgiveness, and the Sierra Leonean culture. Per Sierra Leonean custom, we began each meeting with a prayer. We ended each session with guidance on how to provide forgiveness education to the nearly 150 children of the school. Each day teachers were both participants in the *Forgive for Good* curriculum and facilitators, as they led students through the age adapted curriculum.

Evaluation

Evaluating the effectiveness of our curriculum proved to be challenging for numerous reasons. First, we had to limit our evaluation to the teachers who completed the curriculum. In addition, we would have liked to have evaluated the children both before and after our training. However, the very large number of children involved made it impossible for us to do so. Also, we tried to limit our program to a specific age group, yet the desperate need for intervention at all ages compelled us to include anyone who wanted to participate. Even though we chose our evaluation assessments carefully and piloted them, in Sierra Leone they required greater time to complete than we had anticipated. Therefore we had to prioritize, and we chose to incorporate extra teaching rather than evaluation of children in addition to adults. With these challenges, we did succeed in providing the training to the teachers and children but only evaluated adults' changes in psychosocial variables from pre- to post-intervention.

Participants. Twenty four adult teachers ($M = 33$ years of age) participated in our evaluation effort. Thirteen of these teachers were randomly assigned to participate in the forgiveness training and eleven teachers were randomly assigned to the control group. We had planned that the teachers assigned to the control group would receive the training following the initial evaluation phase; however, due to security threats at the school (i.e., armed robbery), we were unable to complete the second phase of our training work. In the initial evaluation, there were more male (n = 16) than female teachers (n = 7), more unmarried (n = 13) than married teachers (n = 11), and parents of between zero and four children. The education levels of the teachers ranged from junior secondary school (roughly equivalent to middle school in the United States) to greater than a four year college degree. Not surprisingly, monthly income indicated extreme poverty and ranged from \$5 to \$133 (Median = \$60). All participants provided consent and volunteered freely to participate.

Measures. Our approach to assessment was multifaceted. We attempted to assess multiple aspects of psychosocial functioning that might be impacted by our forgiveness education. These included forgiveness, gratitude, and mental well-being (i.e., stress, depression, and happiness). *Forgiveness* itself was assessed using two standard forgiveness assessments. The Heartland Forgiveness Scale (HFS: Thompson et al. 2005) measured dispositional forgiveness, which is the tendency to be forgiving of oneself, others, and situations; the Transgression-Related Interpersonal Motivations Inventory (TRIM: McCullough, Root, and Cohen 2006) measured motivations (i.e., avoidance, revenge, benevolence) toward a specific transgressor. Both instruments use Likert-type response scales and consisted of 18 items. While both the HFS and TRIM have demonstrated acceptable reliability and validity, in the present sample the reliability of these measures was insufficient on four out of the six possible subscales. Only the avoidance and benevolence subscales of the TRIM demonstrated acceptable reliability (αs = .73–84).

Gratitude was assessed using the Gratitude Questionaire-6 (GQ-6; McCullough, Emmons, & Tsang 2002). This scale assesses aspects of gratefulness, appreciation, and feelings about receiving from others. It contains six items that are rated on a Likert-type response scale. Previous research (McCullough et al. 2002) has shown acceptable reliability and validity for this scale. Reliability for pre- and post-assessments of gratitude were acceptable (αs = .65).

Mental well-being was assessed by observing three domains of psychological health: stress, depression, and happiness. *Stress* was measured by the 10-item version of the Perceived Stress Scale (PSS: Cohen, Kamarck, and Mermelstein 1983), the most widely used measure of stress. The PSS measures perceived lack of control and uncertainty in an individual's life. Items are responded to on a Likert-type scale and acceptable levels of reliability and validity have been documented (Cohen, Kamarck, and Mermelstein 1983). In the present sample, the PSS demonstrated acceptable levels of reliability for a short scale (αs = .53–65). *Depression* was measured by a commonly used assessment tool, the Center for Epidemiologic Studies-Depression 10-item Scale (CES-D 10 Radloff, 1977). This instrument measures on a Likert-type scale the frequency an individual experiences the most common symptoms of depression. The CES-D 10 is a psychometrically reliable and valid instrument (Radloff 1977) and in the present study demonstrated acceptable levels of reliability (αs = .60–67). The final domain measured was *happiness*. Happiness was assessed by measuring mood and satisfaction with life. Mood was assessed using the 20-item Positive and Negative Affect Schedule (PANAS: Watson, Clark, and Tellegen 1988), and life satisfaction was assessed using the 5-item Satisfaction with Life scale (SWLS: Diener, Emmons, Larsen, and Griffen 1985). Both measures utilize Likert-type response scales and have been found to have acceptable psychometric properties (Diener et al.; Watson et al.). In the present study the reliability of the negative affect and the life satisfaction scales was acceptable (αs = .63–.76); however, the reliability of the positive affect scale was not.

Analyses. Our analyses compared the control group to the forgiveness education group on levels of forgiveness, gratitude, and mental well-being. We used analyses of covariance (ANCOVA) for these comparisons, which allowed us to control differences between control and forgiveness groups at pretest and to compare differences in adjusted levels of forgiveness, gratitude, and mental well-being at posttest. Due to the pilot nature of this work and the small sample sizes involved in our statistical tests, we decided to apply an alpha level of .10 as significant. We paid special attention to the size of the differences in reporting our results. We did so in an attempt to balance between type I and type II errors (Cohen 1977) and to ensure that the practical value of intervention efforts is not overlooked due to the lack of power to reject the null hypothesis.

RESULTS

Forgiveness and Gratitude

We treated our analyses of forgiveness differently than we did the other data. We computed change scores on the two reliable subscales of the TRIM which represented changes in avoidance and benevolence motivations from pre-to post-intervention. We then used ANCOVA to calculate differences between control and forgiveness groups in changes in avoidance and benevolence while holding constant variations in the length of time since the transgression occurred. We did this because recent evidence (McCullough et al., under review) suggests that forgiveness follows a distinct temporal pattern that is related to the time since the transgression occurred. By using time since the offense as a covariate, we removed the effect of time from our computations, regarding the pre- to post-change in avoidance and benevolence across our forgiveness training. When we conducted this analysis, we found that the control and forgiveness groups did not differ significantly on the avoidance scale, $F (1, 21) = .53$, $p = .48$, $\eta^2 = .02$, but did differ on the benevolence scale, $F (1, 21) = 5.14$, $p = .03$, $\eta^2 = .19$. Furthermore, the size of this difference was large, according to Cohen's rubric for determining effect size (Cohen 1977). Participants in the forgiveness group showed much larger increases in benevolent motivations than those in the control group (see Figure 14.1).

Gratitude and Mental Well-Being

Our analyses of gratitude and mental well-being demonstrated change on each outcome measure. In all cases we used ANCOVA to control for pre-existing levels of the variable and then compared the control and forgiveness groups at posttest. As compared to the control group, those who completed the forgiveness education exhibited lower levels of negative mood, $F (1, 20) = 3.57$, $p = .07$, $\eta^2 = .15$, stress, $F (1, 21) = 3.17$, $p = .09$, $\eta^2 = .13$, and

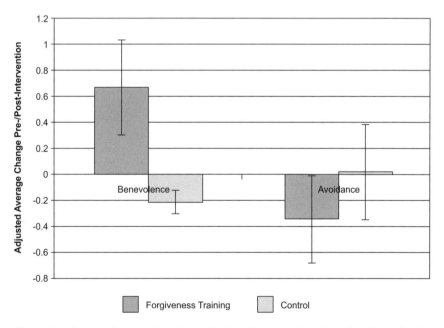

Figure 14.1. Average increases (positive values) or decreases (negative values) in unforgiving motives for forgiveness education and control groups controlling for the amount of time since the offense occurred.

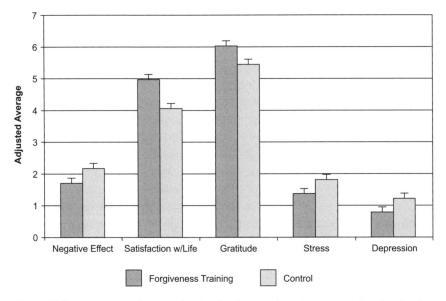

Figure 14.2. Average post-intervention levels of gratitude and mental well-being for forgiveness education and control groups controlling for pre-intervention levels.

depression, $F(1, 21) = 4.99$, $p = .04$, $\eta^2 = .19$, and higher levels of gratitude, $F(1, 21) = 3.73$ $p = .07$, $\eta^2 = .15$, and life satisfaction, $F(1, 21) = 5.17$, $p = .03$, $\eta^2 = .20$ (see Figure 14.2). In all cases, the size of the differences between groups was very large.

ANALYSIS OF RESULTS

The main goal of our forgiveness education intervention was to develop a culturally relevant version of Luskin's (2002) *Forgive for Good* curriculum to use in Sierra Leone and scientifically evaluate its effectiveness. Through the collaborative work of our team and consultants, we developed cultural and age-appropriate versions of the *Forgive for Good* curriculum and successfully delivered them in Sierra Leone. Our evaluation provides support for the effectiveness of this approach. Forgiveness education resulted in improved mental well-being and the development of more benevolent dispositions among adult participants. Importantly, those who participated in the training showed dramatically improved levels of benevolent motives toward their offenders. In sum, these findings are similar to several studies showing important associations between forgiveness and mental health, well-being, and positive effects of forgiveness education in developed countries (for reviews see, Toussaint and Webb 2005; Wade, Worthington, and Meyer 2005).

Given that participants were randomly assigned to the forgiveness education and control groups, threats to the validity of these findings as a result of selection factors are not likely. That is, often in this type of field work the effectiveness of different interventions has to be measured by comparing intervention and control groups where participants were allowed to determine if they wanted to participate in the intervention or not. This causes serious problems in interpreting the effectiveness of the intervention itself, since the results could be due to the fact that those who chose to be in the intervention group may possess characteristics such as higher motivation, commitment, or personal relevance. Our randomized assignment procedure eliminates this confounder.

Two other factors are important to note with respect to our evaluation work. First, our education efforts used excellent assessment tools with long histories of use and strong psychometric characteristics. This is an improvement over studies of this type that often rely on personal anecdotes for evidence of effectiveness (Ross and Rothman 1999). Second, our intervention was based on a standard forgiveness education curriculum. Hence, while small in scale and pilot in nature, our study may be the first randomized, controlled trial of forgiveness education in an impoverished area with a history of civil war.

DISCUSSION

In nations with violent pasts, survivors face the challenge of making sense of these events while simultaneously trying to restore hope for the future. Although many approaches may be used to help people move forward, forgiveness appears to be a particularly hopeful means of coping. In Sierra Leone the devastation and hurt from a decade-long civil war is readily evident and the trauma and grief that Sierra Leoneans endured has not been easy to overcome. Unanswered questions for the provision of psychosocial support and intervention are: (1) Can forgiveness be made culturally appropriate? (2) Can attempts to promote forgiveness be effective in improving individual levels of well-being and peace?

Although cultures may exist where forgiveness interventions may be problematic, our experience in Sierra Leone suggests that attempts to foster forgiveness are culturally appropriate and well-received. Furthermore, we provide scientific evidence that these efforts can be effective agents of change in stimulating hope, well-being, and peace at the individual level. As Sierra Leone's Bishop Joseph Christian Humper stated, "Learning to forgive those who have wronged us is the first step we can take towards healing our traumatized nation" (Humper 2004). Our belief is that forgiveness must begin with individual citizens. Effective strategies that promote forgiveness at the individual level will create a groundswell of forgiveness that can offer resolution and relief that transcend the boundaries of states, nations, and cultures.

ACKNOWLEDGMENT

The work described in this chapter was made possible through the support of the Nena Amundson Lifetime Wellness Program and Study Abroad office at Luther College, a grant from the Davis Projects for Peace program to the third and fourth authors when they were students at Luther College, and by the generosity of numerous individual and organizational donors.

REFERENCES

Chapman, A. 2007. "Truth Commissions and Intergroup Forgiveness: The Case of the South African Truth and Reconciliation Commission." *Peace and Conflict: Journal of Peace Psychology* 13: 51–69.

Cohen, J. 1977. *Statistical Power Analysis for the Behavioral Sciences.* Rev. ed. Hillsdale, NJ: Lawrence Erlbaum Associates.

Cohen, S., Kamarck, T., and Mermelstein, R. 1983. "A Global Measure of Perceived Stress." *Journal of Health and Social Behavior* 24: 385–96.

Diener, E., Emmons, R. Larsen, R., and Griffen, S. 1985. "The Satisfaction with Life Scale." *Journal of Personality Assessment* 49: 71–75.

Dubrow, N., and Peddle, N. 1997. *Trauma Healing and Peace Education Training Manual.* 2nd ed. Chicago, IL: Taylor Institute.

Enright, R. D., and Fitzgibbons, R. P. 2000. *Helping Clients Forgive: An Empirical Guide for Resolving Anger and Restoring Hope.* Washington, DC: American Psychological Association.

Enright, R. D., Knutson, J. A., Holter, A. C., Baskin, T., and Knutson, C. 2007. "Waging Peace through Forgiveness in Belfast, Northern Ireland. II: Educational Programs for Mental Health Improvement of Children." *Journal of Research in Education* (Fall): 63–78.

"Female Genital Mutilation a Vote-Winner in Sierra Leone." 2009. Afrol News (March 5). Available at: http://www.afrol.com/articles/15927.

Ferguson, N., Binks, E., Roe, M., Brown, J., Adams, T., Cruise, S., and Lewis, C. 2007. "The IRA Apology of 2002 and Forgiveness in Northern Ireland's Troubles: A Cross-National Study of Printed Media." *Peace & Conflict* 13: 93–113.

Freedman, S. R., and Enright, E. D. 1996. "Forgiveness as an Intervention Goal with Incest Survivors." *Journal of Consulting and Clinical Psychology* 64: 983–92.

Friedberg, J. P., Adonis, M. N., Von Bergen, H. A., and Suchday, S. 2005. "Short Communication: September 11th Related Stress and Trauma in New Yorkers." *Stress and Health* 21: 53–60.

Holter, A. C., Martin, J., and Enright, R. 2006. "Restoring Justice through Forgiveness: The Case of Children in Northern Ireland." In *The Handbook
of Restorative Justice: A Global Perspective,* eds. D. Sullivan and L.Tifft,
311–320. New York: Routledge.

Humper, J. C. 2004. *Witness to Truth: Report of the Sierra Leone Truth and Reconciliation Commission.* Vol.1. [Foreward]. Accra, Ghana: Graphic Packaging.

Johnson, D. R., Feldman, S. C., Lubin, H., and Southwick, S. M. 1995. "The Therapeutic Use of Ritual and Ceremony in the Treatment of Post-Traumatic
Stress Disorder." Journal of Traumatic Stress 8 (2): 283–98.

Kadiangandu, K. J., and Mullet, E. 2007. "Intergroup Forgiveness: A Congolese
Perspective." *Peace & Conflict* 13: 37–49.

Kalayjian, A. S. 1999. "Forgiveness and Transcendence." *Clio's Psyche* 6 (3):
116–19.

Kaminer, D., Stein, D., Mbanga, I., and Zungu-Dirwayi, N. 2001. "The Truth and
Reconciliation Commission in South Africa: Relation to Psychiatric Status
and Forgiveness among Survivors of Human Rights Abuses." *British Journal of Psychiatry* 178: 373–77.

Luskin, F. 2002. *Forgive for Good: A Proven Prescription for Health and Happiness.* San Francisco: Harper.

Luskin, F., and Bland, B. 2000. *Stanford-Northern Ireland HOPE 1 Project.* Available at: http://learningtoforgive.com/researchfiles/hope1.htm.

Luskin, F., and Bland, B. 2001. *Stanford-Northern Ireland HOPE 2 Project.* Available at: http://learningtoforgive.com/researchfiles/hope2.htm.

Manzi, J., and Gonzalez, R. 2007. "Forgiveness and Reparation in Chile: The
Role of Cognitive and Emotional Intergroup Antecedents." *Peace & Conflict* 13: 71–91.

McCullough, M. E., Emmons, R. A., and Tsang, J. A. 2002. "The Grateful Disposition: A Conceptual and Empirical Topography." *Journal of Personality
and Social Psychology* 82: 112–27.

McCullough, M. E., Root, L. M., Berry, J. W., Tabak, B. A., and Bono, G. [under
review]. "On the Form of Forgiving."

McCullough, M. E., Root, L. M., and Cohen, A. D. 2006. "Writing about the Personal Benefits of a Transgression Facilitates Forgiveness." *Journal of Consulting and Clinical Psychology* 74: 887–97.

Mellor, D., Bretherton, D., and Firth, L. 2007. "Aboriginal and Non-Aboriginal
Australia: The Dilemma of Apologies, Forgiveness, and Reconciliation."
Peace & Conflict 13: 11–36.

Nader, K., Dubrow, N., and Stamm, B. H. 1999. *Honoring Differences: Cultural
Issues in the Treatment of Trauma and Loss.* New York: Routledge.

Peddle, N. 1998. "National Kids in Distress Project." United Nations Chronicle
35: 46–7.

Peddle, N. 2007. "Reflections of a Study on Forgiveness in Recovery from/Resiliency
to the Trauma of War." In *Women's Reflections on the Complexities of Forgiveness,* eds. W. Malcolm, N. DeCourville, and K. Belicki, 187–213. New York:
Taylor & Frances.

Peddle, N., Stamm, B., Hudnall, A., and Stamm, H. 2006. "Effective Intercultural Collaboration on Psychosocial Support Programs." In *Handbook of International Disaster Psychology: Fundamentals and Overview,* 1: 113–26. Westport, CT: Praeger Publishers/Greenwood Publishing Group.

Radloff, L. S. 1977. "The CES–D Scale: A Self-Report Depression Scale for Research in the General Population." *Applied Psychological Measurement* 1: 385–401.

Ross, M. H., and Rothman, J. 1999. *Theory and Practice in Ethnic Conflict Management: Theorizing Success and Failure.* New York: Macmillan.

Schumm, D. H. (1995). "Forgiveness in the Healing Process." In *Healing the Children of War: A Handbook for Ministry to Children Who Have Suffered Deep Traumas.* ed. P. Kilbourne, 267–83. Monrovia, CA: MARC Publications.

Statistics Sierra Leone 2006. *Final Results: 2004 Population and Housing Census.* Freetown, Sierra Leone: GOSL.

Staub, E., and Pearlman, L. 2000. P. Kilbourn, eds. *Healing, Forgiveness, and Reconciliation in Rwanda: Project Summary and Outcome.* Available at: http://www.theworld.com/~gubin/Rwandafiles/Tempfinal.htm.

Staub, E., Pearlman, L., Gubin, A., and Hagengimana, A. 2005. "Healing, Reconciliation, Forgiving, and the Prevention of Violence after Genocide or Mass Killing: An Intervention and its Experimental Evaluation in Rwanda." *Journal of Social and Clinical Psychology* 24: 297–334.

Stein, D., Seedat, S., Kaminer, D., Moomal, H., Herman, A., Sonnega, J., and Williams, D. R. 2008. "The Impact of the Truth and Reconciliation Commission on Psychological Distress and Forgiveness in South Africa." *Social Psychiatry and Psychiatric Epidemiology* 34 (6): 462–68.

Thompson, L. Y., Snyder, C. R., Hoffman, L., Michael, S. T., Rasmussen, H. N., Billings, L. S., Heinze, L., Neufeld, J. E., Shorey, H. S., Roberts, J. C., and Roberts, D. E. 2005. "Dispositional Forgiveness of Self, Others, and Situations." *Journal of Personality* 73: 313–61.

Toussaint, L. L., and Webb, J. R. 2005. "Theoretical and Empirical Connections between Forgiveness, Mental Health, and Well-Being." In *Handbook of Forgiveness,* ed. E. L. Worthington. New York: Brunner-Routledge.

Truth & Reconciliation Commission, Sierra Leone. Available at: http://www. trcsierraleone.org/drwebsite/publish/index.shtml.

2007/2008 Human Development Reports. Available at: http://hdrstats.undp.org/countries/country_fact_sheets/cty_fs_SLE.html.

Wade, N. G., Worthington Jr., E. L., and Meyer, J. E. 2005. "But Do They Work? A Meta-Analysis of Group Interventions to Promote Forgiveness." In *Handbook of Forgiveness,* ed. E. L. Worthington. New York: Brunner-Routledge.

Wagner, R. V., ed. 2007. *Peace and Conflict: Journal of Peace Psychology* 13 (1).

Watson, D., Clark, L., and Tellegen, A. 1988. "Development and Validation of Brief Measures of Positive and Negative Affect: The PANAS Scales." *Journal of Personality and Social Psychology* 54: 1063–70.

Worthington, E. L., Jr. 2006. *Forgiveness and Reconciliation.* New York: Routledge.

Chapter 15

CULTURAL COMPETENCE IN THE TRAUMA TREATMENT OF THAI SURVIVORS OF MODERN-DAY SLAVERY

The Relevance of Buddhist Mindfulness Practices
and Healing Rituals to Transform Shame
and Guilt of Forced Prostitution

Ginger Villareal Armas

"He abused me, mistreated me, defeated me, robbed me." Releasing such thoughts banishes hatred for all time. Animosity does not eradicate animosity. Only by loving kindness is animosity dissolved. This law is ancient and eternal.
—The Buddha, *The Dhammapada*

ABSTRACT

This chapter examines the relevance of Buddhist mindfulness practices and healing rituals in the trauma treatment of Thai modern-day slaves (MDS). Topics of discussion include: (a) the significance of sexual slavery, (b) its traumatic nature, (c) the psychological consequences (e.g., shame, guilt) of forced prostitution, (d) the importance of cultural competence in treating sexual slaves from Thailand, and (e) the pertinence of Zen Master Thich Nhat Hanh's practices to trauma interventions. Sources integrated include writings on general traumatology, modern-day slavery, Southeast Asian refugees, prostitution, battered women, torture, and mindfulness. More literature is needed regarding modern-day slavery: its assessment, psychological effects, and culturally competent treatment with diverse populations. Mindfulness seems to be an appropriate intervention for Thai MDS.

CULTURAL COMPETENCE IN THE TRAUMA TREATMENT OF THAI SURVIVORS OF SEXUAL SLAVERY: THE RELEVANCE OF BUDDHIST MINDFULNESS PRACTICES AND HEALING RITUALS

The majority of Americans believe slavery ended with the Emancipation proclamation, but, recently, awareness of modern-day slavery has been increasing. Traumatic by nature, modern-day slavery denies basic human rights. As a result, MDS need psychological treatment for what they have experienced. Although services are gradually growing for this overlooked population, there is a dire need for more efforts to rehabilitate emancipated MDS. With little or no treatment, those who have been emancipated become incapable of restoring normality to their lives (Zimmerman et al. 2003). Although there have been impressive and meaningful efforts by social activists around the world, rehabilitation services are still in the infancy stage and need to be developed and researched further (Batstone 2007). More literature would be useful for psychologists, who may inevitably encounter MDS during the surging prevalence of modern-day slavery.

Gold (2008) stated that in general the "treatment of trauma-related disorders is a complex and challenging area that requires specialized knowledge and skills" (119). It could be especially daunting and challenging to work with MDS. Diversity is just one challenge a psychologist faces while working with this marginalized population, which is composed of individuals from various countries worldwide. Furthermore, due to the complexities of modern-day slavery, cases are highly individualized. Although there are common themes, each individual typically has a unique, intricate history of captivity. When working with MDS, it is important to diagnose and to formulate a treatment plan with the individuality of each client in mind. Adhering to cultural competence in trauma therapy is a wise first step.

Since modern-day slavery afflicts an extensive and diverse population, this chapter will focus solely on Thai females who are survivors of sexual slavery, either through human trafficking abroad or through the local brothels of Thailand. However, it is evident that more research is needed regarding modern-day slavery, its trauma, and all individuals afflicted— not just women from Thailand. An integration of the current literature led to the conclusion that mindfulness practices may be an appropriate and relevant intervention strategy for this population.

THE TRAUMA OF MODERN-DAY SLAVERY

Challenges of Defining Modern-day Slavery

Occurring worldwide, modern-day slavery is overwhelmingly extensive in its scope. The breadth of current research exposes only a fragment of the wide variety of means and effects of modern-day slavery. Future research could focus on several forms and different aspects encompassing the slave trade (e.g., culture shock, dissociation, Stockholm syndrome). Due to its complexity, there is much confusion about this international problem. Since modern-day slavery is a clandestine, illicit activity, data collection is challenging. As a result, researchers may have trouble reaching a consensus on a consistent theoretical basis for comprehending it (Savona and Stefanizzi 2007). It is difficult to have a concise, clear definition because many areas overlap, such as how some slaves enduring forced labor may also become sexual slaves. In an effort to categorize modern-day slavery, which has overlapping forms, perhaps it would make most sense to list only three types: sexual, labor-intensive, and a combination of sexual and labor-intensive. Sexual slavery, the first form, could include forced prostitution, ritual sex slavery, and personal sexual exploitation. Next, labor-intensive slavery could involve forced soldiering and manual labor jobs. Third, sexual/labor-intensive slavery could include servile marriages and domestic servitude, such as human traffickers coercing maids into households, where they work for indefinite hours and are sexually abused by their employers. All forms may entail human trafficking, which involves the transport of individuals for nefarious activities.

Scope of the Problem

In 1860, at the height of American slavery, there were 3.9 million slaves in the United States (Hadden 2008). Today, there are 27 million estimated slaves worldwide (Bales 2004). In 2000, the increased activity in the slave trade led to the creation of an annual Trafficking in Persons (TIP) Report, which currently estimates: 800,000 individuals are trafficked annually, 80 percent of which are female, and 50 percent are minors (U.S. Department of State 2008, 7). Sexual trafficking is difficult to stop. Socioeconomic risk factors, such as poverty and unemployment, increase an individual's vulnerability to becoming a victim. These socioeconomic factors may also make modern-day slavery more enticing to potential human traffickers. After drugs, human trafficking yields the most profits for organized crime syndicates. The slave trade has been estimated to yield $9 billion in profits annually (Malarek 2003). An Albanian pimp described the moneymaking nature of human trafficking by saying, "I paid $2,500 for her. I made the investment back in a few days" (Malarek 2003). In addition, there are currently little or no consequences for traffickers, who feel they can deny the human rights of slaves with impunity. Human traffickers exploit the vulnerabilities of modern-day slaves, who may be even more vulnerable than their historical counterparts. In his book *Disposable People: New Slavery in the Global Economy,* Bales (2004) stated, "Buying a slave is no longer a major investment [as it was in the old slavery]. Slaveholders get all they can out of their slaves, and then throw them away" (4).

Forced Prostitution of Thai Women

Recruitment. Although prostitution is illegal in Thailand, many girls and young women are forced to work as prostitutes. Thai MDS may be kidnapped or sold by acquaintances, procurers, and even family members and orphanages that have been entrusted with the care of children. With the intention of selling her, a man may feign a romantic interest and pursue a young woman. In other cases, a boyfriend may sell a woman he has already been dating to the slave trade. A procurer may attempt to deceive prospective slaves into believing there is a career opportunity which will lift them out of poverty. However, after accepting false job offers, these new recruits are sold to slaveholders, who use force, fraud, and coercion to make them work as prostitutes. Typically, deceit and betrayal characterize this phase of sexual slavery. It is understandable how the experience of recruitment could lead to "alterations in relations with others," specifically mistrust and fear of intimacy (Herman 1997, 121).

Seasoning and Forced Migration. Once slaves have been recruited, traumatic experiences may begin almost immediately. Human traffickers and slaveholders may start a systematic indoctrination, which is referred to by pimps as seasoning (Farley 2003). This seasoning process asserts the perpetrator's power and involves using multiple means of control, many of which overlap. These methods of force, fraud, and coercion may include emotional and physical abuse, and sexual assault. Emotional abuse is an effective means of destroying a woman's self-esteem. Working to shatter her sense of self, the perpetrator minimizes a sexual slave's worth as a person and commodifies her. In addition, brothel patrons treat her as a sex object, whose sole purpose is to pleasure others. As a result, sexual slaves experience depersonalization and debilitation (Farley 2003; Zimmerman et al. 2003). Physical abuse may further debilitate MDS and cause them to accept their circumstances passively. Abuse may take the form of battering and torture, including burnings, starvation, and social isolation. In addition to physical abuse, survivors of sex trafficking have reported experiencing frequent rapes, including gang rape and forced oral, vaginal, and anal sex (Miller, Decker, Silverman, and Raj 2007; Zimmerman et al. 2003).

Forced continuous migration may also have debilitating effects. The initial and subsequent relocations may be characterized by trauma. During transit, MDS may witness and have horrific experiences. The survival of MDS is linked to human traffickers. The traffickers may reiterate this fact with threats, such as telling the individuals they are transporting that they will die if they are abandoned in the desert through which they are traversing. Human traffickers emphasize the helplessness of MDS. Indeed, human traffickers are in control of every aspect of the journey. They decide when and where MDS will talk, eat, sleep, urinate, defecate, and move. Often, slaveholders will transport modern-day slaves to various locations along a prostitution circuit. They may traffic MDS in order to avoid detection from the authorities, but frequent migration may serve another purpose: as another means in the seasoning process. Constant relocation minimizes the chance that sexual slaves will form meaningful alliances (Batstone 2007). Social isolation could arguably be a form of psychological torture. Furthermore, through isolation, imprisonment, and frequent migration many victims are unaware of their location in a foreign country. As a result, they are hesitant to escape and find the resources they need. If MDS are able to access health services, the traffickers speak for them. If there is an opportunity for the MDS to be alone with the health provider, then they may not speak English or may be too fearful of the trafficker to seek help. Thus, due to fear and cultural barriers, MDS are even more vulnerable.

When victims do go through the health or legal systems, they are not recognized as victims. The majority of Americans assume that workers provide services voluntarily. It does not help that the MDS also do not recognize themselves as victims. Typically, individuals who have been trafficked are unaware they have rights. Fear may also stop them from attempting to get help, and traffickers purposely exacerbate this fear. MDS are often fearful due to past experiences in their native countries, where local police were often complicit with traffickers. Since most of them are living illegally in the United States, many individuals who have been trafficked fear that reaching out to authorities would lead to deportation. Slaveholders take every precaution to strengthen the dependence of MDS upon them. Immediately after recruitment, slaveholders confiscate documents of MDS, such as passports, visas, and identification. In addition, they withhold money. In some cases, slaveholders use debt bondage as a means of denying freedom to MDS. After a procurer promises false jobs to new recruits and a human trafficker transports them across borders, slaveholders claim that these MDS owe them money for the journey and must work to pay off their debts. They also take special steps to assert authority over MDS. Perpetrators may ensure compliance and passivity by forcing or coercing sexual slaves to use drugs and alcohol prior to servicing brothel patrons. The seasoning process is comparable to the psychological consequences experienced by battered women. Research has suggested that women who endure interpersonal violence may develop learned helplessness (Walker 1979). Walker's theory of learned helplessness and battered women relates the learned helplessness model (Seligman 1975) to the process of how abusive partners may perpetrate violence. Walker suggested that "Repeated batterings, like electrical shocks, diminish the woman's motivation to respond. She becomes passive. Secondly her cognitive ability to perceive success is changed. She does not believe her response will result in a favorable outcome, whether or not it might (49)."

Captivity. The seasoning process inures Thai sexual slaves to inhumane living and forced prostitution. Typically, MDS are housed in dilapidated, cramped quarters with others who are enslaved. Although there is some controversy, the majority of literature has suggested that prostitution has a negative psychological impact on commercial sex workers (Farley 2003). It is hoped that the opposing sides of this debate can come to a consensus that forced prostitution unquestionably has deleterious effects on its victims. Forced prostitution entails not only the trauma of sexual exploitation, but also all types of abuse, captivity, terror, and, at times, torture.

THE STAGES OF TRAUMA PSYCHOTHERAPY

Herman (1997) developed a three-stage post trauma psychotherapy model which is commonly used today. Stage 1, Safety, involves making sure that the client is no longer in jeopardy. First, the clinician must assess whether or not the client is still in danger. If so, then a safety plan is created to extricate the client from the dangerous situation. In addition to addressing the client's physical safety, the clinician focuses on psychological stabilization. In other words, with the clinician's help, the client works towards effectively dealing with emotional distress and minimizing compulsive behaviors that serve as ineffective coping skills to traumatic triggers. Teaching the client relaxation techniques will help with this objective. Also helpful is Safe Place Imagery, during which the client uses eight steps to conjure mentally an image of a haven (Shapiro 2001). Until the client reaches stabilization, it is too early to process the trauma. Prematurely attempting to resolve the trauma could be iatrogenic.

Before progressing to Stage 2, Remembrance and Mourning, the clinician must determine that the client has nearly resolved any compulsive, self-harming behaviors. Also, the client must have developed adequate self-care, including self-soothing. There are a variety of methods to facilitate trauma processing, including Eye Movement Desensitization and Reprocessing (EMDR; Shapiro 2001). Shapiro founded this technique after discovering that her disturbing, recurrent thoughts disappeared after a walk in the park. Later, she attributed the reduction of her emotional distress to the coordination of her eye movement and thought loop. EMDR employs the premise that one can become desensitized to distressful cognitions and that the mechanism of rapidly moving one's eyes back and forth can reprocess thoughts. Finally, Stage 3, Reconnection with Ordinary Life, helps the client to find meaning in the traumatic experience and to reengage in quotidian life. This includes reconnection with others. Due to the trauma, the client may have experienced alterations in interpersonal relationships, including mistrust of other people and feelings of isolation.

THE TRAUMA TREATMENT OF EMANCIPATED THAI SEXUAL SLAVES

The Importance of Cultural Competence

Cultural competence is crucial in the treatment of emancipated Thai MDS. In general, failure to practice in a culturally competent manner may lead to secondary & tertiary traumas (Brown 2008). According to Sue and Sue (2008),

> A culturally competent helping professional is one who is actively in the process of being aware of his or her own assumptions about human behavior, values, biases, preconceived notions, personal limitations, and so forth . . . One who actively attempts to understand the worldview of his or her culturally different clieunt . . . One who is in the process of actively developing and practicing appropriate, relevant, and sensitive intervention strategies and skills in working with his or her culturally different client (43–44).

Clinician's Self-Awareness of Biases in Working with Thai Women. For a psychologist from the Western world, it may be difficult to understand the self-sacrificing and self-blaming tendencies of Thai MDS. It is important to acknowledge these cultural biases and to progress with an empathic attitude. It might be iatrogenic and damage rapport if the clinician challenges the survivor's self-blame. It is more effective to address shame and guilt through interventions that are compatible with the background and beliefs of MDS, such as empathic listening and mindfulness practices. According to Mollica (1988), the primary goal of treatment for refugee survivors of violence and torture is to have them tell their trauma stories. Similarly, listening to the trauma stories of Thai MDS is crucial to their healing and recovery. To cultivate a safe environment in which a survivor feels safe enough to reveal her traumatic experiences, it is crucial to develop rapport through empathic listening. By sharing their trauma history, Thai MDS no longer carry their burden alone. The effect of social support has healing effects (Herman 1997).

In order to be effective in working with diverse populations, Sue and Sue (2008) encouraged clinicians to gain self-knowledge. They explained that understanding individuals from different backgrounds requires book learning, self-exploration, and more interactions with multicultural people. Through this independent study, clinicians will most likely experience intense feelings, since the topic of diversity usually elicits strong emotions. Sue and Sue (2008) advocated for acknowledgment of what arises through introspection and other explorations. They also emphasized the importance of open dialogue in developing cultural competence.

Clinician's Knowledge of Thai Culture. When working with Thai women who have endured sexual slavery, it would be prudent to consider the impact of their sociocultural background on their traumatic experiences and worldviews. There are several factors that may predispose Thai females for sexual slavery in Thailand. First, there is an unequal distribution of wealth. Although Thailand has abundant natural resources and is a leading exporter of grains, not all of its provinces have experienced stability and wealth. Unlike the fecund plains of the southern region, the mountainous land in the north is barren. In the midst of Thailand's rapid industrial growth, its northern mountainous region is struggling with abject poverty. By making the job market more competitive, Thailand's burgeoning population has also made it more difficult to survive. According to Bales (2004), due to the struggle for survival, Northern Thai denizens "have been forced to view their own children as commodities" (38). In need of a breadwinner, a female child is sacrificed on behalf of the family. More specifically, a daughter is sold into slavery to ensure a family's survival. Undoubtedly, selling one's child is a desperate act. However, Thai parents would hardly consider selling a son. Influenced by Theravada Buddhist beliefs, Thailand's patriarchal society is another factor that predisposes these parents to sell their daughters. In general, a female should "fulfill triples roles as dutiful daughter, caring wife, and sacrificing mother" (Tantiwiramanond and Pandey 1987, 140–41).

Germane to prostitution are three major Buddhist beliefs: reincarnation, karma, and merit-making. Reincarnation is the belief in a cycle of life, where after a soul dies it is reborn into a new body. The law of karma asserts that your past actions create your current life. Therefore, merit-making is seen as a way to ameliorate suffering. By making merit, one may reap the benefits in future lives. Although there is some controversy, most scholars interpret Theravada Buddhist sacred texts as holding the belief that women are karmically inferior to men; in other words, women may not become enlightened (Bales 2004; Batstone 2007; Keyes 1984; Kirsch 1985). It is believed that if one is born a woman, then one committed bad deeds in order to receive this fate. Similarly, if one is suffering in one's current life, then one feels reprehensible; due to the belief of karma, one attributes suffering to wrong action in a past life. At the same time, it is considered a great blessing to be born, and children who are born are indebted to their parents for life (Bales 2004). Girls, especially, are obligated to provide for their families financially. If they do not fulfill this obligation, then they may risk being born as women again. Being born a male in the next lifetime is the predominant preference. The ultimate objective is to attain enlightenment and to be freed from the cycle of life.

Again, the meaning of Buddhist concepts has been fiercely debated. Some scholars disagree with the interpretation of karma and gender roles just described. However, when working with Thai survivors, it is more important to work with their understanding of Buddhism. It has been well documented that, due to their spiritual beliefs and sociocultural background, these women feel shame and believe they are reprehensible because of their misfortunes (Bales 2004; Batstone 2007; Tantiwiramanond and Pandey 1987). By having knowledge about these beliefs, clinicians may gain more insight into the mentality of Thai survivors of sex trafficking. First of all, Thai women are predisposed to feelings of guilt and shame. Given the responsibility for the livelihood of their families, Thai daughters feel shame when they are unable to earn enough money to rescue their parents from poverty. Influenced by karma, they may also feel ashamed by the forced prostitution they have endured. In Thai society, this would make them unfit to marry. According to a study on attitudes about gender roles, most Thai girls believe that they should preserve their virginity (Fongkaew 1995).

Finally, the last predisposing factor for sexual slavery is Thailand's social acceptance of prostitution in spite of its illegality. The sex industry in Thailand is a thriving business, which is supported by foreigners and local men. The indigenous use of prostitution by Thai men is often overlooked, but their patronage contributes to the demand of sexual slaves. It is socially acceptable for Thai husbands to have outings with male friends, during which they patronize brothels. Thai wives tolerate the infidelity of their husbands with the rationalization that prostitutes are less threatening than mistresses. If a spouse spends the night with a prostitute, it is perceived as a harmless digression from the marital bed. However, if a spouse is having an extramarital affair, the wife could fear that a mistress, or a minor wife, may replace her. In addition to loss of her husband, a wife could fear losing her financial support. Thailand's patriarchal society may perceive that the brothel plays a role in maintaining matrimonial harmony by fulfilling a husband's sexual needs which are not met in the marriage. Plus, prostitution is readily accepted because the lucrative sex industry contributes greatly to Thailand's economy.

Clinician's Development and Practice of Culturally-Sensitive Intervention Strategies. In order to adhere to cultural competence, Sue and Sue (2008) advocated for an emic model, which takes into account the diversity of individuals and their cultural backgrounds. As opposed to the etic or culturally universal perspective, the emic perspective is culturally specific (31). With an emic perspective, it becomes clear that there is not one therapeutic orientation that will work for everyone. Rather, it is important to keep the individuality of each client in mind. Sue and Sue also described how it would be advantageous for a clinician to remain "in the process of actively developing and practicing appropriate, relevant, and sensitive intervention strategies and skills in working with his or her culturally different client" (44). In developing innovative practices, it is beneficial to explore past and other germane research for inspiration. Since there is minimal research on modern-day slavery, looking at past research on counseling Southeast Asian refugees may be relevant. Unlike immigrants who relocate of their own volition and on their own timeline, both refugees and modern-day slaves endure more stress due to life-threatening premigration trauma and forced migration, which is usually abrupt. Refugees escape from persecution due to religion, membership in an ethnic or social group, or political affiliation or views. MDS are forcibly moved across international borders to fulfill the intentions of the human traffickers. After fleeing their native countries, refugees often must live in resettlement camps while waiting for residence in a new country. Thai modern-day slaves are often forced to relocate frequently along the prostitution circuit. In both situations, there is instability and uncertainty about one's next destination. Safety and survival are also concerns. While in transit, both populations may be exposed to a wide variety of traumas, such as sexual assault. In most Southeast Asian cultures, once a woman has been sexually assaulted, she is deemed ineligible for marriage. Most survivors of sexual assault, including refugees and MDS, feel shame and guilt.

For working with refugees, Sue and Sue (2008) recommended normalizing traumatic stress reactions and giving reassurance that symptoms can be treated. When waiting for them to self-disclose, clinicians must also keep in mind the survivors' feelings of shame and guilt. Another consideration is that most Southeast Asian individuals present their emotional distress as somatic complaints. However, somatic symptoms may be indicative of exposure to trauma. It would be wise for clinicians to ask questions about the client's own insights about the presenting problems, past interventions, and expectations for treatment. In addition to psychological literature, the teachings of Zen Master Thich Nhat Hanh might be a useful resource when working with Thai survivors of sex trafficking.

Relevance of Teachings by Zen Master Thich Nhat Hanh to Treatment of Thai MDS

Zen Master Thich Nhat Hanh: A Biography. In 1926, Thich Nhat Hanh was born in Central Vietnam and, at the age of 16, he entered a Zen Buddhist monastery, where he was later ordained as a monk. He coined the term and became one of the leading proponents of Engaged Buddhism, which advocates the application of Buddhist insights to social activism. Dedicated to transforming suffering in individuals and in society, he was industrious in his peacemaking attempts during the Vietnam War. His contributions from the 1960s include the foundation of a grassroots relief organization, a Buddhist University, a publishing house, and a magazine, which was instrumental in promoting pacifism. In an effort to end the Vietnam War, Thich Nhat Hanh traveled abroad in order to share his pacifist views with government officials in Europe and the United States, including the American secretary of defense Robert McNamara. Thich Nhat Hanh's efforts influenced Martin Luther King, Jr. to express publicly his opposition against the war. Afterwards, the latter nominated the former for a Nobel Peace Prize in 1967. In the midst of Thich Nhat Hanh's accomplishments, the Vietnamese government denounced his pacifist endeavors and banished him from Vietnam. As a result, he currently lives in exile at Plum Village, his Buddhist retreat center located in France. Today, Thich Nhat Hanh is an internationally venerated teacher. He is a prolific writer, who frequently lectures around the world. During meditation retreats, he instructs participants on how to live more mindfully and provides them with other mindfulness practices, such as healing rituals like Beginning Anew and Touching the Earth. These transformative lessons could be beneficial for survivors of modern-day slavery, particularly former Thai sexual slaves.

Mindfulness: An Introduction. Mindfulness, an ancient Buddhist practice, involves being more aware without judgments and living in the present moment. These practices could especially be helpful for Thai MDS who are experiencing traumatic stress reactions, like dissociation and depersonalization. Practicing mindfulness may lead to insights about past conflicts. Various practices include: mindful breathing, the use of *gathas,* walking meditation, sitting meditation, Beginning Anew and Touching the Earth.

Mindfulness Practices: An Application to Herman's Model of Trauma Treatment. During Stage 1, which focuses on safety, stabilization, and preparation for Phase 2, it would be helpful to teach the client mindful breathing and *gatha* recitation. When practicing mindful breathing, one is fully conscious of one's inhalation and exhalation. Observing the breath, one returns to the present moment, which can be a helpful practice for MDS who are experiencing dissociative symptoms. Rather than merely having the intention of living in the now, the breath gives one a concrete focus, which is in the present. Providing breathing exercises is one of the steps in Kalayjian's (2002) biopsychosocial and spiritual treatment model for trauma. Because slow breathing has calming physiological effects on the body, this practice is an ideal intervention for emotionally distressed and traumatized individuals (Kalayjian 2002). However, preexisting medical conditions that may contraindicate mindful breathing must be taken into consideration before prescribing this intervention.

Thich Nhat Hanh has also recommended the use of *gathas,* or mindfulness verses. For instance, during mindful breathing, one could mentally affirm, "Breathing in, I know that I am breathing in. Breathing out, I know that I am breathing out" (Hanh 2000, 15). The *gatha* can be eventually shortened to "In/Out." One sitting meditation technique employs the repetition of these verses. Regardless of their locations, clients would be able to return to mindful breathing and the mental recitation of *gathas*. In addition to reciting *gathas* during mindful breathing, movement can be coordinated with the gathas during walking mediation, which is a recommended practice for Stage 1 and Stage 2, Remembrance and Mourning. In other words, as practitioners step with their left feet, they may coordinate the inhalation with the *gatha* "In," and, as practitioners step with their right feet, they may coordinate the exhalation with the *gatha* "Out." The practitioners are encouraged to pay attention to their feet making contact with the ground as they walk. By focusing on tactile sensations in the present moment, this practice may be ideal for moments of dissociation. Also, it is interesting that walking meditation may have similar effects as Shapiro's (2001) walk, during which she founded EMDR.

During Stage 3, Reconnection with Ordinary Life, Beginning Anew and Touching the Earth are recommended practices. Originally written by Master Zhi Xuan (811–883 C.E.) a teacher in the Tang era in China, the Beginning Anew liturgy inspired a traditional Vietnamese ceremony of the same name (Hanh 2008). Translated from the Chinese words *chan hui,* Beginning Anew describes a metaphorically cleansing practice during which one bathes in the water of compassion. The Beginning Anew practitioner expresses regret for past acts and the intention of behaving subsequently in a different manner. The resolution for change is in itself healing. Thich Nhat Hanh (2008) stated, "It means expressing our regret for mistakes we have made . . . coupled with a deep and transforming determination to act differently from now on. Because we know that we can act differently, we do not need to feel guilt" (1).

Based on Beginning Anew, Thich Nhat Hanh developed a practice called Touching the Earth. This transformative ritual involves prostrations done in conjunction with guided meditations, which take the format of a dialogue with the Buddha. The practitioner addresses the Buddha through a script, a bell is invited, and then the practitioner touches the ground while prostrating. During the prostrations, the practitioner symbolically offers his or her negativity to the earth. It is believed that, just as the earth absorbs garbage as compost that nourish flowers and plants, the earth absorbs and then transforms the practitioner's suffering and afflictions. Some of the guided meditations describe the compassionate nature of the earth and how the practitioner must emulate its compassionate nature—to have compassion towards one's self and others. The fundamental premise of this ritual is that compassion has a transformative power. With compassion, one develops insight on how to gain freedom from suffering.

Due to feelings of guilt and shame, it would be helpful to share with these women Thich Nhat Hanh's (2008) words: "Because we know that we can act differently, we do not need to feel guilt" (1). Knowing that they can begin anew may also be helpful to alter the survivor's internalization of society's perception of them as sullied through sexual slavery. Hopefully, through these practices, these Thai women will gain insights, including that their enslavement was not their fault.

One variation of Touching the Earth incorporates a guided meditation entitled The Earth as a Solid Place of Refuge. The meditation script encourages the practitioner to perceive the earth as a sanctuary. This perception would be beneficial for former MDS. In general, past research has shown that fear is a predominant feeling for individuals suffering from trauma (Herman 1997; Kalayjian 2002). A Thai woman can use this meditation to create an atmosphere of safety by taking refuge in the solidity and compassionate nature of the earth. After experiencing betrayal by loved ones and procurers, she can rely on the stability of the earth and allow the earth to absorb her suffering and to transform it. This practice seems compatible with Shapiro's (2001) Safe Place Imagery and could perhaps be used during Stage 1.

Another variation of Touching the Earth includes a guided meditation entitled The River of Life, which involves the visualization of unity with the practitioner's ancestors (Hanh 2008). During the guided meditation script, the practitioner pictures the blood of her ancestors coursing through her own veins. Again, the bell is invited, and the practitioner prostrates while offering past negative experiences with these family members to the earth. This is very compatible with Herman's (1997) Stage 3, which focuses on reestablishing relationships. Similarly, another variation that could be helpful includes a similar guided meditation entitled Oneness with All Beings. The practitioner visualizes oneness with all beings, including not only individuals who have been exploited, but also oneness with the perpetrators of these exploited individuals. At this time, Thai women could visualize those who have wronged them, such as procurers, human traffickers, and slaveholders. Then, during the prostration, the Thai women could offer to the earth all of the suffering they have endured at the hands of the key figures in their enslavement. Touching the Earth may help these Thai women to cultivate a more compassionate nature not only towards themselves, but also towards those who may have betrayed and exploited them, such as family members. Due to the complexities of the sociocultural circumstances of their enslavement, Thai women may have difficulty acknowledging and expressing their anger towards others who were instrumental in their traumatic experiences. This inability to express anger may exacerbate their feelings of shame and guilt. If they are unable to acknowledge the role others played in their enslavement, then they are more likely to place blame on themselves. This could be an innocuous way for Thai women to express and release their anger. Through visualization of unity with the perpetrators of their captivity, Thai women may gain insights about and forgiveness towards these people who have contributed to their suffering. To increase one's capacity for compassion, one script leads the practitioners to visualize these people as innocent, vulnerable children who may have been hurt throughout their lifetime (Khong 1999).

DISCUSSION

In general, traumatology is pertinent to contemporary clinical psychology and requires more attention from practicing professionals. Specifically, modern-day slavery has a high prevalence and needs to be addressed. Thai women are just one group that composes this neglected population. Ideally, the proposed strategies that have been discussed may act as a starting point to inspire more theoretical ideas on how to help these individuals. There are two caveats. First, it is important to keep in mind an emic model of cultural competence, which takes into account within-group differences (Brown 2008). Through interactions with each female client, the clinician may get a sense that one former sexual slave may not be receptive to these mindfulness practices whereas another survivor would be. Second, the use of mindfulness practices as an intervention strategy is only an option and should be presented to Thai modern-day slaves as such. In other words, it must be clear that the clinician is merely offering a suggestion, and, ultimately, it is the survivor's choice to participate. It is empowering to give sexual assault survivors options and to let them reestablish control of their bodies and lives (Mount Sinai Hospital 2006). According to the empowerment approach, control is an important aspect of recovery from sexually traumatic experiences (Ullman and Townsend 2008). When a survivor has endured sexual slavery, control has been taken away from her by several perpetrators: family members (in some cases), procurers, human traffickers, slaveholders, and the patrons of the sex industry.

However, mindfulness practices are, in themselves, empowering. Psychological trauma is characterized by feelings of impotence (Herman 1997). Kalayjian (2002) described the unruly nature of traumatic experiences and offers breathing exercises as a method by which the survivor may regain control over traumatic stress reactions. There are clear advantages to the mindfulness practices described in this paper. According to Zen Buddhist philosophy, living mindfully provides liberation through focusing on the present moment (Hanh 2000; Hanh et al. 2003). Influenced by empirical studies, cognitive-behavioral therapists have recognized the value of introducing mindfulness to their clinical practices (Linehan 1993; Segal, Williams, and Teasdale 2002). The notion that the present moment is liberating could be healing for former slaves, especially because their oppressors have denied them freedom. Due to their focus on compassion and renewal, rituals like Touching the Earth have great potential to address psychological distress specific to Thai women, such as shame and guilt.

However, one might wonder how culturally sensitive it is to give Zen Buddhist practices to women who hold strong Theravada Buddhist beliefs. Since Zen and Theravada are two separate schools of Buddhism, is it inappropriate to offer these interventions? Would this be comparable to offering Roman Catholic teachings to followers of the Seventh-Day Adventist World Church? Understandably, this is a valid concern, because religion can be a delicate matter. However, Thich Nhat Hanh presents his teachings in a religiously neutral tone. He has asserted that his practices may be viewed as practical guidelines for a peaceful life (Hanh 2000). Many of his students belong to various faiths and have provided testimonials of the transformative nature of these practices (Hanh et al. 2003). In addition to sharing his practices, Thich Nhat Hanh teaches MDS by his example. He himself is a refugee who was persecuted by the Vietnamese government for his pacifist beliefs. He has not merely survived through traumatic experiences; he is now perceived as a paragon of peace. For this reason, Thich Nhat Hanh's teachings have made a profound impact on many of his students around the world (Hanh et al. 2003).

When clinicians practice cultural competence, the worldviews of MDS are taken into consideration, and their voices are heard. By listening to their trauma stories, clinicians are no longer inactive bystanders, who are complicit with slaveholders, human traffickers, procurers, and brothel patrons. Psychologists could help even more by developing and systematically researching intervention strategies, such as the mindfulness practices discussed in this chapter. More research is needed, but the advantages of these intervention strategies are clear.

REFERENCES

Bales, K. 2004. *Disposable People: New Slavery in the Global Economy.* Rev. ed. Berkley: University of California Press.

Batstone, D. 2007. *Not for Sale: The Return of the Global Slave Trade—and How We Can Fight It.* Rev. ed. San Francisco: HarperSanFrancisco.

Brown, L. S. 2008. *Cultural Competence in Trauma Therapy: Beyond the Flashback.* Washington, DC: American Psychological Association.

Farley, M. 2003. *Prostitution, Trafficking, and Traumatic Stress.* Binghamton, NY: The Haworth Maltreatment & Trauma Press.

Fongkaew, W. 1995. "Early Adolescent Girls in Transition in a Peri-Urban Northern Thai Community: Perceptions of Gender Role and Sexuality." Doctoral dissertation. University of Washington, 1996. *Dissertation Abstracts International* 56: 4, 834.

Gold, S. N. 2008. "The Relevance of Trauma to General Clinical Practice." *Psychological Trauma: Theory, Research, Practice, and Policy* S (1): 114–24.

Hadden, S. E. 2008. "The Fragmented Laws of Slavery in the Colonial and Revolutionary Eras". In *History of Law in America: Early America—1580–1815.* Vol. 1: ed. M. Grossberg and C. Tomlins, 253–87. New York: Cambridge University Press.

Hanh, T. N. 2000. *The Path of Emancipation: Talks from a 21-day Mindfulness Retreat.* Berkeley, CA: Parallax Press.

Hanh, T. N. 2008. *Touching the Earth: 46 Guided Meditations for Mindfulness Practices.* Rev. ed. Berkeley, CA: Parallax Press.

Hanh, T. N., et al. 2003. *I Have Arrived, I Am Home: Celebrating Twenty Years of Plum Village Life.* Berkeley, CA: Parallax Press.

Herman, J. L. 1997. *Trauma and Recovery: The Aftermath of Violence—from Domestic Abuse to Political Terror.* Rev. ed. New York: Basic Books.

Kalayjian, A. S. 2002. "Biopsychosocial and Spiritual Treatment of Trauma." In *Comprehensive Handbook of Psychotherapy: Vol. 3. Interpersonal/Humanistic/Existential,* ed. F. Kaslow (series ed.) and R. Massey and S. Massey (vol. eds.), 615–37. New York: John Wiley & Sons.

Keyes, C. F. 1984. "Mother or Mistress but Never a Monk: Buddhist Notions of Female Gender in Rural Thailand." *American Ethnologist* 11: 233–41.

Khong, C. 1999. "Touching the Earth." In *Touching the Earth* [cassette]. Dieulivol, France: Plum Village.

Kirsch, A. T. 1985. "Text and Context: Buddhist Sex Roles/the Culture of Gender Revisited." *American Ethnologist* 12: 302–20.

Linehan, M.M. 1993. *Cognitive-Behavioral Treatment of Borderline Personality Disorder.* New York: Guilford.

Malarek, V. 2003. *The Natashas: Inside the New Global Sex Trade.* New York: Arcade Publishing.

Miller, E., Decker, M.R., Silverman, J.G., and Raj, A., 2007. "Migration, Sexual Exploitation, and Women's Health: A Case Report from a Community Health Center." *Violence Against Women* 13 (5): 486–97.

Mollica, R. 1988. "The Trauma Story: The Psychiatric Care of Refugee Survivors of Violence and Torture." In *Post-traumatic Therapy and Victims of Violence,* ed. F. Ochberg, 295–313. New York: Brunner/Mazel.

Mount Sinai Hospital. 2006. *Mount Sinai Sexual Assault and Violence Intervention Program: 2006 Advocate Training Manual.* New York: Author.

Savona, E.U., and Stefanizzi, S., eds. 2007. *Measuring Human Trafficking: Complexities and Pitfalls.* New York: Springer.

Segal, Z.V., Williams, J.M.G., and Teasdale, J.D. 2002. *Mindfulness-Based Cognitive Therapy for Depression: A New Approach to Preventing Relapse.* New York: Guilford.

Seligman, M.E.P. 1975. *Helplessness.* San Francisco: W. H. Freedman.

Shapiro, F. 2001. *Eye Movement Desensitization and Reprocessing,* 2nd. ed. New York: Guilford.

Sue, D.W., and Sue, D. 2008. *Counseling the Culturally Diverse: Theory and Practice,* 5th ed. Hoboken, NJ: Wiley.

Tantiwiramanond, D., and Pandey, S.R. 1987. "The Status and Role of Thai Women in the Pre-Modern Period: A Historical and Cultural Perspective." *SOJOURN* 2 (1): 125–49.

Ullman, S.E., and Townsend, S.M. 2008. "What is an Empowerment Approach to Working with Sexual Assault Survivors?" *Journal of Community Psychology* 36 (2): 299–312.

U.S. Department of State. 2008. *Traffficking in Persons Report 2008.* Washington, DC: Author.

Walker, L. 1979. *The Battered Woman.* New York: Harper & Row.

Zimmerman, C., Yun, K., Svab, I., Watts, C., Trappolin, L., Treppete, M., et al. 2003. *The Health Risks and Consequences of Trafficking in Women and Adolescents: Findings from a European Study.* London: LSHTM.

Chapter 16

EXPLORING LONG-TERM IMPACT OF MASS TRAUMA ON PHYSICAL HEALTH, COPING, AND MEANING-MAKING

Exploration of the Ottoman Turkish Genocide of the Armenians

Ani Kalayjian,
Nicole Moore,
Chris Aberson, and
Sehoon Kim

Never try to reason the prejudice out of a man. It was not reasoned into him, and cannot be reasoned out.

—Sydney Smith

ABSTRACT

Throughout the 20th century, genocide has claimed many lives across the world. Government genocidal policies alone have resulted in over 210 million deaths—80 percent of which were civilian deaths and represent nearly four times the number of individuals killed in combat during international and domestic wars during the same period. Approximately nine decades ago, under the cover of World War I, Turkish armed forces systematically moved to exterminate Turkey's Armenian population.

The present study focuses on how Armenian survivors dealt with the Genocide, what gave them the strength to cope, their level of post-traumatic stress disorder (PTSD), the extent of physical symptomatology, and meanings associated with the trauma, as manifested in selected aspects of survival accounts from 16 Armenian Americans (born before 1917) who had witnessed the Ottoman Turkish Genocide of the Armenians.

Preliminary findings indicate that although these survivors had adjusted and prospered in America, some levels of PTSD persisted. Those who found a positive meaning in their experiences have coped better, and their level of

PTSD and physical symptomatology was lower. This research venture is a follow-up to the study in which Armenian survivors' coping styles and patterns were examined after eight decades. The study revealed that against the backdrop of losses and atrocities outside the scope of conventional life experience, these aged survivors reflected a sense of accomplishment tempered with anger about the perpetrators' denial of how they were victimized.

INTRODUCTION

Although genocides have been perpetrated for several centuries, it was not until 1948, in response to the Jewish Holocaust, that the United Nations Convention on Genocide made genocide a "crime under international law" (Universal Declaration of Human Rights 2000–2008). Retrospectively, genocide should have been recognized earlier by the world at large. Genocide is still going on today as the authors write this chapter. One reason for the growing attention to genocide is the ongoing genocide in Sudan against the people of Darfur. This began in 2003, and has taken at least 1,000,000 lives and displaced 2.3 million people. Educators are relinquishing the mantra "Never Again" and embracing the realization that genocide has not stopped happening. The goals of this chapter are to educate the reader on the history of the Armenian Genocide, demonstrate the long lasting and severe traumatic effects of the genocide on survivors, and present traditional coping methods, such as rituals and religion which enabled the survival of the Armenian people. An additional goal of this chapter is to educate young people about patterns of genocide and how it occurs, so that there is a chance for prevention.

HISTORICAL PERSPECTIVES

Approximately 1.5 million Armenians were massacred from 1915 to 1923 in the Ottoman Turkish Empire at the hands of the Young Turks. Henry Morgenthau, the U.S. Ambassador to the Ottoman Empire at the time, witnessed one of the earliest examples of genocide in the civilized world. With the absence of any international law forbidding the *extermination of a race,* Morgenthau was unable to put an end to the Armenian genocide, in spite of several telegrams sent to the U.S. State Department (Kalayjian et al. 1996). There were no measures taken by the Ottoman Empire to prevent the genocide, and therefore history was bound to repeat itself. Adolph Hitler once said, "Who still talks nowadays of the extermination of the Armenians?" (Armenian National Institute 1998–2008). Galvanizing support for his final solution of the Jewish problem in Nazi Germany, Hitler capitalized on the forgotten genocide of the Armenians.

On March 25, 1915, backed by the ruling Young Turks, Turkish Minister of the Interior Talaat Pasha ordered his final solution for the Armenians living in Ottoman Turkey: *"The duty of everyone is to effect on the broadest lines possible the realization of the noble project of wiping out of existence the well-known elements who for centuries have been the barrier to the empire's progress in civilization"* (World War I Primary Documents 2000–2007).

The vernacular of this order offers insight into the intentions, circumstances, and the meaning of the genocide of the Armenians. The Armenians represented a competitive threat and an ethnic problem for the Ottoman Empire as the Empire was shrinking and losing its political stability. The Armenians, the first group to endorse Christianity, clashed with the nationalist Muslim Turks. Long before the Armenian genocide, they represented a colonial threat to Russia in Transcaucasia, and before that they were invaded by Persia. Traditionally Armenians were successful traders who represented a large sector of the bourgeoisie in Russian Transcaucasia. The Russians benefited from and controlled this trade. The Turks, however, did not care to profit from Armenia's trade; Turks viewed them as a threat and therefore wanted to eliminate them completely and expand into the Armenian territories. "The Turks wanted the Armenians out of the way; they also wanted Armenian wealth and were prepared to kill, torture, and maim to get it. Their motives were old; the means to achieve them were new and chilling" (Winter 2003, 209–10).

By 1914, the combination of Armenia's strong Christian identity, its connection with Russia (whom Turkey had battled with over Armenia), and its overall strong presence in the bourgeoisie prompted the Turks to want to eliminate the perceived Armenian threat. Indeed, Talaat Pasha blamed the Armenians for hindering Turkish expansion. In his orders of deportation, he clearly blamed the Armenians for having been the barrier to the Empire's progress in civilization (Dadrian 1994). The Young Turks would not tolerate a multiethnic empire. In fact, it was the very essence of the Christian Armenian identity that threatened the Turkish Empire. The deportation and killing of 1.5 million Armenians, according to Dadrian, was intended to rid eastern Turkey of an old and prosperous community, whose Armenian residents inspired envy and who were perceived as enemies in time of war. Consequently, when the deportations began, the Turks removed the most influential and powerful male members of the Armenian community ages 18–45, including leaders, clergymen, intellectuals, businessmen, and journalists. The Armenians were feared by the Turkish Ottoman Empire.

Christianity was a pivotal part of the Armenian identity; consequently, the perpetrators attacked Armenian Christianity. According to Balakian

(2004), when an Armenian woman was given her deceased son's bloody clothes, a Turk took her to a Church where he pointed to the cross and said "Kneel down and pray. We'll do it to you like you did it to Christ. Hey Mother, pray to your son. Have you no faith in the resurrection?" Such psychological torment, which so many Armenians faced during the genocide, would haunt survivors for eternity. Balakian, a member of the Armenian Diaspora, reflects on the catastrophic nature of the genocide:

> What did it mean when a people who loved and worked and built a culture on the land where they had lived for three thousand years were destroyed? What did it mean for the culture's legacy? What did it mean for the human race? When a civilization is erased, there is a new darkness on the earth. I could feel dust blowing over dry land, where now blood is part of the rocks, where the water will never run clean again (253).

Balakian asks many important questions about the impact of genocide on its survivors. Indeed, the Turks, like all perpetrators, sought to "destroy the victim's sense of autonomy" (Herman 1997, 77). It is imperative to realize and understand the repercussions of eliminating one's autonomy, particularly its psychological ramifications.

In her book *Trauma and Recovery,* Herman (1997) illustrates the importance of a supportive social environment following mass trauma. In cases of genocide, post-traumatic stress disorder (PTSD) is prevalent in survivors due to a long-term mass trauma generated by witnessing death, destruction, starvation, torture, and forced relocation.

Throughout the 20th century, genocide has claimed many lives across the world. Eastern European Jews during the holocaust, Armenians during the Ottoman Turkish Empire, and Africans from Rwanda and Sudan are just some of those who have suffered. Government genocidal policies alone have resulted in over 210 million deaths—80 percent of which were civilian deaths (170 million)—a figure that represent nearly four times the number of individuals killed in combat in international and domestic wars during this same time period (Robinson 1998; Rummel 1996). These statistics do not include human rights violations, and severely underestimate the additional toll on human life from physical and psychological scarring.

Though less than 10 years old, the 21st century has already demonstrated that it is no more immune or better protected from genocide's deadly wrath. The Darfur area of Sudan is the latest region to host and suffer daily through ethnopolitically motivated massacres. While many continue to die, survivors will be forced to manage traumatic effects long after the conflict ends. In spite of this grim reality, psychology is uniquely qualified to address the consequences of these atrocities (Woolf 2000).

While specific definitions may vary, a common thread among genocides is death and intent to destroy in part or in full an ethnic group (Office of the

Higher Commissioner for Human Rights 2008). Death often results from the physically torturous conditions of exhaustion, starvation, dehydration, and disease (Kalayjian et al. 1996). Clearly, this makes scientific examination of genocide's psychological effects a rather difficult task. Many genocide victims do not survive, and those who do often do not wish to relive their trauma for the purpose of scientific research. In addition to the obvious physical toll, genocide survivors struggle with many lasting psychological effects of their trauma (Kalayjian et al. 1996). In 2001, Athanase Hagengimana administered a survey to Rwandan genocide survivors and found two common constellations of symptoms:

1. Post-traumatic stress disorder (PTSD)

    Ihahamuka, a word the Rwandans created post-genocide, is mainly used for children or people who are easily frightened, have trauma-related nightmares, and often avoid reminders of traumatic events. This applies in the cases of many children and adults who cannot stand seeing soldiers in uniform because they witnessed soldiers murdering their relatives in the 1994 genocide.

2. Chronic traumatic grief

    Traumatic grief was found to be highly prevalent. Since 91 percent of survivors had no chance to bury their relatives or perform mourning ceremonies, this affected the bereavement process. Of interviewed survivors, 88 percent had not yet seen the corpses of their loved ones.

Hagengimana (2001) discovered that survivors' post-genocide habits are called *ihahamuka* as well. These include antisocial behaviors in young people (e.g., promiscuity in young girls or widows), excessive drinking that was not present before the genocide, and excessive aggression and irritability directed toward anyone. The healing of wounds and justice for survivors seem to be unavoidable requirements for reconciliation.

Schiraldi (2000) refers to PTSD as a normal response by normal people to abnormal situations. While PTSD can follow both natural and human-made disasters, the latter may be more difficult to deal with. Frequently, the perpetrators still live in close proximity to victims—thereby providing constant reminders of the past, as well as a threat for the future. Even if the immediate source of the trauma is removed, time does not necessarily heal all wounds. The survivor may, in fact, continue to suffer, to appear frozen in time (Brahm 2003–2007). Survivor guilt has also been a painful symptom associated with genocides and PTSD (Niederland 1981). Danieli (1988) has described coping functions for such guilt among Jewish holocaust survivors in the form of commemoration. Survivors' guilt, she posits, preserves loyalty to nonsurvivors, providing a symbolic cemetery for those who were never allowed a legitimate resting place. Because of the powerful anger created by Turkey's denial, the nature of Armenian survivor guilt is not necessarily the same (Kupelian, Kalayjian, and Kassabian 1998). Comorbidity commonly accompanies PTSD, as 62 to 92 percent of those suffering from PTSD have a previous or concurrent psychiatric disorder compared to only 15 to 33 percent of non-PTSD comparison groups (Helzer, Robins, and McEvoy 1987).

In a study of older adult Armenian genocide survivors, Kalayjian et al. (1996) found that the survivors identified destruction of life, physical harm, deportation, pillaging, and loss of status as the main stressors they were forced to endure. The depth of such trauma may have been compounded by the decision of many survivors not to discuss their experiences prior to the study. There is no consensus as to why survivors choose to remain silent. Some suggest this stems from feelings of humiliation, weakness, and fear (Mazor et al. 1990). Some others stay silent out of fear of repeated torture (Kalayjian and Shahinian 1998). Danieli (1982) found that fear and isolation inhibited holocaust survivors' mourning. This is particularly important given the positive correlation between holocaust survivors' ability to communicate their experiences of traumatic events and their post-traumatic health (Cahn 1987). Common coping methods have included religion, family, work, and denial (Kalayjian et al.).

According to Herman (1997), post-traumatic stress commonly manifests itself in three ways:

- First, hyperarousal arises from continual vigilance in hopes that the experience will not occur again.

- Second, the traumatic memory is omnipresent in the mind of the traumatized. The memory repeatedly occurs as a flashback, which can happen at any time, and the victim is unable to distinguish the memory from actually experiencing the event again.

- Third, traumatized individuals appear to be indifferent in order to mask the feelings of vulnerability and helplessness.

Such trauma affects both individuals and communities. An increase in the prevalence of trauma can lead to a decrease of *trust* within a society. Trauma often spirals out of control in a vicious cycle. Human rights violations create massive trauma, which can, in turn, fuel additional human rights violations, and so on. Feelings of trauma can generate feelings of frustration and revenge, which can produce this *cycle of violence* and perpetuate feelings of victimhood on all sides of the conflict. Shared trauma generates a we feeling but also creates an us versus them mentality (United States Institute of Peace 2001).

Are men, women and children affected differently? Women are more likely to be left behind after husbands and children are killed in conflict

(Kalayjian et al. 1996). Women are often humiliated, feeling that they could do nothing to stop the violence. What is more, the loss of a husband or children can make it difficult for women to provide for their families, thereby adding further humiliation. Children also face particularly difficult trauma. They lack the emotional development and life experience to make sense of the trauma, even more so than adults (Brahm 2003–2007). Jarman (2001) observes that in Chechnya traumatic events often produce rage in teenagers because their lives have been turned upside down, and they have essentially been robbed of their youth. It is no surprise that children rendered orphans by genocide are often immediately recruited as soldiers.

Survivors' children are susceptible to picking up attitudes from adults in their lives, thereby providing the opportunity for trauma to be transmitted across generations. While parents may attempt to shield and protect their children from knowledge of the trauma, children who perceive that a parent is incapable of tolerating certain effects will stop experiencing and expressing them, in an attempt to protect the bond with the parent (Kalayjian 2002).

More than half a century ago, Sullivan emphasized the importance of validation of trauma in achieving resolution and closure (Sullivan 1953). An explicit expression of remorse by a perpetrator to a victim can provide great healing value (Staub 1990). Denial, on the other hand, perpetuates the trauma, and enables perpetrators to evade the consequences of their actions (Hovannisian 1987). In the case of the Turks and Armenians, there has never been a formal acknowledgement of genocide made by the Turkish government. Fittingly, Des Pres has referred to the plight of the Armenians as one marked by "permanent loss and the pain of memory mocked by denial" (Des Pres 1987, 17). In addition to the damage such denial causes the specific victims and their families, it can clearly set a dangerous precedent for future genocidal killing (Smith, Markusen, and Lifton 1995). The most recent evidence of this is found in the series of genocides that continue to occur in various countries in sub-Saharan Africa. The violence in Darfur is occurring less than a decade after the genocide in its neighbor, Rwanda. It seems genocide can beget genocide. "When the extermination of the Armenians was made negligible, the exterminations of the Holocaust were made possible" (Kupelian et al. 1998, 206).

The eight stages of genocide that Stanton (1996) describes are classification, symbolization, dehumanization, organization, polarization, preparation, extermination, and denial. It is through each of these stages that a human population is exterminated. Each of these stages is another layer of foundation that cements the acts of genocide.

The first author of this paper has identified eight phases of healing from a genocide, which are: acknowledgment, validation, reparation, facing negative feelings (such as anger, fear, shame, and humiliation), facing denial and revisionism, gaining acceptance, forgiveness, discovery of new meaning, lessons learned, and closure (Kalayjian 2005).

METHOD

Participants

Participants in this research were older Armenian Americans who were born before 1917, had witnessed the Armenian genocide, and were willing to participate in this research. There were 16 participants (9 female and 7 male). The participants' ages ranged from 79 to 93, with a mean age of 85.3 years. In this group, 50 percent had achieved higher education; 43 percent immigrated to the Unites States between 1912 and 1952; 56 percent had arrived after 1966. All participants had been married, 56 percent had been subsequently widowed, and 87 percent had living children. Occupationally, the largest group (31%) had worked in the garment industry (alterations, tailoring, and dressmaking). The second largest group (25%) comprised either owners or managers of a business. The third-largest group was composed of housewives (12%) and dentists (12%). One person was a teacher, another was a pharmacist, and a third was a telephone operator. With regard to religion, 87 percent had an apostolic religious affiliation and 12 percent had a Catholic religious affiliation.

During the period of 1995 to 2005, all participants were interviewed in their own homes in the New York metropolitan area. Some participants' first language was Armenian and they were asked questions and given the instruments in Armenian. The instruments were translated and then translated back.

Procedure

The interview instrument consists of 23 questions aimed at gathering factual demographic data. The interview's duration was from 30 minutes to 4 hours in length. The Mini-Mental State Exam (MMSE) was given to assess cognitive status and impairment. The instrument assesses orientation, immediate and short-term recall, language, and the ability to follow simple verbal commands. The MMSE has demonstrated validity and reliability in psychiatric, neurological, geriatric, and other medical populations (Folstein, Folstein, and McHugh 1975). Although the instrument only took about 30 minutes to complete, many survivors wanted to talk for a long time, making the interview last as long as four hours. The Brief Symptom Inventory (BSI) is a 53-item self-reported symptom inventory designed to reflect the psychological symptom patterns of psychiatric and medical patients as well as community nonpatient respondents (Derogatis 1993). The BSI is a Likert scale that ranges in raw scores from 0 to 212. The raw scores are then converted into T-scores for each scale. This inventory reports a profile of nine primary symptom dimensions and three global indices of distress (Derogatis). The primary symptom dimensions are: (1) Somatization (SOM), (2) Obsessive-Compulsive (O-C), (3) Interpersonal Sensitivity (I-S), (4) Depression (DEP), (5) Anxiety (ANX), (6) Hostility (HOS), (7) Phobic Anxiety (PHOB), (8) Paranoid Ideation, (PAR), (9) Psychoticism (PSY). The participants yielded T-scores in SOM from 41–80, O-C from 38–72, I-S from 38–74, DEP from 41–61, ANX from 38–72, HOS from 39–70, PHOB from 44–72, PAR from 43–80, and PSY from 46–67.

The global indices are: Global Severity Index (GSI), Positive Symptom Total (PST), and Positive Symptom Distress Index (PSDI). The participants yielded T-scores in GSI from 33–73, PST from 30–70, and PSDI from 30–65. This instrument was chosen due to the high reliability of internal consistency. Alpha coefficients for all nine dimensions of BSI ranged from a low of .71 on the Psychoticism dimension to a high of .85 on Depression (Derogatis 1993). The Life Purpose Questionnaire (LPQ) was used to measure an individual's sense of life meaning. It is a questionnaire that produces scores that range from 0 to 20. Scores can range from having no sense of life meaning to a definite sense of life meaning. The participants yielded scores between 13 and 19. The LPQ was chosen because of its test-retest reliability, which resulted in a .90 correlation. In addition, the LPQ items are designed to be more easily understood and completed by some persons (Hutzell 1987, as cited in Derogatis).

RESULT

Of the respondents, 59 percent were women with an average age of 86.3. The most common education level was primary school education (44%), with the remaining having either middle school (6%), high school (25%), or a post-secondary degree (25%). Most were unemployed at the time of the evaluation (67%). With regard to marital status, 41 percent were married at the time of the interview, and the remaining participants were widowed. The most common religion was Apostolic (88%) followed by Catholic (12%).

1. Gender & PTSD

    Men and women did not differ with regard to PTSD in the past or at the time of the interview. Men's past PTSD ($M = 11.2$) and current PTSD ($M = 10.0$) was nearly identical to women's past PTSD ($M = 11.7$) and current PTSD ($M = 10.4$), $t(15) = 0.5, 0.4$, ns, respectively.

2. PTSD & BSI

In general, higher BSI scores related to greater PTSD. Scores on the BSI overall and GSI were marginally correlated with past PTSD, r (17) = .47, p = .059, and significantly related to current PTSD, r (17) = .67, p = .003.

3. LPQ & PTSD/BSI

Scores on the Life Purpose questionnaire were unrelated to BSI scores, past, or current PTSD, r (17) = −.02, −.04, −.21, all *ns,* respectively.

4. The more countries one was forced to migrate to, the higher levels of PTSD and BSI.

Migration, in terms of the number of countries migrated to, was marginally related to the overall GSI score such that more migration related to lower GSI, r (17) = −.46, p = .061. However migration was unrelated to PTSD, either past or current, and in the LPQ, r (17) = −.14, .01, −.31, all *ns.*

5. The longer a survivor has been in his or her permanent home, the less PTSD and less BSI would be experienced.

Year of entry was unrelated to past and current PTSD, the GSI, and the LPQ, r (17) = .04, −.24, .17, and .15, respectively, all *ns.*

DISCUSSION

It is complicated to study the long-term impact of a mass trauma, such as a genocide that has occurred over 90 years ago, especially since at the time of the genocide and in the years that followed there were limited research findings addressing the psychosocial and spiritual impact of this or any other genocide (since it was the first one recorded in the 20th century). Additionally, participants stated that they had not received mental health or psychological assistance in their lifetime. In looking at the history of psychology and immigrants, there has been a void in areas of immigrants receiving psychological assistance. This can be due to lack of resources, services, and funds, and the cultural stigma that can go along with receiving psychological assistance. In addition, the Ottoman Turkish Genocide has been denied by both the Turkish and American governments. Survivors could not express their feelings and worked to process their feelings; they were unable to talk about them for at least two decades post-genocide due to fear of continued persecution. This persecution continues even today in Turkey, as well as in America. Hrant Dink, a journalist friend of the first author, was brutally killed on January 19, 2007, by a Turkish extremist, for "insulting Turkishness, and violating Article 301" as per Turkish governmental accusations. In article 301, if anyone talks about his own ethnicity, about genocide, or about the government's human rights violations, he is considered the enemy. Dink was murdered for his views on human rights and minority rights, and for stating his Armenian identity.

In a previous study with another sample of survivors from the Ottoman Turkish Genocide, Kalayjian et al. (1996) found that survivors did not talk about their feelings until the time of the interview, which was approximately 75 years post-genocide. Survivors expressed fear of further persecution, and kept silent for decades.

The results of this study revealed that a larger percentage (60%) of survivors who had talked about their negative experiences with family members had lower levels of PTSD. Although this was in a paraprofessional environment, the survivors felt comfortable enough to share such traumatic memories and experience catharsis. In the process of talking about their trauma they received some validation from their family members, and ultimately began working on gaining meaning from the experience. Communication is significant because it allows people to process their experiences, and would provide an opportunity to discover a new meaning. Establishing communication with people allows survivors to share their stories with others who may have had similar experiences, or with people who could help them process their experiences.

COPING METHODS IN FORM OF ARMENIAN RITUALS AND RELIGION

Armenian roots in Christianity, Christian rituals, and Armenian rituals go back to the fourth century. Armenia renounced its Eastern or Persian influenced past when in 301 A.D., King Tiridates established Christianity as the sole religion in Armenia, which made it the first Christian state in the history of the world (Babayan 2001–2002).

Before and during the time of the genocide, which started on April 24, 1915, the Armenians were being attacked, looted, raped, and exterminated. The survivors of the genocide used their Armenian and Christian rituals to cope with the horrible atrocities. One of the strongest Christian rituals was prayer. However, Armenian rituals were very important too, as they included sharing family stories, Armenian religious education, cooking, kin-keeping (bringing and keeping family together), and serving others.

The rituals and traditions that the Armenians practiced were the legacy of their ancestors. This legacy was passed on from generation to generation, changing along the way and adopting to the times and events of history such as the genocide (Kaprielian-Churchill 1990). Rituals and legacies were used to help family members articulate and relay family identity, learn family history, and provide succeeding generations with information about family culture.

Religion

The Armenian churches preserved religious traditions, such as going to church as a family and participating in social hours, as connections to other Armenians were greatly valued and therefore encouraged (Manoogian, Walker, and Richards 2007).

Attending Sunday school is and has always been of the utmost importance for Armenians. The education begins with the spiritual, moral, and social teachings and canons of the Armenian Church and ends with its extensive humanitarian, evangelical, and education activity in Armenia. Christian education is a priority within the scope of the Armenian Church's mission of faith. Armenians believe religious education will make a presence in the individual and community by following it through with a process of spiritual and intellectual development and formation. The Armenian belief in the importance of their faith gave them the strength to live on after the genocide (Kalayjian et al. 1996).

Prayer was a significant Christian ritual that the survivors practiced before, during, and after the genocide. One survivor stated, "On our march, I would constantly be praying and that kept me going." Even after the Armenians witnessed or experienced rape, torture, and death, they used the ritual of prayer to cope and persevere. The Armenians prayed for answers too, as they could not understand why they were being prosecuted for their beliefs in Christianity. Many Armenians stated, "I prayed for answers, how could such Christian people be punished liked this?"

Rituals

The survivors who were interviewed spoke about the significance of passing on information from one generation to the next. Intergenerational transmission, both material and symbolic, such as cherished possessions, family stories, language, values, norms, roles, morals, and rituals, is important, as it shapes individual and family identities (Csikszentmihalyi and Rochberg-Halton 1981; Pratt and Friese 2004, as cited in Manoogian, Walker, and Richards 2007).

The ritual of sharing family stories validates and gives meaning as well as identity to the family and can encourage family bonding. In practicing storytelling, the Armenians were able to continue and celebrate their history and collective identity. They had very few material possessions to pass on to the next generation and thus sharing family tales was of the outmost importance. The family stories reflect themes of unity, respect, strength, and endurance (Chaitin 2002, as cited in Manoogian, Walker, and Richards).

The retelling of genocide experiences became a ritual that showed the new generations that their ancestors persevered and did not give up. This was supposed to encourage hope for the future and made people's will and efforts to maintain family traditions and their culture even stronger (McAdams 2004).

Cooking was another Armenian ritual which was significant to carrying on their identity, ethnicity, and culture in the new world after the genocide (Manoogian, Walker, and Richards 2007). In some ways, it kept the memories of their parents and grandparents alive. One woman stated, "I enjoyed cooking with my grandmother when I was a child; that is my last memory of my grandmother alive before the march. I honor her and the Armenian culture by cooking and teaching my granddaughter how to cook." Cooking also brings the Armenian family and community together. This gives them a greater sense of their roots and identity.

Kin-keeping (*bringing and keeping family together*) was another practice that was and is still used after the genocide. The Armenians had to rebuild their families and they all became an extended family. Kin-keeping is a family need and a cultural necessity to preserve the Armenian identity (Manoogian, Walker, and Richards 2007). Families and community members were encouraged to go to church, marry other Armenians, gather for birthdays and holidays. One way of keeping the family together was teaching the Armenian language to the new generations. In some cases there was only one survivor of a family, and families developed from there. The Armenians now felt a greater importance in their new countries to nurture and facilitate their family connections.

Another ritual was *serving others*. As the Armenians arrived in different countries, most of them were helped by other people. This act of kindness in assisting others became a prominent practice for all Armenians, even more so after the genocide. One man states, "If it was not for the assistance of a friend, I would not have had the opportunity to work." The Armenians realized that they were refugees entering a new country without any paper work and that the world did not acknowledge the genocide. They were very grateful for the help they received in establishing themselves and the emphasis on serving others became a daily ritual and a permanent place in their culture.

RESILIENCE

Genocide survivors had to create new lives for themselves in their respective new countries in the Diaspora. They had to compartmentalize their experiences and memories in order to move forward with their lives. Survivors had no opportunities to secure jobs or living quarters in advance of the genocide and neither did they have any legal papers or documents from their past lives. The survivors moved forward by placing emphasis on excelling in their current host country and prospering. Their primary focus was survival through work, family, cultural connection through church, and procreation (Kalayjian et al. 1996).

MIGRATION

During the genocide the survivors had no choice but to walk from country to country until they found a satisfactory situation. In that time period in the Middle East and Europe, these countries were just coming out of World War I. Therefore, they too were plunged into poverty, and their citizens into economic and emotional depression. These challenges added to the survivors' distress and made the environment unsafe and void of nurturance.

INTERVIEWS

The interviews lasted longer than the allocated time for each question. The majority of survivors used the interview time to process unresolved feelings as they talked about their traumatic memories. In the qualitative portion of the questionnaire, symptoms of PTSD were expressed: extreme distress, crying, sobbing, expression of anger regarding denial, and talking about nightmares and flashbacks they had experienced. The professionals who conducted the interviews spent time processing and offering coping skills and supportive therapeutic techniques to alleviate survivors' pain and suffering. Survivors were also given personal referrals, and the opportunity to follow up during the subsequent days and weeks.

PTSD AND BSI

In general, higher BSI scores related to greater PTSD. Scores on the BSI overall GSI were marginally correlated with past PTSD, $r(17) = .47$, $p = .059$, and significantly related to current PTSD, $r(17) = .67, p = .003$. Research has shown that the body keeps score of the trauma. The body is negatively affected by the trauma.

Scientific research in the past decade reinforced these findings, stating that cells have memory (van der Kolk 1994). Research findings indicate that when trauma strikes, the immune system becomes occupied by a fight-or-flight response, thus leaving the body with little defense to protect physical health. Therefore, trauma survivors often express more physical symptoms and illnesses such as high blood pressure, ulcers, migraine headaches, backaches, skin problems, and other infections. Genocide survivors can benefit from being mindful of the impact of the trauma on their physical health. If one is unaware of this phenomenon, these physical symptoms may continue manifesting and transmitting to one's emotional and psychological state (van der Kolk).

As indicated in the research conducted by Kolb (1987), excessive stimulation of the central nervous system at the time of the trauma results in permanent neuronal changes that have a negative effect on learning, habituation, stimulus discrimination, and physical symptomatology. The abnormal startle response is characteristic of PTSD symptoms (American Psychiatric Association 1994). The failure of the abnormal acoustic startle response to have habituated suggests that traumatized people have difficulty in evaluating sensory stimuli and mobilizing appropriate levels of physiological arousal (Shalev and Rogel-Fuchs 1993). Thus, survivors with PTSD could not properly integrate memories of the genocide trauma; instead, they were mired in the continual reliving of the past and were misinterpreting physiological stimuli as threats.

Genocide as a mass trauma is experienced as an intense level of stress. Intense stress releases endogenous stress-response neurohormones such as catecholamines (e.g., epinephrine, norepinephrine, and serotonin), and hormones of the hypothalamic-pituitary-adrenaline variety, endogenous opiates. These stress hormones help survivors mobilize the energy required to deal with mass trauma in ways ranging from increased glucose release to enhanced immune function. In a normal stress-free person, stress produces rapid and effective hormonal responses. However, genocide as a mass trauma causes chronic and persistent stress, which inhibits the effectiveness of the stress response and induces desensitization (Axelrode and Reisine 1984).

Although there was no statistical relationship discovered among the LPQ, PTSD, and BSI, anecdotal findings shared by the survivors indicated that those who had resolved their trauma and had achieved a peaceful inner state discovered more meaning in life and found meaning in their daily tasks. Others who had expressed a lot of expectations from the perpetrators (such as acknowledgment of the genocide, reparation, and getting their homes and lands back) shared high levels of anger and resentment towards the Turkish government were more symptomatic and had less meaning in their lives, and no clear-cut goals in their daily tasks. The latter reinforces a sense of helplessness. Although Sullivan (1953) states that acknowledgment, validation, and reparation are essential for closure for a traumatic experience, in their absence, one is able to validate oneself and create the peace within by practicing forgiveness (Kalayjian 2009).

Although the authors hypothesized that if survivors had permanent homes and were not forced to migrate from country to country they would score lower on BSI, indicating less symptomatology, and low scores on PTSD; the findings revealed the year of entry as well as number of countries forced to immigrate were unrelated to levels of BSI and PTSD. Perhaps when survivors finally immigrated to the United States and felt comfort, financial security, and the benefits of a democracy, their arrival may have made the travels worth going through. Since the majority of survivors ended the interview with gratitude and the notion of "God bless America," indicating their level of joy and gratitude.

LIMITATIONS

These survivors were children at the time of the genocide, and the interviews took place approximately 70 years after the atrocities. These children suffered throughout their lives without any therapeutic interventions.

The nature of the interview questionnaire elicited traumatic memories; therefore, many survivors did not want to be subjected to the retraumatization inherent in the interview, which resulted in a small sample size. In addition, many survivors' families were not willing to have them participate due to the increase arousal of their parents after such interviews. A daughter of a survivor stated "I know it is for a good cause, but I am the one who will suffer with my mother all night when she is having nightmares and flashbacks after the appointment." This exemplifies the pain of a severe and long-term unresolved trauma.

Limitations of age, sample size, and having to use a convenience sample (since not enough survivors are living at this time, as the Genocide occurred around 1915), are all limitations to this study.

RECOMMENDATION FOR FURTHER RESEARCH

Future research can benefit from focusing on current genocides and their immediate impact on the survivors. Emphasis should be placed on healing interventions, coping strategies, and psychosocial and spiritual rehabilitation.

Most importantly, future research can benefit from studying the creative efforts and therapeutic interventions utilized in conjunction with perpetrators—perhaps then, and only then, can humanity prevent genocides.

ACKNOWLEDGMENT

Special gratitude to the following people for their unconditional support: Yuki Shigemoto, Ginger Armas, and Abigail Ortega.

REFERENCES

American Psychiatric Association. 1994. *Diagnostic and Statistical Manual of Mental Disorders.* 4th ed. Washington, DC: Author.

Armenian National Institute. 1998–2008. *Chronology of the Armenian Genocide 1939.* Available at: http://www.armenian-genocide.org/1939.html.

Axelrode, J., and Reisine, T.D. 1984. "Stress Hormones: Their Interaction and Regulation." *Science* 224: 452–59.

Babayan, Y. 2001–2002. *Armenian History: Christianization.* Available at: http://www.armenianhistory.info/.

Balakian, P. 2004. *The Burning Tigris: The Armenian Genocide and America's Response.* New York: Harper-Collins.

Brahm, E. 2003–2007. *Trauma Healing.* University of Colorado. Available at Beyond Intractability Knowledge Base Project Web site: http://www.beyond intractability.org/essay/trauma_healing/.

Cahn, A. 1987. *The Capacity to Acknowledge Experience in Holocaust Survivors and Their Children.* Paper presented at the 95th annual convention of the American Psychological Association, New York.

Csikszentmihalyi, M., and Rochberg-Halton, E. 1981. *The Meaning of Things: Domestic Symbols and the Self.* Cambridge, UK: Cambridge University Press.

Dadrian, V.N. 1994. "Documentation of the Armenian Genocide in German and Austrian Sources." In *Genocide: A Critical Biographic Review.* Vol. 3, ed. I. Charney, 77–125. New Brunswick, NJ: Transaction Publishers.

Danieli, Y. 1982. "Therapists' Difficulties in Treating Survivors of the Nazi Holocaust and Their Children." *Dissertation Abstracts International* 42 (12): 4, 927.

Danieli, Y. 1988. "Treating Survivors and Children of Survivors of the Nazi Holocaust." In *Post-Traumatic Therapy and Victims of Violence,* ed. F.M. Ochberg, 278–94. New York: Brunner/Mazel.

Derogatis, L.R. 1993. *The Brief Symptom Inventory (BSI): Administration, Scoring, and Procedures Manual-III.* Minneapolis, MN: National Computer Systems.

Des Pres, T. 1987. "Introduction: Remembering Armenia." In *The Armenian Genocide in Perspective,* ed. R.G. Hovannisian, 9–17. New Brunswick, NJ: Transaction.

Fiese, B.H. and Pratt, M.W. 2004. "Metaphors and Meanings of Family Stories: Integrating Life Course and Systems Perspectives on Narratives." In *Family Stories and the Life Course,* ed. M.W. Pratt and B.H. Fiese, 401–18. Mahwah, NJ: Erlbaum.

Folstein, M., Folstein S., and McHugh, P. 1975. "Mini-Mental State: A Practical Method for Grading the Cognitive State of Patients for the Clinician." *Journal of Psychiatric Research* 12: 189–98.

Hagengimana, A. 2001. *After Genocide in Rwanda: Social and Psychological Consequences.* Available at: http://www.isg-iags.org/oldsite/newsletters/25/athanse.html.

Helzer, J.E., Robins, L.N., and McEvoy, L. 1987. "Post-Traumatic Stress Disorder in the General Population." *New England Journal of Medicine* 317 (26): 1630–1634.

Herman, J.L. 1997. *Trauma and Recovery.* New York: Basic Books.

Hovannisian, R.G. 1987. "The Historical Dimensions of the Armenian Question, 1878–1923." In *The Armenian Genocide in Perspective,* ed. R.G. Hovannisian, 19–42. New Brunswick, NJ: Transaction.

Imber-Black, E. 2002. "Family Rituals, from Research to the Consulting Room and Back Again: Comment on the Special Section." *Journal of Family Psychology* 16: 445–46.

Jarman, R. 2001. "Healing as Part of Conflict Transformation." *Committee for Conflict Transformation Support Newsletter* 12. Available at: http://www.c-r.org/ccts/ccts12/healing.htm.

Kalayjian, A.S. 2002. "Biopsychosocial and Spiritual Treatment of Trauma." In *Comprehensive Handbook of Psychotherapy, Vol. III: Interpersonal, Humanistic, Existential,* ed. F. Kaslow, 615–37. New York: John Wiley & Sons.

Kalayjian, A.S. September, 2005. "Eight Stages of Healing from Mass Trauma." Paper presented at the UN 58th Annual DPI/NGO Conference, *Our Challenge: Voices for Peace, Partnership and Renewal,* New York.

Kalayjian, A.S. 2008. "Forgiveness when Denial Persists: The Case of Generational Transmission of Ottoman Turkish Genocide of the Armenians." In: *Forgiveness: Pathways for Conflict Transformation and Peace Building,* ed. A.S. Kalayjian and R. Paloutzian, 1–25. New York: Springer Publishing.

Kalayjian, A.S., Shahinian, S.P. 1998. "Recollections of Aged Armenian Survivors of the Ottoman Turkish Genocide: Resilience through Endurance, Coping, and Life Accomplishments." *The Psychoanalytic Review* 85 (4): 489–504.

Kalayjian, A.S., Shahinian, S.P., Gergerian, E.L., and Saraydarian, L. 1996. "Coping with Ottoman Turkish Genocide: An Exploration of the Experience of Armenian Survivors." *Journal of Traumatic Stress* 9 (1): 87–97.

Kaprielian-Churchill, I. 1990. "Armenian Refugees and their Entry into Canada: 1919–1930." *Canadian Historical Review* 71 (1): 88–108.

Kolb, L. 1987. "A Neuropsychological Hypothesis Explaining Post-traumatic Stress Disorder." *American Journal of Psychiatry* 144: 989–95.

Kupelian, D., Kalayjian, A.S., and Kassabian, A. 1998. "The Turkish Genocide of the Armenians." In *International Handbook of Multigenerational Legacies of Trauma,* ed. Y. Danieli, 191–210. New York: Plenum Press.

Manoogian, M.M., Walker, A.J., and Richards, L.N. 2007. "Gender, Genocide, and Ethnicity: The Legacies of Older Armenian American Mothers." *Journal of Family Issues* 28: 567–89.

Mazor, A., Gampel, Y., Enright, R.D., Orenstein, R. 1990. "Holocaust Survivors: Coping with Post-traumatic Memories in Childhood and 40 Years Later." *Journal of Traumatic Stress* 3: 1–14.

McAdams, D.P. 2004. "Generativity and the Narrative Ecology of Family Life." In *Family Stories and the Life Course,* eds. M.W. Pratt and B.H. Fiese, 235–57. Mahwah, NJ: Erlbaum.

Niederland, W. 1981. "The Survivor Syndrome: Further Observations and Dimensions." *Journal of the American Psychoanalytic Association* 29 (2): 413–25.

Office of the Higher Commissioner for Human Rights. 2008. *Convention on the Prevention and Punishment of the Crime of Genocide.* Available at: http://www.unhchr.ch/html/menu3/b/p_genoci.htm.

Robinson, M. 1998. *Opening address.* Paper presented at the Genocide and Crimes Against Humanity: Prevention and Early Warning Conference, United States Holocaust Memorial Museum, Washington, DC.

Rummel, R. 1996. *Death by Government.* New Brunswick, NJ: Transaction.

Schiraldi, G. R. 2000. *The Post-Traumatic Stress Disorder Sourcebook.* Los Angeles: Lowell House.

Shalev, A. Y., and Rogel-Fuchs, Y. 1993. "Psychophysiology of the Post-traumatic Stress Disorder: From Sulfur Fumes to Behavioral Genetics." *Psychosomatic Medicine* 55: 413–23.

Smith, R. W., Markusen, E., and Lifton, R. J. 1995. "Professional Ethics and the Denial of the Armenian Genocide." *Holocaust and Genocide Studies* 9 (1): 1–22.

Stanton, G. 1996. *The Eight Stages of Genocide.* Available at: http://www.genocidewatch.org/8stages1996.htm.

Staub, I. 1990. *Denial of the Armenian Genocide: Compounding the Crime.* Paper presented at the Armenian Center at the School of International Affairs, Columbia University, New York.

Sullivan, H. S. 1953. *The Interpersonal Theory of Psychiatry.* New York: W. W. Norton.

United States Institute of Peace. December, 2001. *Training to Help Traumatized Populations* (Special Report 79). Washington, DC: Author.

Universal Declaration of Human Rights. 2000–2008. *Fifth Anniversary of the Universal Declaration of Human Rights 1948–1998.* Available at: http://www.un.org/Overview/rights.html.

van der Kolk, B. 1994. *The Body Keeps the Score: Memory and the Evolution Psychology of Post-traumatic Stress.* Boston: Harvard Medical School.

Winter, J. 2003. "Under Cover of War: The Armenian Genocide in the Context of Total War." In *The Specter of Genocide: Mass Murder in Historical Perspective,* eds. R. Gellately and B. Kiernan, 189–213. Cambridge, MA: Cambridge University Press.

Woolf, L. 2000. *Incorporating Genocide, Ethnopolitical Conflict, and Human Rights Issues into the Psychology Curriculum.* Available at: http://www.lemoyne.edu/OTRP/teachingresources.html.

World War I. 2000–2007. *Primary Documents: Talaat Pasha's Alleged Official Orders Regarding the Armenian Massacres, March 1915-January 1916.* Available at: http://www.firstworldwar.com/source/ armenia_talaatorders.htm.

Chapter 17

GENDER AND GENOCIDE

Armenian and Greek Women Finding Positive Meaning in the Horror

Artemis Pipinelli and
Ani Kalayjian

The dead cannot cry out for justice; it is a duty of the living to
do so for them.

—Lois McMaster Bujold

Violence against women is one of the most intractable violations of human rights. The mission of the international women's human rights movement is to raise awareness of women's human rights violations and to challenge the injustice of threats, abuse, and humiliation against women. This chapter describes Armenian, Greek, and Cypriot gendercide and rape, and presents a historical documentation of sexual abuse, humiliation, and murder of women under Turkish rule. The horrors of rape and sexual abuse were part of a campaign against women which included genocide and ethnic cleansing. A model called "the persona of meaning" (Pipinelli 2006) and Kalayjian's seven-step Biopsychosocial and Eco-Spiritual Model (Kalayjian 2002a) based on Viktor Frankl's logotherapeutic (1962) work for meaning-making, is discussed and recommendations are given for future studies. This seven-step model is used globally in over 25 outreach projects and is founded on the premise that after mass trauma one needs to express one's feeling, find validation and empathy, then move into discovering a new meaning, incorporating forgiveness, and use breath for self healing. Only with forgiveness can one release one's paralyzing past. Forgiveness enables one to envision a future without judgment, resentment, anger, or sadness. Although forgiveness by women who were violated would require, at minimum, the perpetrators' acknowledgment, apology, and making amends to the greatest extent possible (Sullivan 1953), even without this acknowledgment or in the absence of the culprit, this seven-step model has helped women achieve integration and closure. This chapter also discusses authentic rituals, religious practices, and other forms of healing.

INTRODUCTION

From the beginning of time to today's war zones of Bosnia, Rwanda, Sierra Leone, and Darfur, rape has been used as a weapon of violence and humiliation especially against women, particularly during conflicts, genocides, and ethnic cleansing. Rape is documented and condemned by Nongovernmental Organizations (NGOs) as well as states within the United Nations as a crime against humanity. However, rape still occurs. The objective of the perpetrators is ethnic cleansing, which they in part achieve by terrorizing and publicly humiliating women, which then humiliates the entire family, community, and the nation. Consequently, women are too ashamed to return to their homes, and therefore the perpetrators claim their lands and ultimately achieve their goal of ethnic cleansing. The crime of rape (or first-degree sexual assault in some states) generally refers to nonconsensual sexual intercourse committed by physical force, threat of injury, or other duress. Lack of consent can include the victim's inability to say no to intercourse, thus feeling powerless and helpless against the aggressors.

Historically the crime of rape can be found in antiquity (the rape of the Sabine women and incidents in the Bible) as well as in mythology (Europa and Leda by the god Zeus in ancient Greece). In ancient Rome a raped woman would, like Lucretia, remove the stain on her honor by committing suicide. In every conflict and society throughout history, women have been violated sexually as a way of being dominated or forced to submit or as a prelude to being killed or ethnically cleansed by an aggressor. Such events have been well documented in historic records for posterity, but few if any forms of protection or safety have ever been enacted to help victims. Only recently, on September 2, 1998, the United Nations International Tribunal for Rwanda declared rape a war crime (Obote 2007). The International Criminal Tribunal for Rwanda (ICTR) in fact considered rape committed under certain circumstances to be (part of) genocide: see Chesterman (2001), who stated that "rape and sexual violence, constitute genocide in the same way as any other act, as long as the violence is committed with the specific intent to destroy, in whole or in part, a particular group, targeted as such. Indeed, rape and sexual violence . . . are even . . . one of the worst ways of inflicting harm on the victim as he or she suffers both bodily and mental harm . . . . Sexual violence was an integral part of the process of destruction, specifically targeting Tutsi women and contributing to their destruction and to the destruction of the Tutsi group as a whole . . . . Sexual violence was one step in the process of destroying the Tutsi group—destroying the spirit, the will to live, and life itself." In Rwanda, violence against women remains one of the most intractable violations of human rights. Sadly, rape persists not only in times of war but also in times of relative peace. Women are often beaten in their homes by intimate partners; raped or sexually assaulted by soldiers during times of civil unrest; sexually assaulted by law enforcement personnel while in their custody; raped in refugee camps by other refugees, local police or military personnel; and targeted for sexual violence based on their low social status. Several decades of work by the women's human rights movement culminated in 1998 with gains in governmental actions by law to deter violence against women in a handful of countries. This chapter provides a review of literature that addresses rape as a weapon of humiliation. Concurrently, this chapter emphasizes meaning-making and recovery based on a model that has been proven to be therapeutic and effective in over 25 mass traumas.

DEFINITIONS

The *Oxford English Dictionary* (2008) defines genocide as "the deliberate extermination of a race of people." According to the United Nations, genocide means the methodical intent to destroy, in whole or in part, national, ethnic, racial, or religious groups, and its primary crime does not relate to war conflicts but instead constitutes a crime against humanity. The partial or total annihilation of a national, racial, or religious group matches Article 2 of the Special Convention, which was passed by the General Assembly of the United Nations in 1948 (UN 1948).

According to Jones (2004), the term *gendercide* is used to acknowledge organized, gender-selective mass killing, a common feature of war, ethnic cleansing, genocide, and other human-induced conflicts. The term was first used by Mary Anne Warren (1985) in her book on *Gendercide: The Implications of Sex Selection.* Warren drew an analogy between the concept of *genocide* and what she called *gendercide.* The goal of these mass killings is the annihilation of real or imagined opponents and/or reproductive powers and group coherence as a distinct part of a more thorough genocidal design, or *root-and-branch extermination* (Jones 2004).

HISTORICAL PERSPECTIVES:
OTTOMAN GENDERCIDE

According to a United Nation report (UN 2006), violence and discrimination against women have reached epidemic global and social proportions. The horrors of rape and sexual abuse were part of a campaign against women during the Armenian and Greek genocides of 1895–1923 and Cypriot ethnic cleansing of 1974. Armenian and Greek females were targeted for physical destruction, sexual abuse, slavery, and forced assimilation. They were taken from their homes, forced into death marches, were raped and abused both physically and mentally.

After the Russian victory over the Ottoman Empire in the Russo-Turkish War of 1877–78, the Russians seized a large swath of territory inhabited by the Armenians, but ceded much of it after signing the Treaty of Berlin on June 13–July 13, 1878 (Douglas and Campbell 2006). The Russians claimed that they were protectors of the Christians within the Ottoman Empire. The weakening control of the Ottoman government over its empire during the next 15 years deluded many Armenians to believe that they could gain independence. However, this ultimately led to the Armenian genocide. From 1894–1896, under the rule of Sultan Abdul Hamid, some 300,000 Armenians were systematically murdered (Kalayjian et al. 1998). The international confusion created by World War I (1914–1918) compelled Turkish rulers to declare Armenians as enemies of the Ottoman Empire. From 1915–1918, over 1.5 million Armenians were slaughtered under the jurisdiction of the Young Turks in the Ottoman Empire. The Turkish government however, denies any wrongdoings and claims that the Armenian deaths were the result of interethnic strife, disease, and famine during World War I. While a number of Turkish, Western, and Armenian scholars consider the Ottoman Turkish Genocide the first major genocide of the 20th century, the Armenian genocide has used the term gendercide (Dadrian 1994). Genocide in this case appears as a power for the radical resolution of the conflict over Anatolia, occupied by Ottoman Turkey. The collapse of moral values occurred so rapidly that the abuses committed against both the Armenians and Greeks took place publicly, including but not limited to brutalization through warfare (Dadrian 1994).

The *Hellenic Genocide* was the systematic torture, massacre, and ethnic cleansing of one million Hellenes (Greeks) perpetrated by the Turks in Asia Minor. Most of the victims were massacred between the years of 1895 (much earlier than World War I) and 1955 (much after World War II). The present estimate is that some 2 million Greek men, women, and children were killed during that period (Evdokas 1976).

In the same place and often at the same time, 1.5 million Armenians were also massacred. From 1915 to 1923, over 353,000 Pontian Greeks were murdered. Mustafa Kemal (1881–1938) was behind the modernization and industrialization of the Republic of Turkey as well as its militarization. His many Westernizing reforms have deflected criticism of Turkey's record on human rights and discrimination against its Christian and Kurdish minorities. Since Mustafa Kemal was the consummator of the Assyrian, Armenian, and Greek genocide, his role in these horrors has been significantly downplayed due to Turkish pride. It goes against Article 301 (recently revised, Turkey Central 2009) of the Turkish Penal Code which bans "denigrating the Turkish Identity." However, no one can deny that the Assyrian, Hellenic, and Cyprus Genocides were an organized and a systematic torture, massacre, and ethnic cleansing of several million Hellenes perpetrated by the Turks in Asia Minor. In 1994, the Greek Parliament adopted legislation marking May 19 as a day of commemoration of the genocide of the Greeks of Pontus. In 2001, the Greek Parliament also adopted legislation marking September 14 in commemoration of the 1922 Genocide of the Greeks in Asia Minor. Turkey was angered by this decree and Prime Minister Bulent Ecevit declared, "Nobody with the slightest bit of sense could ever take those claims seriously" (Malkidis 2007).

The truth is, as noted by Bjørnlund (2006), that hundreds of Armenian women were systematically murdered after being raped, representing the symbolic rape and humiliation of the entire community. Beautiful daughters of Armenian families were sexually assaulted, raped, and murdered. Reports demonstrate that female relatives of male torture victims were raped in front of their relatives, as part of their humiliation and punishment (Jones 2004). A great number of Armenian women and children were abducted and sent to be Turkified or adopted into Kurdish households, in a system which worked to secure the loyalty of local tribesmen and villagers. Further sexual violence was a routine of war and was often encouraged as a by-product of the overall genocidal campaign. Rape as a weapon of dehumanization was a deliberate attempt to weaken and force women and children to accept the Muslim faith.

CYPRUS GENDERCIDE

In 1959, after negotiations in Zurich and London, Cyprus was proclaimed an independent republic. Britain, Greece, and Turkey were appointed to be its guarantors. Racial tensions were endemic to the Cypriot Constitution and Greek and Turkish Cypriots had little to say about the drafting. Once in Cyprus, instead of restoring the state of affairs under the 1960 constitution and protecting the human rights of all the people of Cyprus, Turkey extended its invasion (European Commission); to the credit of the contending communities, however, Cyprus did not slip into civil war.

Despite a number of United Nations resolutions calling for an end to outside interference, the Turkish occupation and de facto partition of the island into two areas continues to this day (Pan Cyprian Committee 2006). By August 18, 1974 the Turkish army had drawn a line (aptly called the Attila line) across the island, which still remains intact. Turkey then violated a UN ceasefire and three days later declared the restoration of the democracy by invading Cyprus again on August 14, 1974. Even now, Turkey occupies 38 percent of the island's territory after the ethnic cleansing of 200,000 Greek Cypriots in 1974, during which 5,000 were killed, and over 1,619 Greek Cypriots were abducted and remain missing (Pan Cyprus Press 2006). Their whereabouts were never disclosed by the Turkish authorities. The Turkish army was specifically designed to brutalize and terrify local Greek Cypriots. Moreover, the Turkish army was trained to drive thousand of Cypriots out of their homes. A witness gave evidence of two mass killings at Palekythron. In each case, between 30 and 40 Cypriot soldiers who had surrendered to the advancing Turks were shot. At Trimithi, eye-witnesses told of the deaths of several men (Argyros 2007).

On November 1, 1974, the UN General Assembly unanimously passed a resolution calling on all states to respect the independence of the Republic of Cyprus, and urging the speedy withdrawal of all foreign troops (Cyprus Press 2006). Even now, Turkey still refuses to comply with over 100 UN Security Council resolutions demanding the immediate withdrawal of Turkish troops from Cyprus soil and to facilitate the return of the refugees to their homes (Argyros 2007). The European Commission on Human Rights found violations of a number of Articles of the Convention (UN 2007). Such violations were exclusively directed against members of the Greek Cypriot community. The Commission outlined the violent attack of the Turkish troops and specifically included the rapes of 1000 women, from ages 12 to 71. Rape victims suffered severe gynecological problems as well as psychological trauma. In some cases, women were forced into prostitution. Many were collected from different villages and held in separate rooms of empty houses where they were repeatedly raped by Turkish soldiers. In other cases, members of the same family were repeatedly raped, some in front of their children. Rapes also occurred in public before spectators. The brutality of these violent sexual attacks was followed by extreme physical trauma, including near suffocation. Children and pregnant or mentally-retarded women were not spared. Testimonies included that of a man whose wife was stabbed in the neck while resisting rape; and his 6-year-old granddaughter who was stabbed and killed by Turkish soldiers attempting to rape her. A Red Cross worker who cared for 38 injured women said that the women had been raped and abused, many in front of their husbands and children. The European Human Rights Commission, in a 12 to 1 vote, found that incidents of rape constitute "inhuman treatment" and thus were in violation of Article 3 for which Turkey is responsible under the Convention (Argyros 2007). These are indications that the goal of Turkish forces was the dispersion of the Cypriot population. Rape is among the systematic weapons that are used for terror against women: "Instances that have included sexual infringements against women are apparently part of an inclusive pattern of war" (Stiglmayer 1994).

As of 2009, 40,000 Turkish troops remain in Cyprus as a presence that prevents securing the human rights of the Greek Cypriots. Turkey has been found guilty of mass violations of human rights by the European Commission and the Court of Human Rights, including the right to life, the right to property, liberty, and security of person, freedom of thought, conscience, and religion, and the prohibition of discrimination.

EFFECTS OF THE TRAUMA OF RAPE AND POST-TRAUMATIC STRESS DISORDER (PTSD)

The psychosocial impact of the continued occupation of Turkey is severe. The first and second generation survivors of the Armenian, Greek, and Greek-Cypriot genocide and gendercide have suffered mass trauma, death of loved ones, and forced relocation. According to Kalayjian (2002a), the majority of the adults and older adults suffered from moderate to severe post-traumatic stress disorder (PTSD). The majority of women who were raped also experienced severe PTSD. The variables that helped survivors cope with PTSD included: (a) familial ties, (b) religious and spiritual awareness, and (c) the continued collective struggle for freedom from Turkish occupation. Armenians, Greeks, and Greek-Cypriots still have feelings of anger (a) directed outward toward Turkey and the world's silence, and (b) directed inward. Often, the anger directed inwards results in domestic violence and addictions. PTSD is not the only condition that resulted from the mass trauma. Other diagnoses included: generalized anxiety disorder (GAD), depression, addiction, and phobic disorders (Kalayjian 2002a).

In conclusion, recovery from the trauma of rape, and specifically genocidal rape, is complex and its negative impact is ongoing. The negative impact of the mass trauma can be detrimental to those who do not have the internal control and/or psychological factors to manage their feelings of helplessness and hopelessness. Some women do undergo a healing process while others may become victims trapped in the deep abyss of emotional turmoil (Kalayjian 2002a).

PROGRESS IN THE INTERNATIONAL
ARENA ON RAPE AND SEXUAL ABUSE

Historically, sexual assault was tacitly accepted as a necessary evil of warfare used to stabilize and/or promote military combat morale. Rape was considered the bonus of war, after its dangerous employments. Violence against women demonstrated the control that male opponents had over their victims and the forceful weapon they could wield against the social structure of the attacked society. If women survived the war, they felt victimized, ashamed, and remained silent.

Human Rights Watch reveals that international governments have not focused enough legislative attention on violence and sexual assaults against women. From Bosnia to Peru, South Africa to Russia, and even today in Darfur, authorities treat violence against women as a lesser crime and discourage women from reporting it. Other reports indicate that slow progress is being made for women in some western countries.

For example, in 1998 public education programs in Egypt were implemented to communicate the health risks associated with the practice of female genital mutilation. However, regardless of such programming, many Egyptians still violated the ban against mutilation. In Peru, victims of abuse were scrutinized by police, as if they had provoked their attacks. Sexual violence victims still face many obstacles and biases in the legal system in many Middle Eastern, African, Indian, and Latin American countries. In countries like Peru, Russia, Africa, Turkey, and Pakistan, victims of sexual violence must first undergo a forensic exam in order to gather evidence supporting their rape claims; however, such exams prove inadequate to provide compelling evidence of sexual assault. Soldiers, militia, and their sympathizers continue to sexually assault women with impunity in armed conflicts around the globe, including in Sierra Leone, Chechnya, Kosovo, Bosnia, and Angola. Despite international recognition of rape and sexual assault during armed conflict as horrific crimes, governments and the international community at large rarely respond vigorously to investigate and punish such violence. To date, international research studies on rape as a weapon of war remain inadequate (HRWWR 2001).

THE ARMENIAN CASE

While interviewing Armenian survivors to explore coping reactions, resilience and meaning-making, we came across many horrifying stories about the atrocities committed by the Ottoman Turkish Empire (Kalayjian et al. 1996). The following is one of many cases where gendercide was used to humiliate women, their families and communities.

THE STORY OF MRS. H

Mrs. H (Argyros 2007) is from the village of Urfa, in Anatolia, which is currently considered to be part of Turkey. Mrs. H described how on one day all the men were collected from her neighborhood. Some men were told that they were going to the army, while others were told that they would be given special promotions. Regardless, all were killed. The Turks either shot them, or if they did not want to waste the bullets, they burned them, all tied together in the church courtyard. Then, the Turkish gendarmes came for the women and children. Before evicting them, they first selected the most beautiful of women to be enslaved or forced into prostitution. Next, they came for the rest. In an attempt to save their daughters, mothers slathered mud on their girls to make them look less attractive. Mrs. H reported that on that day, a group of Turkish gendarmes forced a few young girls out of their homes, ripped their clothes off and in front of all their neighbors began taking turns raping them, while the girls screamed for their mothers, fathers, and God. After each Turkish soldier had taken his turn, the girls were set on fire. No one was able to run to their rescue as the Turkish soldiers watched from the sidelines and if anyone dared to try to rescue the girls, they were shot to death. The Turkish soldiers repeatedly said that they did not want to waste bullets on Armenians; they wanted them to die burning, screaming, yelling, and crying.

THE CYPRIOT CASE: MRS. M

Mrs. M (Argyros 2007) was sexually assaulted during the Turkish invasion of her village of Palekynthro in 1974. She was 20 years old at the time. Today, she is a grandmother. Mrs. M is still brought to tears when she recalls the horrible acts committed against her and still harbors anger against the perpetrators. However, she is thankful that she did not get pregnant. Others were not so lucky.

Mrs. M was assaulted by three Turkish soldiers who held her down at knifepoint. She testified: "because I did not resist, I am now alive. Other women in her village resisted and were shot. Turkish soldiers broke open the door of my home and hurled themselves toward me. In front of my mother, I was violated multiple times by multiple soldiers. Then, gun shots were heard. Other Turks were warning their comrades that Greek-Cypriot troops were approaching. With this, the Turks left and ran. The Greek-Cypriots took me to a shelter near the Red Cross. This is how I survived. I know women who got pregnant and had abortions. They did not want to carry the children of their perpetrators. Archbishop Makarios gave us permission to get abortions at that time."

It was very difficult for Mrs. M to recall such painful memories. She was asked if she could forgive those who hurt her and she replied "No never." "I pray to Jesus to find peace. Also, I am angry at those who started all that, those big greedy powers." Mrs. M expressed her frustration regarding the injustice and her anger toward the United Nations for not intervening. "Even the Anan plan cut us short," she said. Mrs. M drew strength from her family. "I am a survivor and not a helpless victim." She enjoys taking care of her two grandchildren. They are the meaning and purpose of her life.

In the case of Mrs. M, forgiveness on the personal level will require some time. In theory, although forgiveness is easier to achieve when the perpetrator acknowledges, apologizes and/or shows remorse, forgiveness is still possible without these things. In order to forgive, Mrs. M will have to make a conscious choice to shift her perception from paralyzing fear to envisioning a future without anger, resentment, sadness, or pain. However, this will take time. Also, repentance can pave the way for forgiveness, which may, in turn, lead to reconciliation.

RAPE AS A MAJOR TRAUMA

The experience of rape can be manifested in a variety of psychological symptoms such as major depression, general anxiety, and substance abuse as well as physiological and spiritual symptomatology. According to the DSM-IV (American Psychiatric Association 2000) post-traumatic stress disorder (PTSD) (309.81) is categorized among anxiety disorders. Those who are diagnosed with PTSD meet the following six criteria:

1. The person must experience or witness a traumatic event that is marked by a threat to well-being of self or others, and strong feelings of intense fear, helplessness, or horror

2. The person must constantly re-experience or relive the traumatic event. Re-experiencing the event includes images, thoughts, and perceptions; recurring flashbacks, reliving the experience, illusions, hallucinations, and dissociative flashback dreams or nightmares. Psychological and physiological distress on exposure to internal or external cues that symbolize or resemble an aspect of the traumatic event

3. There is an intense desire to avoid all stimuli that seem even slightly related to the event. In addition, there is a lack of general responsiveness

4. The person must feel a persistent increased arousal in at least two of the following ways: insomnia, irritability, difficulty concentrating, hypervigilance, or unnecessary and disproportionate startle responses

5. The symptoms mentioned above must last longer than a month
6. The symptoms must negatively affect the individual's social and occupational functioning

Frankl (1962) was the first to note that positive meaning can be made even out of mass trauma. The role of the therapist in logotherapy (meaning-oriented therapy) is to help a rape survivor discover a unique personal meaning in relation to a traumatic experience, thus transforming the pain of the trauma into meaningful awareness and perhaps encouraging the person to make positive and active contributions to their family, community, and to the greater global community (Kalayjian 2002a).

SOCIAL IMPLICATIONS AND MORAL RESPONSIBILITY

Social awareness of the issues of rape during times of war can help individuals as well as non-governmental organizations (NGOs) highlight such issues for political solutions. The goal of the international women's human rights movement is to raise awareness on women's human rights violations and to eliminate threats, abuses, and humiliation against women across the globe. The Armenian, Greek, and Cypriot survivors of rape can attempt to forgive. Without the perpetrators' acknowledgment and acceptance of responsibility, full reconciliation among parties cannot take place at the state level. However, even without acknowledgement of the wrongdoing, women can work through their issues by finding meaning through the Bio-psychosocial and Eco Spiritual Treatment Model (Kalayjian 2002b).

One way to prevent such atrocities is through public awareness. Human Rights Watch reports that international governments do not focus enough legislative attention on domestic and sexual violence against women. After mass human-induced traumas such as gendercide and genocide, not only is legislative action needed but acknowledgment, validation, and reparation are imperative for survivors to achieve closure. A similar case is the Jewish Holocaust; in December 1995, Edgar Bronfman, President of the World Jewish Congress, met with then Senator D'Amato, chairman of the senate Banking Committee, to discuss Holocaust compensation payments and the global search for justice for victims of Nazi persecution (Huber 2002). This acknowledgement is, as one commentator put it, "the moral of this story is a story of the moral."

Nadler (2001), a researcher at Tel Aviv University, focuses on the changing themes in psychological theory in regards to post-traumatic stress disorder. It was found that the perceptions of Israeli Holocaust survivors have been changing over the past 20 years. On a societal level, the suffering of a few has become the collective memory of the many, and the emphasis was extended beyond the survivors and directed on to the survivor's families and on Israeli society as a whole. Nadler argues that psychological theory makes the distinction between individual and social trauma. However in the case of *Gendercide* rape, the trauma is both individual and societal, since it affects the entire community and/or nation.

Since reparative efforts have been absent with respect to the Turkish Genocide and gendercide against the Armenians, Greeks, and Cypriots, it is critical, then, to focus on international awareness. Forgiveness releases people from their paralyzing pasts by allowing them to envision a future without judgment, resentment, anger, or sadness. According to Kalayjian et al's (1996a) research, conducted 80 years after the Ottoman Turkish Genocide of the Armenians, resentment and anger were still carried by many survivors due to the ongoing Turkish denial of the Genocide. This persistent Turkish governmental denial has evoked intense anger in many survivors, mainly because of the government's lack of validation and reparation. Individual case studies in psychotherapy practices have revealed that harboring resentment is detrimental to one's physical, mental and spiritual health. Despite the many positive findings on the effectiveness of practicing forgiveness, victims experience confusion regarding forgiveness when perpetrators do not express remorse or if they completely deny their crimes. Forgiveness comes from relinquishing the anger that may be as destructive as the trauma itself. At the same time, the anger can serve as a motivating force to fight injustice. This positive channeling of anger then creates new meaning and purpose in the lives of survivors and provides spiritual awareness (Kalayjian 2002a). However, forgiveness is a personal choice that requires a shift in one's attitude. Forgiveness requires courage, a decision to let go, strong internal control, capacity for resilience, and a willingness to learn lessons.

HEALING AND MEANING-MAKING
AFTER TRAUMA

Since rape victims face fear, anger, shame, and other negative emotions related to the trauma, they are even more vulnerable to depression immediately following the trauma. Joiner and Blalock (1995) assert that females show higher lifetime prevalence for depression. However, only a few studies have looked at the relationship between gendercide and depression. Because of biological variables and greater vulnerability due to genetic factors and the reproductive cycle, females are more susceptible to depressive symptoms than males (Buss 1996). Yet, other research asserts that women more openly express their symptoms, as compared to men, who in extreme cases may rely more on substance use such as alcohol or express emotions through aggression (Holdcraft, Iacono, and Mcgue 1998). Rape victims will most likely suffer from feelings of loss of control, hopelessness, and helplessness that are directly tied to depressive symptoms and trauma. In certain cases of rape the use of alcohol plays a distinct role for victims and perpetrators of rape (Larimer et al. 1999).

Research has demonstrated that the traditional female role increases dependence and helplessness among women (Buss and Plomin 1984). Moreover, stressors resulting from lower socioeconomic status leave women vulnerable to depressive symptoms. Gendercide survivors are usually depressed, ashamed, and horrified by what happened to them. Beck (1972) found that females displayed more symptoms of depression, low self-esteem, and self-blame than did males. Thus, one can imagine the effects of rape on the psychological well-being of the female victim. These gender differences should be examined in future studies.

Another line of investigation looks at the relationship between cultural and spiritual factors and trauma. Abernethy et al. (2006) applied a multicultural model (Atkinson, Morten and Sue 1998) for cultural competence and factors in the treatment of African American families. They discussed three different cultural perspectives: spiritual, womanism, and trauma. The concept of womanism is a way for many women to "affirm themselves as black, while simultaneously owning their connection with feminism and with the African American community." The spiritual perspective highlights the integration of spiritual values into the therapist's treatment process. A great number of traumatized women receive the social support they need by relying on prayer, the Holy Bible, and the church community, as well as by attending religious services while others receive trauma counseling (Kalayjian et al. 1996).

The global community needs to understand the spiritual needs of women, specifically those who have been abused and traumatized by rape, in order to assist them in reaching an inner peace through spirituality and meaning-making. While women had no control over the horrible events of *gendercide* and rape, the recovery that comes from the healing process can help them choose whether they want to live as victims or survivors. The damage caused by gendercide rape is often long and painful, making recovery a laborsome process. However, the essential first steps involve developing personal meaning, which is defined as purpose in life, sense of direction, sense of order, and/or reason for existence. Meaning should promote hope and optimism (Reker, Peacock, and Wong 1987), after which the healing of trauma can then follow (Kalayjian 1996). Meaning of life is understood as the extent to which individuals hold personal beliefs and convictions that permeate their lives with meaning, and give them a sense of hope and optimism (Chang and Shanna 2001). This transformation from pain to meaning is exemplified in the case of Rwandan survivor Immaculee Ilibagiza (2008) as described in her book entitled *Left to Tell: Discovering God amidst the Rwandan Holocaust.* In spite of the death of her entire family, she found an inner peace and sense of hope through forgiveness and spirituality (Koenig and Larson 2001).

Frankl (1962), an existential humanistic psychiatrist, concurred with earlier existential philosophers who believed that people are free to make choices. The core of the human experience is to search for meaning and purpose. Therefore, the major constructs of Frankl's theory are: the will for making meaning, the existential vacuum (a feeling that life has no meaning or purpose), realities and potentialities, personal choice, and death transcendence. Frankl believed that meaning was often the outcome of love, work, and suffering. Humans could transcend their biological and social circumstances to a level of spirituality that allowed them to create meaning in their lives. He believed that when the search for meaning is inhibited, individuals develop an "existential vacuum" in which they experience feelings of boredom, indifference, apathy, and meaninglessness that could possibly lead to suicide. For Frankl, the existential vacuum was often the product of today's complex and impersonal world, rather than a specific pathology within an individual. Frankl believed that life has no meaning or purpose in and of itself. Instead, purpose in life is specific to a person and comes from life circumstances. Individuals, life experiences, and environments can all change, resulting in either an existential vacuum or in meaning and purpose in life. A person finds meaning through the biological world in relation to self and others. In turn, the biological world and the world from within (personality and locus of control) influence the search for purpose. Therefore, women who have been traumatized by rape may find meaning by working on their inner strength, control, and their self-image. Pipinelli (2006) presented a meaning-making model that may be applied to trauma and rape victims. Based on her research, there were two primary variables: meaning of life; and strong (internal) locus of control, indicating how people live their lives. These variables constitute the "Epikratiki persona" (*epi* in Greek means on; *krato* means to hold), or persona of meaning. This persona of meaning helps the trauma survivors change their self perception, from helpless and hopeless victims to individuals who have survived brutality and acquired the experience to live free of psychological suffering. Kalayjian (2005) has also offered a model for healing from the mass trauma of genocide. This model has eight stages in total: (1) acknowledgement, (2) validation, (3) reparation, (4) facing fear, anger, shame, and humiliation, (5) facing denial and revisionism, (6) acceptance and forgiveness, (7) discovery of new meaning, and (8) lessons learned and closure. She has utilized this model in the Armenian-Turkish reconciliation dialogue groups from 1999–2007 with relative success (Kalayjian 2009).

SPIRITUAL PRACTICES AMONG GREEKS AND ARMENIANS

Spirituality has been an important part of the Greek and Armenian cultures since ancient times. Unlike the Greek goddesses that were powerful and independent but still inferior to male gods, mortal women were mainly responsible of bearing children. Zeus raped Europa in order to produce sons. This rape seems to serve as a mechanism for producing offspring with the blood of Zeus. In addition, this rape was violent, *not* consensual and was camouflaged as a nonviolent rape where a woman succumbed to the power of the male patriarch or conqueror. Such rapes were seen as part of the patriarchal powers dominating the matriarchal powers. Much later, the Greek ancient deity was translated into the new Christian religion. Armenia was the first nation to accept Christianity in 301 A.D. The Greek and Armenian ancient gods and goddesses became angels, temples became churches and festivals and holidays were renamed. For hundreds of years, Armenian and Greek women who experienced trauma have worn black clothes to demonstrate their feelings of anger, sadness, and depression, like the old furies in ancient tragedies who had severe pain and wanted liberation through the good deeds of the sufferer. The rape victims seek liberation through prayer and being part of the community that condoned the perpetrators and ask God for forgiveness.

Greek ancient pottery depicts women pulling their hair as an expression of mourning and inflicting more pain on themselves. One may observe similar practices in Modern Greek funerals. However in the same ancient art, men assumed the dominant role; they were self controlled and unemotional. Currently, fathers of victims show more of their feelings of sorrow and even tears at the loss of loved ones.

From the rape of Persephone (Debloois 1997) to the ancient young priestesses who were raped by powerful Greek men in the temples, today's rape victims wash their bodies not in the rivers, but in their own private baths to wash away the rapist's clues and memories. Baptism in the Greek Orthodox Church cleans the person from his sins and agiasmos (Greek holy water, specially prepared and prayed over by a group of priests in the church during mass), and Myron (for Armenians) becomes the symbolic healing agent that cleans and alleviates the sufferer from his physical and psychological trauma. These spiritual rituals are effective as they connect the victims/survivors with their community, for social support (Vaux 1988) and meaning (Frankl 1962; Kalayjian 2002a; Pipinelli 2005).

CONCLUSION

In conclusion, violence against women is still one of the most intractable violations of women's human rights. The goal of the international women's human rights movement is to raise awareness of women's human rights violations and to challenge the injustices of threats, abuses, and humiliation against women around the world. Rape is one of many brutal weapons of war, as well as a weapon of mass destruction. Its aim is to humiliate, punish, control, instill fear, and drive women and entire communities from their land. The horrors of rape and sexual abuse were part of a campaign against women during the Armenian and Greek Genocides and Cypriot ethnic cleansings of the 19th and 20th centuries. The victims were as young as 12 and as old as 71. In addition to merciless public rapes, victims endured severe gynecological problems as well as psychological trauma. Rape victims who experienced fear, anger, shame, and other negative emotions related to the trauma were more vulnerable to depression immediately after the trauma. According to Kalayjian et al. (1996), resentment and anger persisted in the hearts of many survivors because the Turkish government denied the genocide. The Armenian, Greek and Cypriot victims of rape will never forget their trauma. However, Kalayjian (2002b) and Pipinelli (2006) offer two models for healing the wounds of mass trauma, which include processing their negative feelings and practice forgiveness on both interpersonal and intrapersonal levels as well as creating a sense of peace within.

Human Rights Watch reports that international governments do not focus enough legislative attention on domestic and sexual violence against women. Rape and violence against women still constitutes a serious crime against women and should not be tolerated or taken lightly. Education and respect for the cultural dignity of individuals and societies may raise awareness of the problem and lead to resolutions of such conflicts in this globalized era.

REFERENCES

Abernethy, A. D., Houston, T. R., Mimms, T., and Boyed-Franklin, N. 2006. "Using Prayer in Psychotherapy: Applying Sue's Differential to Enhance Culturally Competent Care." *Cultural Diversity and Ethnic Minority Psychology* 12 (1): 101–14.

American Psychiatric Association. 2000. *Diagnostic and Statistical Manual of Mental Disorders*. 4th ed. rev. Washington, DC: Author, 467.

Argyros, A. 2007. *Case of Cyprus vs. Turkey Registry of the European Court of Human Rights* F-67075. Available at: www.greekgenocide.org and http://www.argyros.argyrou.btinternet.co.uk/cyprus/Quotes.htm.

Atkinson, D., Morent, G, and Sue, D. W. 1998. *Counseling American Minorities,* 5th ed. New York: McGraw-Hill, vii, 391.

Beck, A. T. 1972. "Measuring Depression: The Depression Inventory." In *Recent Advances in the Psychobiology of the Depressive Illnesses,* eds. T. A. Williams, M. M. Katz, and J. A. Sheilds, 299–302. Washington, DC: U.S. Government Printing Office.

Buss, A. H. 1986. *Social Behavior and Personality.* Hillsdale, NJ: Erlbaum.

Buss, A. H., and R. Plomin. 1984. *Temperament: Early Developing Trait.* Hillsdale, NJ: Erlbaum.

Bjørnlund, M. 2006. "A Fate Worse than Dying." Presented in conference on *War and Sexuality in Twentieth Century Europe.* Europæisk Konflikt-og-Identitetshistorie (CONIH), Esbjerg: 28–30.

Chang, E. C., and Shanna, L. J. 2001. "Optimism, Pessimism, and Positive and Negative Affectivity in Middle-Aged Adults: A Test of a Cognitive-Affective Model of Psychological Adjustment." *Psychology and Aging* 16: 524–31.

Chesterman, S., ed. 2001. *Civilians in War.* (International Peace Academy Occasional Paper). International Peace Academy.

Dadrian, V. N. 1994. "Documentation of the Armenian Genocide in German and Austrian Sources." In *The Widening Circle of Genocide: A Critical Biographical Review,* Vol. 3, ed. Israel Charny. New Brunswick, NJ: Transaction Publishers.

Debloois, N. 1997. "Rape, Marriage or Death? Gender Perspectives in the Homeric 'Hymn to Demeter'." *Philological Quarterly* 76 (3): 245 et seq.

Douglas, G., and Campbell, A. 2006. *The Eastern Question from Treaty of Paris 1856 to the Treaty of Berlin 1878 and the Second Afghan War.* Vol. 1. Chestnut Hill, MA: Elibron Classic Series: Adamant Media Corporation.

European Commission of Human Rights and Continuing Violations by Turkey, 9, 86. *Human Rights: Turkey's Violations of Human Rights in Cyprus.* Available at: http://www.mit.edu/~petros/Cyprus/Euro_HRCommission_Report2. html.

Evdokas, T. 1976. "A Representative Research. The 200,000 Refugees of Cyprus; and Pan-Hellenic Committee for Solidarity with Cyprus: Cyprus Witness." *Socio-Psychological Research Group.*

Frankl, V. 1962. *Man's Search for Meaning.* New York: Pocket Books.

Holdcraft, L., Iacono, W. G., and McGue, M. K. 1998. "Antisocial Personality Disorder and Depression in Relation to Alcoholism: A Community-Based Sample." *Journal of Studies on Alcohol* 59 (2): 222–26.

Holy Bible English Standard Version (ESV). 2007. Crossway Bibles, Kindle Eds.

Huber, T. 2002. "Holocaust Compensation Payments and the Global Search for Justice for Victims of Nazi Persecution." *The Australian Journal of Politics and History* 48 (1): 85.

Human Rights Watch World Report 1998. 2001. *The Women's Rights Project. Women's Human Rights.*

Ilibagiza, E., Erwin, S., and Warren, R. 2008. *Led by Faith; Rising from the Ashes of the Rwandan Genocide.* Carlsbad, CA: Hay House.

Joiner, T. E., and Blalock, J. A. 1995. "Gender Differences in Depression: the Role of Anxiety and Generalized Negative Affect." *Sex Roles: A Journal of Research.* 33: 91–101.

Jones, A., ed. 2004. *Gendercide and Genocide.* Nashville, TN: Vanderbilt University Press.

Kalayjian, A. 2002(a). "Biopsychosocial and Spiritual Treatment of Trauma." In *Comprehensive Handbook of Psychotherapy, Vol. 3—Interpersonal/Humanistic/Existential,* ed. Florence Kaslow, 615–37. New York: Wiley.

Kalayjian, A. 2002(b). "Ninety Years Post Ottoman Turkish Genocide of the Armenians: Lesson Learned and Challenges to Overcome." Armenian American Society for Studies on Stress and Genocide (AASSSG) Annual Conference, Fordham University, New York.

Kalayjian, A. 2005. *Eight Stages of Healing from Mass Trauma.* UN presentation. New York, September 7–9, 2005.

Kalayjian, A. 2009. "Forgiveness in Spite of Denial, Revisionism, and Injustice." In *Forgiveness and Reconciliation: Psychological Pathways to Conflict Transformation and Peace Building,* eds. A. Kalayjian and R. Paloutzian. New York: Springer Publishing.

Kalayjian, A. S., and Shahinian, S. P. 1998. "Recollections of Aged Armenian Survivors of the Ottoman Turkish Genocide: Resilience through Endurance, Coping and Life Accomplishments: The case of Ottoman Turkish Genocide of the Armenians." *Psychoanalytic Review* 85 (4): 489–504.

Kalayjian, A. S., Shahinian, S. P., Gergerian, E. L., and Saraydarian, L. 1996. "Coping with Ottoman Turkish Genocide: An Exploration of the Experience of Armenian Survivors." *Journal of Traumatic Stress* 9 (1): 87–97.

Koenig, H. G., and Larson, D. B. 2001. "Religion and Mental Health: Evidence of an Association." *International Review of Psychiatry* 13: 67–78.

Larimer, M. E., Lyndum, A. R., Britt, K., Anderson, K., and Turner, R. 1999. "Male and Female Recipients of Unwanted Sexual Contact in a College Student Sample: Prevalence Rates, Alcohol Use, and Depression Symptoms." *Sex Roles: A Journal of Research* 40 (3–4): 295.

Nadler, A. 2001. "The Victim and the Psychologist: Changing Perceptions of Israeli Holocaust Survivors by the Mental Health Community." *History of Psychology* 4 (1): 159–81.

Obote, O. 2007. *Understanding and Fighting Genocide Ideology.* International Criminal tribunal for Rwanda. The 13th Commemoration of Rwanda Genocide. African Union headquarters, Addis Ababa-Ethiopia, 7 April, 2007. United Nations Organization. Available at: www.un.org.

Oxford English Dictionary. 2008. Concise ed. Oxford, UK: Oxford University Press.

Pan Cyprian Committee 2006. *Disappearances: The Case of the "Missing" Cypriots.* Published by the Pan Cyprian committee of parents and relatives of undeclared prisoners of war and missing persons. Nicosia, Cyprus: Republic of Cyprian Press.

Pipinelli, A. 2006. *Psychological Variables and Depression among Nursing Home and Adult Care Facility Residents.* Doctoral dissertation. Walden University, 2005. UMI Dissertation Services. Available at: www.il.proquest. com.

Press and Information Office Republic of Cyprus 2006. *The Refugees of Cyprus.* 3rd. ed. Nicosia, Cyprus: Press and Information Office.

Reker, G. T., Peacock, E. J., and Wong, P. "Meaning and Purpose in Life and Well-Being: A Life Span Perspective." *Journal of Gerontology* 42: 44–49.

Turkey Central. 2009. www.turkeycentral.com/forum/index.php?showtopic=2955
UN. *Convention on Genocide,* 1948. Convention on the Prevention and Punishment of the Crime of Genocide. Adopted by the General Assembly of the United Nations on December 9, 1948. www.tragicmountains.org/ id20.html.

United Nations. 2006. *New Report Says Violence Against Women Is a Human Rights Violation.* Available at: http://www.un.org/womenwatch/daw/vaw/ index.htm http://webapps01.un.org/vawdatabase/home.action.

Vaux, A. 1988. *Social Support: Theory, Research, and Intervention.* New York: Praeger.

Warren, M. A. 1985. *Gendercide: The Implications of Sex Selection.* Lanham, MD: Rowman & Littlefield Publishers.

Chapter 18

PSYCHOSOCIAL AND SPIRITUAL IMPACT OF 9/11 TERRORISM ON MENTAL HEALTH PROFESSIONALS IN AMERICA

Ani Kalayjian,
Beverly Musgrave, and
Chris Aberson

> Never look down on anybody unless you're helping him up.
> —Jesse Jackson

INTRODUCTION

The sacred dust of 9/11 has an eternal home in the hearts, bodies, minds, and memories of all who witnessed terrorism carefully synchronized and devastatingly effective, in our backyard. This dusk symbolizes that we now live in a different New York, and a different Washington, DC; ultimately, we now live in a different United States, and in a different world.

This research, conducted several months after 9/11, explores the impact and the effects of trauma on the lives of mental health professionals who were not pastoral counselors, as well as the latter, and how this tragedy influenced them and their clinical work. Some of the professionals both lived and worked in New York City, others were not in the immediate vicinity; however, all faced the enormity of the suffering of the terrorist attack.

On September 11, 2001, beginning at 9:10 A.M., the horror occurred in the New York City metropolitan area. This was the first time Americans were faced with a human-made trauma on their own soil. This shocking incident was signified by trembling floors, dark smoke, loud explosive sounds, dust, and debris. The unfathomable sight of bodies falling out of windows and people running from flames that engulfed the World Trade

Center (WTC) shocked the world. At 9:30 A.M. the American Airlines Boeing 757, carrying 58 passengers and 6 crewmembers, crashed into the Pentagon, which set off a state of emergency in the nation's capital. These two attacks constituted the most deadly terrorist attacks on U.S. soil in American history as approximately 3,000 individuals were killed and several thousand more injured. Numerous individuals were vicariously traumatized in rescue efforts as the cleanup continued for a year after the disaster.

DEFINITION OF TERRORISM

The United States faces two major kinds of terrorism: Islamic terrorism and terrorism from the Christian white supremacist and patriot movements. Terrorism, according to Egan (2001), is about atrocity or the threat of atrocity. It is a well designed and executed plan to terrorize a targeted population for political, social, economic, or ideological gain. The word terrorism is rooted in the French Revolution (1789–1799), where the new revolutionary government openly engaged in a brutal systematic purging of the *ancien regime*, its supporters, and those whose dedication to the new order was questionable (Egan 2001). Terrorists are not crazy, nor are they insane. Instead, they are misguided intellectuals with deep and often hopeless levels of frustration. According to Hoffman (1998), terrorists are violent intellectuals and altruists with deep seated political, economic, cultural and/or religious beliefs. While the primary goal of terrorism is to sway public opinion, it is ironic how little is known about the public's opinion of this problem. According to Takooshian and Verdi (1993), there are at least two reasons for this: first, with few exceptions, researchers have acknowledged the difficulty of defining terrorism; second, there are few psychometrically sound instruments with which to access opinions regarding terrorism.

According to Crenshaw (2000), and Hoffman (1998), merging ethnic and religious sensibilities, the widening gap between rich and poor, the status of the United States as the only superpower, links to organized crime, access to the Internet, and the availability of weapons of mass destruction, will likely expand the scope and impact of terrorism in the 21st century (Crenshaw 2000).

The most often cited definition of terrorism is the one adopted by the U.S. State Department, Department of Defense, and Central Intelligence Agency: The term terrorism means premeditated, politically motivated violence perpetrated against noncombatant targets by subnational groups or clandestine agents, usually intended to influence an audience (Office of the Coordinator for Counter Terrorism (1994, 19).

According to the United Nations, terrorism is the act of destroying or injuring civilian lives or the act of destroying or damaging civilian or government property without the expressly chartered permission of a specific government, by individuals or groups independently of governments on their own accord and belief, in the attempt to affect some political change (United Nations 2002).

It is important to note that terrorism is a term invariably applied to an individual or group by others, rather than being self-designated. The same individual (e.g., Osama bin Laden) who is declared a terrorist by an attacked group (e.g., Americans) may be viewed as a hero by those whose interests he represents (e.g., Taliban Muslims). Therefore, yesterday's terrorist may become tomorrow's hero, as in the case of Nelson Mandela.

REVIEW OF LITERATURE

The psychological impact of human-made trauma is one of the most important public health problems in the world. When faced with life-threatening traumatic experiences like 9/11 our primary focus is on survival and self-protection. A hallmark of trauma is a profound loss of the familiar. Terrorism challenges the natural need of humans to see the world as predictable, orderly, and controllable. Studies have shown that deliberate violence creates longer lasting mental health effects than natural disasters or accidental ones (Hamblen 2009).

Reactions to terrorist attacks can have several manifestations: post-traumatic stress disorder (PTSD), major depression, substance abuse, generalized anxiety, and other psychiatric disorders. Other people may demonstrate effective strategies of coping with no apparent adverse effects (Tucker et al. 2000). The main characteristic of PTSD is "the development of characteristic symptoms following exposure to an extreme traumatic stressor involving direct personal experience of an event that involves actual or threatening death or serious injury, or the threat to the physical integrity of another person, or learning about unexpected or violent death, serious harm, or threat of death or injury experienced by a family member or other close associate (Criterion A1)" (APA 2000, 463). Descriptions of what constitutes a traumatic event (i.e., Category A (criterion) in the DSM-III-R description of PTSD) clearly indicate that the mere knowledge of another's traumatic experiences can also be traumatizing.

Most people have the potential to develop PTSD but there are great individual differences among people's reactions to a disaster. Some people are more vulnerable than others; some are more resilient. The reasons for this are varied and multiple. It may be due to biological predispositions as well as an individual's history of stress (Yule, Williams, and Joseph 1999).

Several factors are associated with the likelihood of an individual to develop PTSD, such as the proximity of the traumatic event, the individual's appraisal of the event, individual's emotional and coping responses to the event, and in the post-event period, coping responses, the responses of others, and the social context (Nightingale and Williams 2000); additionally depending on the meaning associated with the event (Kalayjian 1995).

One significant factor, as mentioned previously, is the severity of trauma and the degree of exposure (Tucker et al. 2000). Mental health professionals who listen to eye witness accounts of trauma become a participant and/ or a co-owner and co-witnesses of the traumatic event. Through listening, mental health professionals come to experience the trauma partially themselves (Laub 1992). *Webster's Encyclopedic Unabridged Dictionary of the English Language* (1989) defines compassion as "a feeling of deep sympathy and sorrow for another who is stricken by suffering or misfortune, accompanied by a strong desire to alleviate the pain or remove its cause" (299).

Figley (1995) defines secondary traumatic stress (STS) as the natural consequent behavior and emotions resulting from knowledge about a traumatizing event experienced by a significant other or from helping or wanting to help a traumatized person. He also uses the term "compassion fatigue," to describe people working in crisis situations. Figley (1999) states that there are several kinds of trauma, namely: *(a) simultaneous trauma,* which takes place when all members of the system are directly affected; *(b) vicarious trauma,* when a single member is affected by way of contact with other members (e.g., helping after 9/11); *(c) intrafamilial trauma,* when a family member causes emotional injury to another member; and *(d) chasmal or secondary trauma,* when the traumatic stress appears to infect the entire system after first appearing in only one member. The last phenomenon most clearly parallels what Figley calls secondary traumatic stress (STS) and secondary traumatic stress disorder (STSD).

Researchers have documented that crisis workers are front-line responders for whom potential exposure to occupational trauma is a fact of daily life (Hartsough and Myers 1985; Mitchell and Bray 1990; Stratton, Parker, and Snibbe 1984). Research with mental health professionals working with trauma is limited; however, trauma literature clarifying the inescapable transference and unconscious reenactment of traumatic relational paradigm dynamics is well documented (Blank 1985b; Chu 1992; Courtois 1988; McCann and Pearlman 1990b; van der Kolk 1989; Waites 1993).

The work of McCann and Pearlman (1990) documented the devastating effects of conducting trauma therapy on the identity, world view, psychological needs, beliefs and memory system of psychotherapists. After experiencing such trauma, life is changed, and the therapist may experience vicarious traumatization: *vicarious traumatization is the transformation in the inner experience of the therapist that comes about as a result of empathic engagement with clients' traumatic material* (Pearlman and Saakvitine 1995). Vicarious traumatization is a process rather than an event. It results from the accumulative assault to one's affect and defenses against affect, as well as beliefs about one's safety, control, predictability, and attachment. Given the impact of 9/11, it is safe to say that beliefs about safety, control, and attachment were shattered. Therefore, it is important for mental health workers to address vicarious traumatization and its impact on their lives. Vicarious traumatization and counter-transference affect one another. "Vicarious traumatization represents changes in the most intimate psychological workings of the self of the therapist. The self of the therapist is the context for all her/his counter-transference responses, thus, vicarious traumatization invariably shapes counter-transference" (Pearlman and Saakvitine 1995, 33).

The aftermath of trauma is reflected not only in PTSD but in major depression, generalized anxiety and substance abuse (Karem 1991; Kulka, Schlenger, Fairbank, et al. 1990; Rundell et al. 1989). Trauma, in this case post 9/11, has the potential to overwhelm an individual's customary coping responses. "Traumatic events shatter the sense of connection between individual and community, creating a crisis of faith" (Herman 1992). Bessel Van der Kolk (1987) emphasizes this fact when he says:

> The essence of psychological trauma is the loss of faith that there is order and continuity in life. Trauma occurs when one loses the sense of having a safe place to retreat within or outside oneself to deal with frightening emotions or experiences. This results in a state of helplessness, a feeling that one's actions have no bearing on the outcome of one's life. Since human seems to be incompatible with sense of meaninglessness and lack of control, people will attempt to avoid this experience at just any price . . . Much of human endeavor, in religion, art, and science, is centrally concerned with exactly these grand questions of meaning and control over one's destiny (*Psychological Trauma* 31).

Gender is another variable that is related to levels of PTSD and symptomatology after a mass trauma. There have been many studies that suggest that women are more vulnerable to developing PTSD after a traumatic event. A study of the 9/11 terrorist attacks by Silver et al. (2002) stated that 17 percent of the U.S. population outside of New York City reported symptoms of 9/11-related post-traumatic stress two months after the attacks; 5.8 percent did so even 6 months after the attacks. High levels of post-traumatic stress symptoms were associated with females (odds ratio {OR}, 1.64; 95% confidence interval {CI}, 1.17–2.31). In addition, in an assessment of 182 direct victims of the Oklahoma City bombing six months post-disaster, women reported having twice the rate of PTSD than men (North, Nixon, Shariat, et al. 1999). However, Abenhaim, Dab and Salmi (1992), found that there were no significant differences of PTSD itself between men and women.

Finding meaning and rediscovering a new purpose in the aftermath of a mass trauma is a necessary condition for healing (Frankl 1978). For Frankl, meaning can be found in any situation, even a traumatic one. According to Frankl, each life situation is unique, and the meaning of each situation must therefore also be unique. He asserts that psychotherapists can never define what is or is not meaningful for others; meaning is often found in a self-transcendent encounter with the world; in fact the trauma can become this encounter.

METHOD

This research project was designed to explore the levels of PTSD of mental health practitioners who were not pastoral counselors, and those who were pastoral counselors. Concomitantly, the study explored coping styles used in this particular situation, and how meaning and purpose impact the counselor's levels of PTSD.

The participants were individuals who voluntarily attended a conference on coping methods in the wake of the 9/11 terrorist attacks for mental health practitioners, held in New York City, and another conference for Pastoral Counselors held in Williamstown, Massachusetts. Completing the questionnaire was voluntary and a debriefing session was offered to all participants.

INSTRUMENT

The Post-traumatic Stress Reaction Index Scale, developed by Calvin J. Frederick (1986) and revised by Kalayjian (1995), was utilized. The first section of the questionnaire asked participants to rate their emotional responses to the terrorist attacks retrospectively. The answers were scored on a five-point scale; 0 = none of the time, 1 = a little of the time, 2 = some of the time, 3 = much of the time, and 4 = most of the time. These 20 questions were related to PTSD symptoms such as flashbacks, numbing, sleep disturbances, and loss of interest in daily activities.

The second section of the questionnaire consisted of demographic items such as age, gender, ethnicity, marital status, education levels, employment, and so on. There were also a few open-ended questions added by the authors to elicit the degree of severity of the trauma experienced,

extent and severity of impact, meaning of trauma, clinical preparation, and what facilitated clinicians' preparedness both personally and
professionally.

PROCEDURE

The questionnaire was handed out to the individuals who attended the two
conferences. The completed forms were collected from each individual.

RESULTS

Of the 78 respondents, 34 were mental health practitioners, and 44 were
pastoral counselors. Forty-two respondents (54%) were women and 36
were men (46%). Most held graduate degrees (85%) and were currently
employed (90%). In terms of marital status, 30 (39%) reported being single, 32 (42%) were married or partnered, 9 (11%) were divorced or separated, four (5%) were widowed, and two (3%) did not give their marital
status. The most common age was 50 to 59 (35; 45%), followed by 60
and over (19; 24%), 40 to 49 (11; 14%), 30 to 34 (8; 10%) and 20 to 29
(2; 3%). Three (4%) participants did not report their age.

PTSD. Mental health practitioners who were not pastoral counselors
(M = 22.2) and pastoral counselors (M = 20.6) exhibited similar levels of
PTSD, t (68) = 0.6, p = .53, η^2 = .01. Examining PTSD categories revealed no differences between the groups. Non-pastoral practitioners
reported similar levels of avoidance (M = 4.4), arousal (M = 7.7), and
re-experiencing (M = 3.9) as did pastoral counselors (M = 4.0, 6.5, 4.4), t
(72) = 0.6, p = .57, η^2 = .00; t (73) = 1.3, p = .19, η^2 = .02; and t (74) = 0.7,
p = .50, η^2 = .00, respectively.

Helpful interventions. The two groups differed only in seeking pastoral
assistance. Not surprisingly, pastoral counselors (25%) were more likely to
seek pastoral assistance than were the nonpastoral counselors (6%), Ξ^2 =
5.0. p = .03. Pastoral counselors (40.9%) most commonly sought religious
assistance (23.8%), followed by psychological assistance (16.7%), other
assistance (9.5%), financial (4.8%), social welfare (2.4%), and medical
(2.4%) assistance. The majority of pastoral counselors reported seeking
no assistance (59.1%).

Nonpastoral counselors most commonly sought psychological assistance (25%), followed by other assistance (12.5%), medical (9.4%), and
financial assistance (9.4%). A greater majority of the nonpastoral counselors reported seeking no assistance (65.6%).

Gender. Men (M = 18.8) reported significantly less PTSD than women
(M = 23.3), F (1, 66) = 4.5, p = .03, η^2 = .06. Gender differences were

similar for pastoral and nonpastoral counselors (i.e., no interaction between gender and group), $F (1, 66) = 2.2$, $p = .14$, $\eta^2 = .03$.

Marital Status. Marital status was found not to be related to PTSD. Individuals reporting being married or partnered (M = 21.1) reported similar levels of PTSD as those who were single/divorced/widowed/separated (M = 21.5), $F (1, 64) < 1$. Again, these relationships did not differ between pastoral counselors and nonpastoral counselors, $F (1, 64) < 1$.

Age. Individuals who were under 50 years of age (M = 25.5) reported higher levels of PTSD than individuals who were 50 years old or older (M = 19.6), $F (1, 64) = 4.8$, $p = .03$, $\eta^2 = .07$. Again, this relationship did not differ by group, $F (1, 64) < 1$.

Meaning and Purpose. PTSD was not related to ratings of having discovered clear cut goals and satisfying life purposes for either the nonpastoral group, $r (25) = -.08$, $p = .70$, or the pastoral group, $r (41) = -.10$, $p = .53$. Similarly, there was no relationship between ratings of ability to find meaning and purpose in life and PTSD for either group, $r (25) = -.05$, $p = .81$ for nonpastoral, $r (42) = -.12$, $p = .48$ for pastoral counselors.

However, in the pastoral group there was a significant relationship between PTSD and facing daily tasks as a pleasure. In this group, greater PTSD was associated with viewing daily tasks as painful and boring, $r (41) = -.50$, $p = .001$. This relationship did not exist for nonpastoral mental health practitioners, $r (25) = -.26$, $p = .21$.

Reports of friends and families being affected either negatively or directly by the attacks were similar for pastoral counselors (25%, 39.5%) and mental health counselors (21.2%, 38.2%), $\Xi^2 = 0.2$, $p = .70$, $\Xi^2 = 0.0$, $p = .91$, respectively.

DISCUSSION

The demographic factors, including ethnicity, education level, marital status, and employment, did not show any significant differences in levels of PTSD symptoms. The only area of significance was in gender, where men reported less PTSD than women in both groups. This is consistent with previous research (North et al. 1999). The second area of significance was age, where older participants reported lower levels of PTSD than did their younger counterparts.

Using Figley's framework, the first kind of trauma is *simultaneous trauma.* In this situation, all members of the system were impacted by the same trauma. Both the caregivers and the caretakers were impacted simultaneously, in differing degrees.

The second kind of trauma is *vicarious traumatization,* which is experienced by therapists as a result of empathic engagement with their clients.

The ability to deal with personal traumatic experiences and be available to attend to the needs of the people they serve was a major challenge in this event. The implications for vicarious traumatization were everywhere after 9/11, not only in the faces of loved ones but in the faces of strangers on the street. The impact of dealing with personal loss and listening to the pain and distress of clients, providing a holding environment while attending simultaneously to one's personal pain, offers clinicians an interesting view into the challenges of clinical psychotherapeutic work. The findings revealed no apparent additional traumatization or vicarious traumatization, since their levels of PTSD were moderately low. The study conducted by Galea, et al. (2002) indicated higher than normal prevalence of PTSD in New York City around the same time.

As pertaining to gender, men reported lower levels of PTSD as compared to women. This finding is consistent with previous research findings that indicate higher levels of PTSD in women (Silver et al. 2002). North et al. (1999) studied the impact of Oklahoma City trauma six-month post disaster and found that woman had twice the rate of PTSD as did men. Other research findings reinforce that although women have higher levels of PTSD men have higher levels of drug/alcohol use/abuse. As noted by Yule, Williams and Joseph (1999), most people have their own unique response to disaster, and there is a wide range of individual differences. This notion was reinforced in this study, illustrated by pastoral counselor responses to three open-ended questions: (1). Were you clinically prepared for the event? What would assist you in becoming more prepared? (2). What helped you the most as a pastoral counselor? (3). What did you find most helped your clients?

Pastoral counselors each had their own individual, unique response to the trauma of 9/11. Approximately 41 percent of pastoral counselors sought out personal assistance. Most commonly sought was religious assistance, followed by psychological assistance. As for nonpastoral counselors, only 25 percent sought psychological assistance and they sought no pastoral assistance. This was described as attending to psychological, emotional, and spiritual distress. The following responses describe how pastoral counselors dealt with the stress of the trauma: prayer, faith in God, understanding the disaster in the light of faith, theological reflection, and use of previous trauma both to inform and to cope with the present events. Over half of the pastoral counselors noted the importance of sharing their experience with others, as a way of finding strength and meaning. The use of religious rituals in the community was a source of strength to many.

It is important to note that many pastoral counselors stated that their understanding and information about trauma and training in PTSD was most significant in helping them clinically. Sixty percent of the pastoral counselors reported that they were clinically prepared to deal with the challenges of this trauma. The 40 percent who did not feel as prepared stated that further training in crisis intervention and critical incidents was needed.

MEANING-MAKING AND USE OF RELIGIOUS RITUALS

Most of the pastoral counselors said that their ability to assist clients and others in their ministry was reflected in the following ways: Their ability to be present, offering support and comfort, addressing fears and contextualizing the clients' issues in light of the present events, non-anxious presence, the power of prayer, sacraments and liturgy, community solidarity, joining in legitimizing the magnitude of the disaster, offering a safe space to speak, and providing relational connection.

The work of Davis and Nolen-Hoeksema (2001) focuses on how people make sense of loss. The tragedy of 9/11 challenged the world, especially Americans, to find meaning in the midst of horror. Pastoral counselors in this study confirm the work of Davis and Nolen-Hoeksema as well as the research of Dull and Skokan (1995) by their struggle to make sense of the loss and their focus on the importance of religion to provide a comforting explanation for the events that could not be otherwise explained. The response of the pastoral counselors in this study suggests the power of religion and/or spiritual beliefs in facilitating rediscovery of meaning. Interactions with others and the environment expressed by rituals support and reinforce a person's global meaning system. Sometimes, rituals also aid people in transforming their views of the world. This was observed in New York City by the large turnout at church services and by the hundreds of recognized places where family and friends left candles, flowers, pictures, and poems about their lost loved ones.

Finding meaning and coping with tragic and/or difficult life events was the main thesis of Viktor Frankl, a Viennese psychiatrist and a Holocaust survivor. According to Frankl, meaning can be recovered under any circumstances, even tragic ones. His pioneering work in logotherapy or existential analysis is the core for most human behavior. In his writings, Frankl (1978) consistently points out that human beings readily sacrifice safety, security, and sexual needs for things that are meaningful for them. He further elaborates by stating that just as people differ in their perceptions of trauma and in the ways that they cope with it, they also differ in the meanings they attribute to the same situation. Meanings and meaning potentials can be clouded, covered, and/or repressed due to a fear of responsibility, and as a reaction to trauma. Meaning repressions will ultimately lead to a meaning vacuum or an existential vacuum. This vacuum is then filled by the development of some forms of anxiety, depression, substance abuse, phobias, and compulsive sexual behavior (Kalayjian 2002).

Pastoral counselors reported seeking pastoral counseling and prayers as a main mode of coping and meaning-making. Similarly, mental health practitioners also relied on prayers, meditation, and other self-care and release exercises such as: deep tissue massages, body work, exercising more vigorously, staying fit and mindful. Both groups reported being shocked and disbelieving of what they had witnessed in the aftermath of the trauma itself. Both groups also reported appreciating their families, reconnecting with them if they were separated, contacting them more often than before the trauma, and valuing the family as an important support system for their wellbeing and resilience. Some reported exercising religious rituals such as special prayers after a week, then again after 40 days and finally a year after the trauma. These special prayers and rituals involved going to church, lighting a candle, praying for the souls of those who died, for the survivors and their families, for their own families, friends and loved ones, and wishing them safety, health and peace.

The majority of the respondents who were not pastoral counselors stated new meanings in their lives. They made statements such as, "In the midst of terrible tragedy and suffering, compassion and creativity has emerged," "I learned that our lives are of tremendous importance to ourselves and to others: No more bickering about mundane things," "This is an opportunity to examine our personal prejudices," and "I learned to look more within." Others echoed the wisdom of Nietzsche: "He who has a why to live for can bear almost any how." The following statements exemplify those kinds of beliefs: "If I survived through this, I can survive through anything," "I am now stronger and more aware of the important things in life," and "I am now profoundly committed to peace."

Meaning has also been explored by Park and Folkman (1997). These authors note the diversity in conceptualization and operational approaches to meaning in the context of coping and adjustment to extremely stressful situations. The tragic events of 9/11 called forth the basic question of meaning in most people. The responses to this research in response to the meaning of this terrorist attack are summarized in the following categories:

a. Global Responses: Issues of vulnerability, world view, hope for the future, and trauma captivated the minds and hearts of the respondents. The following responses are significant: "This is a call for all people to get together and care for one another, or we will destroy civilization as we know it," "Hope comes from the human spirit, it was demonstrated everywhere," "9/11 was a devastating event illuminating evil, not only in terrorists but in ourselves and in our indifference to global needs," "The illusion of invulnerability was always false and we Americans have much to learn about the global situation," and "This calamity has unified us on many levels as human beings."

b. Positive and Negative Responses: The desire to look beyond, as well as within, oneself in order to come to a new understanding of a personal and a collective world view was apparent. The following statements exemplified this notion: "We are now aware of our desperate need to learn to think differently, to live justly in order to walk the walk of tolerance, especially for those who are different from us," "Flowing from this is the need to explore our personal and collective prejudice and hatred for self and others, for hatred can destroy our democracy and our civilization." Negative responses include the following: "I have found no meaning in this destruction," "We are so vulnerable" and "I don't understand why others hate us this much?"

c. The Role of the United States: The role of the United States was reflected in several responses: "It is a wake up call for the U.S. to join the world community collegially instead of in a spirit of dominance." It was also noted that we have a golden opportunity as a country to look at our priorities and identify (possibly in a new way) the role of our great country in the disadvantaged third world countries. The need for a keen sense of the country's vulnerability, as well as, its strength, might assist the United States to become more humble. The hatred of other countries toward us and our use of power and domination is a wake up call—can we hear the bells ringing? Ninety-five percent of the respondents stated that only a profound faith and spiritual strength can inspire us as a country and personally to deal with the depth of these issues.

d. Importance of Relationships: The value and meaning of our personal and collective lives is noted by everyone as important. Our need to work together in a complex world starts in our personal relationships, at home, work, and in our local communities. Here is a statement echoing this notion: "I now have realized my personal priorities: less material and more human interactions."

LIMITATIONS OF THIS RESEARCH

A limitation of this study is related to its generalizability. This study drew on a sample of social workers, psychologists, and pastoral counselors who attended either a conference in New York or in Williamstown, Massachusetts. Therefore, the data reflects responses limited to the New York and Massachusetts areas. The use of only one measure was also a limitation of this study. It should be noted that while all participants completed the Reaction Index Scale, only the pastoral counselors had the additional three open-ended questions. In hindsight, if both groups had used the same specific questions, the responses might have been richer and comparisons could have been drawn more consistently.

FUTURE RESEARCH

Future research is recommended to examine how mental health therapists are able to work with clients in trauma, while simultaneously attending to their own personal response to the terror. Concomitantly, can the research examine how trauma impacts a psychotherapist or pastoral counselor? The importance of religion/faith as a coping mechanism was stated, but the exact kind of prayer, amount of prayer, frequency of church attendance, and so on was not collected in this research. Future research can collect more comprehensive data regarding rituals used for resilience and coping, assessment of religiousness, and specify the role of religion in coping in times of crisis, and the longitudinal impact.

Additional research in collecting data on trauma-training needs of mental health clinicians, as well as follow-up research examining the degree to which the professional community is now more prepared to cope with a catastrophe is recommended. Also, future research can explore the lessons learned.

ACKNOWLEDGMENTS

Authors express gratitude to the following: Abigail Ortega, Taleen Babayan, Ben Bensadon, Debbie Sachs, Yuki Shigemoto, Miryam Nadkarni, Elissa Jacobs, and all the mental health professionals and pastoral counselors who took part in this study.

REFERENCES

Abenhaim, L., Dab, W., and Salmi, L. R. 1992. "Study of Civilian Victims of Terrorist Attack (France 1982–1987)." *Journal of Clinical Epidemiology* 45: 103–9.

American Psychiatric Association. 2000. *Diagnostic and Statistical Manual of Mental Disorders*. 4th ed., rev. Washington, DC: Author.

Blank, A. S. 1985. "The Unconscious Flashback to the War in Vietnam Veterans." In *The Trauma of War: Stress and Recovery of Vietnam Veterans,* ed. S. M. Onnenberg, A. S. Blank, J. A. Talbot, 295–308. Washington, DC: American Psychiatric Press.

Chu, J.A. 1992. "The Re-Victimization of Adult Women with a History of Child-hood Abuse." *Journal of Psychotherapy: Research and Practice* 1 (3): 259–69.

Courtois, C. 1988. *Healing the Incest Wound: Adult Survivors in Therapy.* New York: Norton.

Crenshaw, M. 2000. "The Psychology of Terrorism: An Agenda for the 21st Century." *Political Psychology* 21: 405–20.

Davis, C.G., and Nolen-Hoeksema, S. 2001. "Loss and Meaning." *American Behavioral Scientist* 44 (5): 726–41.

Dull, V.T., and Skokan, L.A. 1995. "A Cognitive Model of Religion's Influence on Health." *Journal of Social Issues* 51 (2): 49–64.

Egan, A. 2001. *Dealing with Terrorism.* Available at: http://www. americamaga zine.org/content/article.cfm?article_id=1052.

Figley, C.R. 1995. *Compassion Fatigue: Secondary Traumatic Stress Disorder in Those Who Treat the Traumatized.* New York: Brunner Mazel.

Figley, C.R. 1999. "Compassion Fatigue: Toward a New Understanding of the Costs of Caring." In *Secondary Traumatic Stress: Self Care Issues for Clinicians, Researchers and Educators,* ed. S.B. Hudnall, 3–28. Baltimore, MD: Sidran Press.

Frankl, V.E. 1978. *The Unheard Cry for Meaning.* New York: Simon & Schuster.

Frederick, C.J. 1986. "Children Traumatized by Catastrophic Situations." In *Post-Traumatic Stress Disorder in Children,* ed. S. Eth and R. Pynoos, 71–99. Washington, DC: American Psychiatric Press.

Galea, S., Ahern, J., Resnick, H., Kilpatrick, D., Bucuvalas, M., Gold, J., et al. 2002. "Psychological Sequelae of the September 11 Terrorist Attacks in New York City." *New England Journal of Medicine* 346: 982–87.

Hamblen, J. 2009. *What Are the Traumatic Stress Effects of Terrorism?* Available at: http://www.ncptsd.va.gov/ncmain/ncdocs/fact_shts/fs_terrorism.html.

Hartsough, D.M., and D.G. Myers. 1985. *Disaster Work and Mental Health: Prevention and Control of Stress among Workers.* Rockville, MD: National Institute of Health.

Herman, J. 1992. *Trauma and Recovery.* New York: Basic Books.

Hoffman, B. 1998. *Inside Terrorism.* New York: Columbia University Press.

Kalayjian, A.S. 1995. *Disaster and Mass Trauma: Global Perspectives in Post Disaster Mental Health Management.* Long Branch, NJ: Vista Publishing.

Kalayjian, A.S. 2002. "Biopsychosocial and Spiritual Treatment of Trauma." In *Comprehensive Handbook of Psychotherapy,* ed. R. Massey and S. Massey, 615–37. New York: John Wiley & Sons.

Karem, E.G. October, 1991. *The Lebanon Wars.* Paper presented at the 7th Annual Meeting of the International Traumatic Stress Society, Washington, DC.

Kulka, R.A., Schlenger, W.E., Fairbank, J.A., Hough, R.L., Jordan, B.K., Marmar, C.R., et al. 1990. *Trauma and the Vietnam War Generation.* New York: Brunner/Mazel.

Laub, D. 1992. "Bearing Witness or the Vicissitudes of Listening." In *Testimony: Crises of Witnessing in Literature, Psychoanalysis and History,* ed. S. Felman and D. Laub, 57–74. New York: Routledge.

Mitchell, J.T., and Bray, G.P. 1990. *Emergency Services Stress: Guidelines for Preserving the Health and Careers of Emergency Services Personnel.* Englewood Cliffs, NJ: Prentice-Hall.

Nightingale, J., Williams, R.M. 2000. "Attitudes to Emotional Expression and Personality in Predicting Post-Traumatic Stress Disorder." *British Journal of Clinical Psychology* 39: 243–54.

North, C.S., Nixon, S.J., Shariat, S., Mallonee, S., McMillen, C., Spitznagel, E.L. et al. 1999. "Psychiatric Disorders among Survivors of the Oklahoma City Bombing." *Journal of the American Medical Association* 282: 755–62.

Office of the Coordinator for Counterterrorism. 1994. *Patterns of Global Terrorism 1994* (U.S. Department of State Publication No. 10136). Washington, DC: US Department of State.

Park, C.L., and Folkman, S. 1997. "Meaning in the Context of Stress and Coping." *Review of General Psychology* 1 (2): 115–44.

Pearlman, L.A., and Saaakvitn, K.W. e. 1995. *Trauma and the Therapist.* New York: Norton.

Rundell, J.R., Ursano, R.J., Holloway, H.C., and Silberman, E.K. 1989. "Psychiatric Responses to Trauma." *Hospital and Community Psychiatry* 40 (1): 68–74.

Silver, R.C., Holman, E.A., McIntosh, D.N., Poulin, M., and Gil-Rivas, V. 2002. "Nationwide Longitudinal Study of Psychological Responses to September 11." *Journal of the American Medical Association* 288 (10): 1235–1244.

Stratton, J.G., Parker, D.A., Snibbe, J.R. 1984. "Post-Traumatic Stress: Study of Police Officers Involved in Shootings." *Psychological Reports* 55: 127–31.

Takooshian, H., and Verdi, W.M. 1993. "U.S. Attitudes toward the Terrorism Problem." *Journal of Psychology and the Behavioral Sciences* 7: 83–87.

Tucker, P., Pfefferbaum, M., Nixon, S.J., and Dickson, W. 2000. "Predictors of Post-Traumatic Stress Symptoms in Oklahoma City: Exposure, Social Support, Pre-Traumatic Responses." *Journal of Behavioral Health Services and Research* 27: 406–16.

United Nations 2002. *Terrorism.* Available at: http://www.inlink.com/civitas/mun/res9596/terror.htm.

van der Kolk, B.A. 1987. *Psychological Trauma.* Washington, DC: American Psychiatric Press.

van der Kolk, B.A., 1989. "The Compulsion to Repeat the Trauma: Re-Enactment, Re-Victimization, and Masochism." *Psychiatric Clinics of North America* 12 (2): 389–411.

Waites, E.A. 1993. *Trauma and Survival: Post-Traumatic and Dissociative Disorders in Women.* New York: Norton.

Webster's Encyclopedic Unabridged Dictionary of the English Language. 1989. New York: Random House.

Yule, W., Williams, R., and Joseph, S. 1999. "Post-Traumatic Stress Disorders in Adults." In *Post-Traumatic Stress Disorders: Concepts and Therapy,* ed. W. Yule, 1–24. Chichester, England: John Wiley & Sons.

NOTE

Correspondence and reprint requests should be addressed to 139 Cedar Street, Cliffside, NJ 07010. Home: (201) 723–9578, Fax: (201) 941–2266. E-mail: drkalayjian@gmail.com.

Chapter 19

HEALING INTERGENERATIONAL TRAUMA AMONG ABORIGINAL COMMUNITIES

Sarah Thompson,
Christine Kopperud, and
Lewis Mehl-Madrona

May the stars carry your sadness away,
May the flowers fill your heart with beauty,
May hope forever wipe away your tears,
And, above all, may silence make you strong.
                                                    —Chief Dan George

INTRODUCTION

Intergenerational trauma is defined as the transmission of emotional injuries from one generation to the next. This transmission of trauma occurs at the interpersonal level (from parent to child) expanding to the intergenerational level (from a generation of parents to a generation of children) when enough individuals are impacted, thus affecting an entire group or culture. This trauma may be transmitted directly, when parents treat their children in the same abusive or negligent ways in which they were treated, or indirectly, when children learn coping behaviors from their parents that make the children behave as if they suffered the same trauma that their parents experienced (even though they did not). Mental health professionals are focused upon those coping styles which are not effective, since it is the people who cope poorly who seek help. Those who learned resiliency and transcendence from their parents are less likely to enter the offices of mental health professionals, though the study of these individuals is crucial for our efforts to prevent long-term sequelae from trauma.

The less effective coping styles of those who have been directly or indirectly traumatized result in overwhelming feelings of fear, anxiety, and helplessness, leading to the behaviors underlying alcoholism, family discord, and high suicide rates (Bryant-Davis 2007; Duran 2006). Historical examples of intergenerational trauma can be seen, for example, among the children of Jewish Holocaust survivors and many others. The length and extensiveness of the trauma experienced by aboriginal people in North America is the focus of this chapter; concomitantly, the chapter focuses on rituals and meaning-making for resilience and emotional healing.

LITERATURE REVIEW

The New World trauma began early. Mann (2006 1491) described the extensive impact upon New World peoples of European diseases. For example, just before 1620, 90 percent of the estimated 100,000 Wampanoags of Cape Cod and Eastern Massachusetts died from hepatitis A, making the tribe ready prey to the Narragansett, their traditional enemies, and motivating them to relax their 100-year-old prohibition against Europeans staying any longer than the time required to trade, leading in turn to the formation of Plymouth Colony. Epidemics and the killing of traditional food (the bison) set the stage for treaties in which North American aboriginal people were confined upon designated spots of land; that is to say, they were made second or third class noncitizens on the land that they had once occupied in an ownership/stewardship capacity. Lux (2004) describes the starvation conditions of early reservations/reserves and the residential school phenomenon in which generations of aboriginal children were forcibly taken from their families and sent to boarding schools, where they were stripped of their language and cultural heritage and forced to learn a substandard curriculum only suitable for domestic help or farm labor.

With the implementation of the Indian Act in 1876 in Canada, European concepts of patriarchy were forced onto aboriginal cultures and cultural ceremonies were banned.

FROM INTERPERSONAL TO INTERGENERATIONAL TRAUMA

Interpersonal trauma sets the stage for a larger scale phenomenon—intergenerational trauma. When faced with trauma, we depend on those around us to help us cope and to provide comfort. The stronger the support system, the more resilient we are in the face of stress and trauma.

Interpersonal trauma occurs when our distress is caused by a caretaker. When this happens, we become confused, as we want to go to our caretaker for support and comfort, but also want to push him or her away for causing distress. This approach-avoidance paradigm leads to further stress with a net negative impact on resiliency (Cozolino 2006).

Children who are exposed to this approach-avoidance paradigm by their parents tend to model the same type of behavior. If our parents view the world as dangerous and fearful, we will incorporate this view as we model our parents' behavior, thereby behaving as if we had been traumatized in the same way our parents were.

Mothers who are low in self-efficacy, who do not believe in their parenting abilities, tend to give up when parenting becomes difficult, and may become depressed. Trauma, and especially the residential school experience, had that effect upon parents.

Brody and colleagues, in a study of single-parent African-American families, reported that success in the upbringing of the children was related to the goals of mothers, such as being well educated and well behaved. These goals that predicted parenting practices were ultimately linked to children's ability to regulate their own behavior and to plan ahead. Mothers who have been traumatized and taught to devalue themselves through the residential school experience would not be expected to have self-efficacy or to set positive goals for their children. Consequently, their children would not benefit from these potentially positive effects on mood and behavior.

Experiencing interpersonal trauma, specifically in childhood (whether it takes the form of physical abuse, sexual abuse, or neglect) actually alters the structure and functioning of one's brain. As such, our brain becomes shaped for protective purposes—that is, instead of being open and welcoming of others, individuals may become suspicious, defensive, and uncooperative. Victims of trauma are looking out for themselves, trying to avoid distress instead of connecting and bonding with others. Their regulatory systems become trained to remain on high alert at all times. This negatively impacts essential emotional, social, and intellectual development, leading to brain abnormalities in areas that are developed through social experiences, the corpus callosum, cerebral cortex, and hippocampus (Cozolino 2006).

Imagine a scenario in which an entire population is subjected to this ambivalent style of attachment, where generations of children are taken from their homes and raised in strict environments where their primary care giver is an authority figure from the dominant class, who sees them as savages. Imagine their primary caregivers (multiple figures in aboriginal culture) losing their sense of identity and cultural pride. The new caregiver, who is supposed to provide love, comfort and protection, is instead causing trauma, insecurity, and fear. Children then develop insecure attachments with their caregiver (which alters the structure of their brain), which may lead to their developing an insecure attachment with their children. Consider the following quotation from a woman who experienced this:

> It was always hard for us to tell one another "I love you" because we were taught that to love was wrong . . . they told us that love was wrong and it was the devil's work; we couldn't even hug our own brothers . . . it took me a lot of years until I was able to tell my boys that I loved them (Annett 2007).

Although the aforementioned atrocities happened in the past, it is important to note that these historical losses still plague aboriginal people today. A good illustration of this point can be seen in a study conducted by Whitbeck, Adams, Hoyt, and Chen (2004), which used focus groups of aboriginal elders to determine factors contributing to the perception of historical loss. The primary goal of the study was to identify types of historical loss perceived and experienced by the people. Commonly stated was the loss of language, which was attributed to residential schools. Parents who went to boarding schools did not want to teach their children their native language for fear that the children would be punished for not speaking English. Some expressed a sense of guilt for not passing the language down to their children. Elders grieved for the loss of traditional community practices as well as the closeness of aboriginal communities in which people would visit each other frequently.

Broken treaty promises and land confiscation were also a concern. Elders felt concerned for the many aboriginal youth addicted to substances—feeling that drugs were more powerful than their culture had the strength to fight.

A subsequent review by Struthers and Lowe (2003) examined intergenerational trauma within nursing protocols and conceptual models. The results led the authors to suggest that intergenerational trauma had profound effects on health and well-being. Adding to the negative effects of residential schools has been the failure of the U.S. and Canadian governments to acknowledge this trauma. Only in June 2008 did Prime Minister Steven Harper issue a formal apology in which he said, "The government now recognizes that the consequences of the Indian residential schools policy were profoundly negative and that this policy has had a lasting and damaging impact upon Aboriginal culture, heritage, and language" (Martineau 2008).

THE CASE OF RESIDENTIAL SCHOOLS

The primary method employed to implement colonization in the 1800s and early 1900s was the residential school (Shepard, O'Neill, and Guenette

2006), initiated by the Canadian government, and the Anglican, and Roman Catholic missionaries, all of whom shared the common goal of civilizing the aboriginal populations (Shepard et al. 2006).

In the 1960s, 10,000 aboriginal students were attending 60 residential schools across Canada. Children ranging in age from 3–18 were forced from their homes, and required to attend residential schools which were situated far away from their families. Students spent 10 months of the year at these schools and were only permitted to go home for holidays (Kirmeyer et al. 2007). While at the boarding schools, children were not allowed to practice their native ceremonies, or even to speak their traditional language (Barton et al. 2001).

Residential schools were an attempt at forced assimilation, and were detrimental to the well-being of both the children attendees and aboriginal communities. Their distance from the reserves resulted from a calculated effort to limit contact between the child and other family members, as it had been recognized that the aboriginal culture thrived on community and socialization. Some schools permitted children to correspond with their parents; however, all communications were screened to ensure that children were not reporting the adverse conditions to which they were exposed to on a regular basis. The schools were built to be economical with the cheapest construction materials. They were often poorly constructed, lacking proper ventilation and fire escapes (Kirmeyer et al. 2007). The schools' primary aim was not to educate the children, but to teach them labor skills (Milloy 1999, as cited by Kirmayer et al. 2007).

The curriculum for the aboriginal children was far less challenging than it was for students in mainstream classrooms, which was related to the commonly held belief that aboriginals were savages and lacked the intellectual capacities of Europeans. The material they were taught was critical of their culture and the style of instruction was contrary to what they had received in their own communities which had placed great emphasis on respect, sharing, and cooperation. Children were exposed to harsh punishments and humiliated in the residential schools on a regular basis in order to correct this problem, become more civilized, and eradicate traditional behaviors and values (Milloy 1999, as cited by Kirmayer et al. 2007).

For instance, upon arriving at the residential schools, a child's hair would be cut (this was humiliating, as long hair was important), and they were assigned a number which would serve as their new identity (a procedure duplicated today in prisons). When school faculty felt the children were misbehaving, for example when they were caught speaking their native language or practicing native traditions, common punishments included physical beatings, withholding food, public humiliation, and solitary confinement in closets and bathrooms (Milloy 1999, as cited by

Kirmayer et al. 2007). The following quotation is from a former residential school survivor:

> I cannot forget one painful memory. It occurred in 1932 when I was 15 years old. My father came to the Portage la Prairie residential school to tell my sister and I that our mother had died and to take us to the funeral. The principal of the school would not let us go with our father to the funeral. My little sister and I cried so much, we were taken away and locked in a dark room for about two weeks.

In too many instances, residential school attendees were subjected to sexual abuse. Abusers were often nuns, priests, faculty, and sometimes students themselves. In such cases, older children who were victims of sexual abuse began assaulting younger children.

Aboriginal beliefs, traditions, values, and practices were denigrated by the educators at the residential schools, which had a negative effect on the children's cultural identity. They were not allowed to practice their own language. Some children had no prior exposure to English, and thus had to learn a completely new language. Food was typically rotten or below standards, resulting in malnourishment. Corporal punishment was widely accepted, which was especially upsetting for aboriginal children as it was not practiced in their culture. The conditions of the residential schools impeded students' performance both academically and cognitively. As schools were underfunded, they typically employed underqualified teaching staff and depended on the children for labor. A significant portion of the day was spent doing chores as opposed learning in the classroom. This lack of time doing academic activities limited children's ability to learn. Residential schools only educated children to a grade eight level, as the rest of the time was spent teaching students the skills necessary for society's menial jobs.

The maltreatment and abuse under which children who attended residential schools suffered led to loss of cultural knowledge, low self-esteem, poor self-concepts, a breakdown in family structure and customs due to cultural derogation transmission, all of which was passed on from generation to generation (Barton et al. 2001; Kirmayer et al. 2007). Residential schools only prepared students for manual labor jobs, which prevented them from finding more prestigious employment within the dominant society. Due to the suppression of their culture, they had troubles fitting in with traditional aboriginal communities, and thus became marginalized. Maladaptive behaviors were passed on to subsequent generations.

As a result of these harsh living conditions, survivors of residential schools often had troubles adjusting when they were released from those schools. Suicide rates were high. As a direct consequence of years of maltreatment, ambivalent attachments, inadequate living conditions, and loss of connection with one's family, symptoms such as anxiety, hypervigilance, and a tendency to mistrust others were not uncommon (Duran et al. 1998, as cited by Shepard et al. 2006). Survivors' stories often describe feelings of dissociation and distorted memories of their experiences, as well as the inability to remember large portions of them. They also tended to experience a shutting down of emotions due to inconsistent, ambivalent interpersonal relationships at the residential schools. Other common psychological effects included difficulty concentrating or remembering, as well as feeling numb, depressed, and/or anxious. Also common was the tendency to distrust the dominant group, who had been the perpetrators of their suffering for generations (Bryant-Davis 2007).

Research focusing on intergenerational trauma has emphasized that this problem still negatively impacts the wellbeing of aboriginals. For instance, First Nation's women tend to experience a lower life expectancy than non-First Nations men, and are also shown to have higher rates of illness and hospitalization rates, and struggle finding employment (Waldram, Herring, and Young 2006; Shepard et al. 2006). In 2000, suicide and self-injury were the leading cause of death for aboriginals in Canada.

A telling article written by Tracy Whattam (2003) examines her experience of intergenerational trauma brought on by her mother's experience at a residential school. She opens by saying, "you young people, you have that daylight in your minds. Us, they put curtains around our minds, they tried to keep us in the dark, they wanted to keep us stupid, make us their slaves." Whattam was raised not knowing her native tongue or much about her culture as her mother tried to assimilate her and her siblings. Her mother survived residential schools and then focused on assimilating into the dominant culture in an effort to prevent her children from enduring the same hardships that she had as a child.

This caused Whattam to grow up with a sense of loss. In school she was ridiculed merely for being aboriginal, as well as for being smart and enjoying school. As a way to cope with the stress, she began associating with the wrong crowds and took drugs and alcohol to numb her pain. After grade nine, she dropped out of school and began working, but was fired from every job when she sabotaged her own efforts. Finally, she decided to go to rehab, which proved to be a positive life-changing decision. While she was there, she met some aboriginal people; this was significant for her because her life had been spent assimilating and trying to make friends with non-aboriginals. She came to learn that she was not alone, and that there were many other aboriginals just like her, going through the same struggles.

It was from these newfound friends that she learned about sweats, smudging, Sun dance, and fasting—the cultural traditions that she desperately wanted to learn as a child but was denied. Learning these cultural traditions made her feel a sense of belonging, and as if she could finally begin to grow and mature. The story illustrates one way intergenerational trauma is passed to the next generation, and how reconnecting with one's heritage may lead to a sense of happiness.

THE CASE OF THE INDIAN ACT

Another aspect of colonization responsible for intergenerational trauma is the Indian Act of Canada of 1876, which introduced the concept of blood quantum, specifying that one had to have a certain percentage of native blood to be considered aboriginal in the eyes of the law. This concept fed upon the new theories of Mendel and genetic inheritance flowing from Europe to the Americas and was foreign to the concepts of belonging intrinsic to the indigenous people of North America in which what is now recognized as genetics played a minimal role. The United States followed suit with a similar act in 1904.

Because the Act stated such strict regulations for determining status, many aboriginal people actually lost their status and suffered from loss of identity. This Act changed aboriginal lifestyle to one of institutionalized patriarchy (Shepard, O'Neill and Guenette 2006). This resulted in the disassembling of aboriginal women's roles in their communities, as decision-makers, leaders, producers of food and caregivers of children (Shepard et al. 2006). For example, the Act denied First Nations women the right to vote in tribal issues. Marriage and property rights among the natives were established (Anderson 2000; as cited by Shepard et al. 2006) which took power away from aboriginal women, as it no longer allowed them equal status to men within their communities. Furthermore, aboriginal women's statuses were determined by their husband's blood quantity, as opposed to their own. In essence, an aboriginal woman born to aboriginal parents could lose her Indian status in instances such as intermarriage and moving away from the reserve, independent of her cultural practices, her language, or her family (O'Nell 1996). If an aboriginal woman was not living on a reserve, the measure of her blood quantum was performed differently (in order to detect a smaller amount) than an aboriginal woman living on a reserve. Women were seen as the primary caregivers for children in most aboriginal communities; thus, the oppression and identity crises these women faced were inevitably passed down to their children, and subsequent generations, manifesting in such maladaptive behaviors as alcoholism, family discord, and high suicide rates (Bryant-Davis 2007; Duran 2006).

The concept of formal enrollment was a consequence of the Indian Act, which presented a need for the distinguishing between real Indians and non Indians; this also furthered the problems that aboriginals faced regarding their identities. If an aboriginal was formally enrolled in a tribe, she would receive benefits from the Federal government, including health care, preferred status in hiring decisions for positions within the tribal government, twice-yearly per capita payments, assistance with funeral expenses, exemption from paying certain taxes, some kinds of educational assistance, access to restricted areas of the reservations, eligibility to receive welfare assistance, and services for the elderly (O'Nell 1996). Without the formal enrollment required to receive these benefits, aboriginals without Indian status suffered not only emotional and identity consequences, but also negative economic and community effects, all of which would likely lead to intergenerational trauma.

The Indian Act also banned participation in cultural ceremonies such as the potlatch, a gift-giving cultural ceremony that served to distribute goods equally among one's tribe and establish status within aboriginal communities. As cultural ceremonies can have a positive influence on one's identity, aboriginals' identities were oppressed through these legal changes.

TREATING INTERGENERATIONAL TRAUMA

The attachment style formed with a caregiver can set the stage for interpersonal trauma. The affected individuals desperately want to connect with others but, at the same time, fear this closeness, and get caught in an approach-avoidance paradigm; in turn, passing this coping style on to their offspring who continue it. However, the effects of early ambivalent attachments are not irreversible (Cozolino 2006). The ability to push one's personal boundaries and develop a secure attachment later in life will enable the individual to develop secure attachments with his or her child, thus ending the transmission of trauma from one generation to the next.

In order for counselors, therapists, and health care professionals to help aboriginals deal with the effects of intergenerational trauma and to develop a therapeutic relationship which will allow for the formation of a secure client-therapist attachment, they must first understand, acknowledge, and empathize with what aboriginals have endured at the hands of Americans and the Europeans. Counselors should be educated about intergenerational trauma; that is, they should have an understanding of what effects are associated with this form of trauma, of the needs of these individuals, and of possible interventions (Bryant-Davis 2007). Therapists should understand the impact of oppression and discrimination, be educated about the beliefs and traditions of the culture and approach the situation from an unbiased stance.

The therapeutic setting should involve a safe and comfortable environment where clients can feel safe in disclosing personal information from their lives. The counselor should also delve into the experience of the trauma, as well as the effects they had on the individual, and acknowledge these feelings as legitimate. Bryant-Davis and Ocampo (2005; in press, as cited by Bryant-Davis 2007) suggest that counselors should give attention to the client's anger, feelings of self blame, loss and grief, and coping strategies, as this will give recognition for the losses their people faced. Thus, in order to heal these wounds, they first must be acknowledged, recognized, and empathized.

Family therapy is one method for dealing with intergenerational trauma as everyone has a chance to mourn and to heal together. This may be difficult at first because each family member may handle the trauma differently, and some individuals are not willing to talk about their problems (Abrams 1999).

Liberation discourse involves taking into account the effects of colonization on aboriginal peoples in an attempt to create new narrative healing methods (Duran 2006). Standard counseling approaches cater to the dominant class, and may not be beneficial to aboriginals who have different cultural values. Therefore the therapeutic setting must not focus on dominance, superiority, or self-enhancement and actualization, but instead must incorporate a sense of connectedness with one's community and family (Shepard et al. 2006). Duran defines hybridism as the existence of two or more forms of knowledge which can exist independently without one having to dominate the other. This method would be beneficial in the healing practices of aboriginals, as treating aboriginals requires decolonization, which can be achieved through liberation discourse (Duran 2006).

VICTIMIZATION

While understanding and treating intergenerational trauma within a social and historical context is very important, there can be a fine line between the acknowledgment of the cultural genocide that took place and viewing the consequences as racial problems specific only to aboriginals. In other words, it is very important for the dominant cultural group and counselors/therapists/health professionals alike to avoid viewing the problems aboriginals face (i.e., substance abuse, etc.) as a racial problem (Struthers and Lowe 2003). Here the consequences of intergenerational trauma are considered to be linked to the very essence of being aboriginal as opposed to being understood as simply the results of generations of trauma without healing or resolve. In essence, mainstream society can be in danger of blaming aboriginals for aboriginals' circumstances if it is not careful. This would involve seeing the victimized group (i.e., Canadian aboriginals) as less capable, less desirable, more troubled, and defected (Struthers and Lowe). In turn, further marginalization and racism occurs because the dominant group may take action to separate and marginalize the others. It is important for counselors to take the issues of victimization into account when participating in healing sessions for aboriginals suffering from the effects of intergenerational trauma. This can be accomplished by incorporating aboriginal traditional methods of healing into a counseling session, such as including storytelling, utilizing indigenous traditional healers, and narrative medicine.

TREATMENT OF ABORIGINAL WOMEN AND INTERGENERATIONAL TRAUMA

In regards to the specific treatment of intergenerational trauma for aboriginal women, special considerations should be taken, especially concerning colonialism, residential schools, the Indian Act, and the current states of aboriginal populations. Aboriginal women once had the highly respected status of primary caregiver, but since colonization, aboriginal women's lives are now marked by illness, early death, and domestic violence, all of which translate to forms of intergenerational trauma (Napoli 2002). As such, aboriginal women participating in counseling or treatment for intergenerational trauma should be welcomed in an environment that facilitates healing and acknowledges the effects of the past and of intergenerational trauma.

A review by Sherry Grace (2003) considers the physical and mental health risks that aboriginal women face presently. Based on Statistics Canada, aboriginal women's mortality rates are much higher than Canadian women in general (Mao, Semenciw, and Morrison 1992, as cited in Grace). Aboriginal women's health conditions were rated especially low in terms of mental health, including depression. Also, suicide rates were found to be especially high for aboriginal adolescent girls, where an adolescent status Indian is 7.5 times more likely to commit suicide than adolescent women in the total Canadian population (Grace). There are also higher ratios of depression for women compared to men in Aboriginal communities; where over 9 percent of Aboriginal women report depressive symptoms (Grace). A survey developed by MacMillan, Jamieson, Walsh, Wong, Faries, and McCue (2003) and MacMillan and Offord (2008) found that 15 percent of the women (all were status-declared aboriginals) acknowledged depressive symptoms.

Walters and Simoni (2002) present an indigenous model of stress-coping for aboriginal women in their commentary *Reconceptualizing*

Native Women's Health: An "Indigenist" Stress-Coping Model. This model addresses intergenerational trauma and conceptualizes its effects on aboriginal women, acknowledging both the historical and current contexts that influence women and their stress-coping abilities. They understand the consequences of intergenerational trauma (i.e., the health issues that have been listed in this paper) as outcomes of aboriginal women's coping with the stress of the traumas they have either experienced themselves, or seen in the lives of their primary caregivers.

According to Napoli (2002), in order to enter into a healing relationship (between patient and practitioner) with an aboriginal woman, trust, empathy, acceptance and understanding must be established. Taking the time to engage in casual conversation, sharing a meal, and participating in cultural activities and ceremonies together can be helpful. Engaging in ceremonies together can promote a sense of vulnerability for each participant, which would increase the level of trust (Napoli) and an aboriginal women's receptivity to her counselor if her counselor was from the dominant, conventional, Western perspective.

Napoli (2002) also discusses how aboriginal women gather together to participate in activities and show support for each other. The purpose of the group discussed in the review was to offer opportunities for the women to deal with physical and emotional pain, and to experience intimate connections with one another. In regards to treating intergenerational trauma, a similar approach would thus be appropriate when pursuing healing with aboriginal women specifically. This would include aspects of storytelling, sharing meals, going on walks or even participating in yoga, as the group in the review did. Napoli describes the journey a practitioner takes with a client as a path of transformation for both the client and the health practitioner. It should be noted that this is not only true for the treatment of intergenerational trauma for aboriginal women; empathy, support, and participation in cultural events could contribute to the client-health practitioner relationship between any two people or groups from different backgrounds.

NARRATIVE MEDICINE AS AN INDIGENOUS TRADITIONAL HEALING METHOD

Human experience is highly influenced by the act of comprehending and producing stories. We are insatiable narrative consumers, as attested by the constant consumption of celebrity stories, movies, novels, news items, and gossip of all kinds. The affinity for narrative emerges at a very young age, when we develop deep and long-lasting emotional attachments to the storybooks and movies that surround us at childhood (Alexander,

Miller, and Hengst 2001). Stories do have the power to change our beliefs about the real world.

Reader attitudes shift to become more congruent with the ideas expressed in a narrative after exposure to fiction (Green and Brock 2005; Green, Brock and Kaufman 2000; Prentice, Gerrig, and Bailis 1997). Humans are prolific story producers, predominately using a distinctly story-like structure to communicate with others (Miller 1995; Schank and Abelson 1995). Creating a coherent story of a traumatic event and incorporating it into one's self-representation is fundamental for the successful treatment of PTSD and for resolving intergenerational trauma (Brewin, Dalgleish and Joseph 1996; Herman 1992; van der Kolk and Fisler 1995). Storytelling is a native element of our social interactions, as well as a necessity to maintain health.

Narrative methods for healing involve the human capacity to tell and create stories within the context of communities in which everyone is invested in the stories about an individual who is suffering. The significance of a narrative element appears to be determined by the goals and intentions of story characters. The most basic elements of a story include a setting and an agent who holds a certain goal and whose progress towards that goal is impeded or facilitated by certain events (Peterson 1999).

With crafted narratives it is often partly left to the audience to infer the significance of its elements. Comprehending literary narratives entails the reverse of certain processes employed in real-world experience. Ordinary interaction directs our attention to the assessment of the immediate goals of those whom we interact with (Yantis 1996), while narrative comprehension requires the inference of intentions and goals through interpretation of the objects and episodes selected by the author. If a well-crafted story contains an event or character, it is assumed that this element is in some way relevant to the goals of the protagonist. It is only in stories that we witness the creation of an imagined world which mirrors our own realm of experience (Bruner 1986; Gerrig 1993; Graesser, Mills, and Zwaan,1997; Oatley 1999).

Identity can be conceptualized as a life story constructed by the individual within a social context (McAdams 1988). Healing can occur through reconstruction of that identity. Gardner (1977) developed a narrative technique in which therapist and client write a story. The therapist listens to the symbols the client uses, adds to them within the session and introduces healthier resolutions of the conflicts that have been exhibited in the client's story.

Narrative approaches recognize that the past is only relevant as it is repeated in the stories told in the present. For the context of intergenerational trauma, we must ask what stories are being told in the present about those traumas. Children may tell stories heard from parents that did not actually happen to them. Lehrer (2007) explained that Proust realized that the moment we finish eating, for example a cookie, we begin warping this memory to fit our own personal narrative (82). Our memories feel true regardless of whether they ever occurred (83).

Stories, whether in novels or movies, promote therapeutic change by offering deepening emotion, providing role models, enhancing client strengths, reframing problems, improving communication, and re-prioritizing values (Hesley 1998; Lampropoulos 2004).

Psychotherapy involves putting together a story that will explain and organize major life events causing distress (Pennebaker 1999). A constructed story is a type of knowledge that helps to organize the emotional effects of an experience as well as the experience itself (1249). Pennebaker coordinated an experiment in which participants were instructed to write about traumatic events for 15 minutes a day for four consecutive days without stopping to check spelling, grammar, or sentence structure. Ninety-eight percent of participants stated that the writing experience had been helpful and they would do it again.

Omer and Alon (1996) explained that clients come to therapy with often bleak self-portrayals, inexorable plots, narrow themes, and demoralized meanings. The therapist's role is to help build together a new story as a co-narrator to help the client present, unfold, and develop new life themes that construct self-healing attitudes instead of self-defeating meanings.

Retelling the story becomes a new form of memory and its process becomes a rewriting.

CASE STUDY

Janelle was a 14-year-old Cree woman whose parents drank heavily, leaving her to fend for herself. Janelle also drank, attended school only intermittently, was sexually active with several boys, got pregnant once and had a miscarriage. Her grandparents had attended residential school. They drank heavily until death in their mid-50s and beat their children. Janelle's parents did not beat her, but neither did they protect her. She was occasionally suicidal when drunk and did not believe her life amounted to much.

She came to clinical attention when she attempted suicide by hanging one night and was found by her parents. One of us (LMM) was called to see her for a psychiatric consultation.

While involving elders often improves difficult family situations, this was not an option as the family had minimal connections to traditional cultures and wanted Janelle to be fixed without their involvement. What are we to do in such a situation?

All LMM could think of doing was to meet with Janelle, who did not really want to. He began these meetings with storytelling as a means of entertaining and engaging her. He chose to tell her stories in which young aboriginal women, both traditional and contemporary ones, were heroes. He told her the story of the woman who fell from the stars and saved the people from starvation by rescuing the buffalo from where they had been trapped by the North Wind (Mehl-Madrona 2003, xx). LMM believed in the idea that hearing a story changes its listener, and at least Janelle was entertained, though she wondered what the point of all these stories was. When we can do nothing else, perhaps all we can do is to tell stories. This storytelling could be perceived as a kind of hypnosis, though Janelle would have never accepted such terminology.

Slowly Janelle's view of herself changed. She stopped being sexually promiscuous and started attending school more regularly, although nothing had changed at home. LMM never asked her to change or confronted her with choices. He believed she would have fled had he done that. He was warm and accepting and entertained her with stories while, at the same time, commiserating with her about the hopelessness of her situation.

After two years, she was en route to high school graduation and her at-risk behavior with sex, alcohol and drugs decreased. LMM learned that she graduated Grade 12 and left the community to attend a technical school in Prince Albert to learn a trade.

CONCLUSIONS

Healing intergenerational trauma is a complex process where active acknowledgment and participation in one's cultural worldview should occur. For a health practitioner, engaging in a narrative medicine approach to healing would include listening to, interpreting, and constructing the stories that surround those who are suffering. A health practitioner should also be considerate of past historical contexts, such as the genocide perpetrated on the aboriginal peoples, and show sensitivity and support in order to build a trusting relationship with the individual and his or her family/community. If a health practitioner is not of the same cultural background as the patient, then treating intergenerational trauma would require special attention to the treatment suggestions made in this paper, such as incorporating an indigenous healer, participating in cultural activities and ceremonies together, and adopting a narrative medicine approach.

REFERENCES

Abrams, M. S. 1999. "Intergenerational Transmission of Trauma: Recent Contributions from the Literature of Family Systems Approaches to Treatment." *American Journal of Psychotherapy* 53 (2): 225–31.

Alexander, K. J., Miller, P. J., and Hengst, J. A. 2001. "Young Children's Emotional Attachment to Stories."Availableat:http://eric.ed.gov/ERICWebPortal/Home. portal?_nfpb=true&_pageLabel=ERICSearchResult&_urlType=action& newSearch=true&ERICExtSearch_SearchType_0=au&ERICExtSearch_ SearchValue_0=%22Alexander+Kristin+J.%22.Miller,P.J.http://eric.ed.gov/ ERICWebPortal/Home.portal?_nfpb=true&_pageLabel=ERIC SearchResult&_urlType=action&newSearch=true&ERICExtSearch_ SearchType_0=au&ERICExtSearch_SearchValue_0=%22Miller+Peggy +J.%22. Hengst, J.A. http://eric.ed.gov/ERICWebPortal/Home.portal?_nfpb= true&_pageLabel=ERICSearchResult&_urlType=action&newSearch= true&ERICExtSearch_SearchType_0=au&ERICExtSearch_SearchValue_ 0=%22Hengst+Julie+A.%22.

American Psychiatric Association. 2000. *Diagnostic and Statistical Manual of Mental Disorders.* 4th ed. rev. Washington, DC: Author.

Annett, A., and Sinclair, S. 2007. *Indigenous Perspectives on the Cultural, Political, Social, Economic Determinants of Mental Health and Wellness; Aboriginal Women and Postpartum Depression.* Available at: https://www. attachmentnetwork.ca/docs/conferences/2009–02–13%20Past%20 Event%20SC%20Influences%20on%20Maternal%20Depression.pdf.

Barton, S. S., Thommasen, H. V., Tallio, B., Zhang, W., and Michalos, A. C. 2001. "Health and Quality of life of Aboriginal Residential School Survivors, Bella Coola Valley, 2001." *Social Indicators Research* 73 (2): 295–312.

Berk, L. E., and Shanker, S. G. 2006. *Child Development.* Toronto, ON: Pearson Education Canada.

Brewin, C. R., Dalgleish, T., and Joseph, S. 1996. "A Dual Representation Theory of Post-traumatic Stress Disorder." *Psychological Review* 103: 670–86.

Brock, T. C., and Green, M. C. 2005. *Persuasion: Psychological Insights and Perspectives.* 2nd. ed. London: SAGE Publications.

Brody, G. H., and Flor, D. L. 1998. "Maternal Resources, Parenting Practices, and Child Competence in Rural, Single-Parent African American Families." *Child Development,* 69 (3): 803–16.

Bruner, J. 1986. *Actual Minds, Possible Words.* Cambridge, MA: Harvard University Press.

Bryant-Davis, T. 2007. "Healing Requires Recognition: The Case for Race-Based Traumatic Stress." *Counseling Psychologist* 35 (1): 135–43.

Cozolino, L. 2006. *The Neuroscience of Human Relationships.* New York: W. W. Norton and Company.

Duran, E. 2006. *Healing the Soul Wound: Counseling with American Indians and Other Native Peoples.* New York: Teachers College Press.

Gerrig, R. J. 1993. *Experiencing Narrative Worlds.* New Haven, CT: Yale University Press.

Grace, S. L. 2003. "A Review of Aboriginal Women's Physical and Mental Health Status in Ontario." *Canadian Journal of Public Health* 94: 173–75.

Graesser, A. C., Mills, K. K., and Zwaan, R. A. 1997. "Discourse Comprehension." *Annual Review of Psychology* 48: 163–89.

Green, M. C., Brock, T. C., and Kaufman, G. F. 2004. "Understanding Media Enjoyment: The Role of Transportation into Narrative Worlds." Communication Theory, 14 (4): 311–27.

Herman, J. L. 1992. *Trauma and Recovery.* New York: Basic Books.

Hesley, J. W., Hesley, J. G. 2001. *Rent Two Films and Let's Talk in the Morning: Using Popular Movies in Psychotherapy.* 2nd ed. New York: Wiley.

Kirmayer, L,. Brass, G. M, Holton, T., Paul, K., Simpson, C., and Tait, C. 2007. *Suicide among Aboriginal People in Canada.* Ottawa, ON: Aboriginal Healing Foundation.

Lampropoulos, G. K. 2004. "Psychologists' Use of Motion Pictures in Clinical Practice." *American Psychological Association* 35 (5): 535–41.

Lehrer, J. (2007). *Proust Was a Neuroscientist.* New York: Houghton-Mifflin. Available at: http://www.amazon.com/exec/obidos/search-handle-url/ref= ntt_athr_dp_sr_1?%5Fencoding=UTF8&search-type=ss&index= books&field-author=Jonah%20Lehrer.

Lux, M. 2004. *Medicine that Walks.* Toronto, ON: University of Toronto Press.

MacMillan, A. B., and Offord, D. R. 2008. "First Nations Women's Mental Health: Results from an Ontario Survey." *Archive of Women's Mental Health* 11: 109–15.

MacMillan, H. L., Jamieson, E., Walsh, C. A., Wong, M.Y.Y, Faries, E. J., and McCue, H. 2003. "The Health of Ontario First Nations People: Results from the Ontario First Nations Regional Survey." *Canadian Journal of Public Health* 94 (3): 168–71.

Mann C. 2006. *The Americas before Columbus.* New York: Granta Books.

Martineau, J. 2008. *Canadian PM Apologizes to First Nations for Residential Schools.* Press Release. June 11. Available at: http://www.nowpublic.com/ world/canadian-pm-apologizes-first-nations-residential-schools.

Mehl-Madrona, L. 2006. "Healing Relational Trauma through Relational Means: Aboriginal Approaches." In *Trauma, Truth and Reconciliation Healing Damaged Relationships,* ed. N. Potter, 393–413. Oxford, UK: Oxford University Press.

Mehl-Madrona, L. 2007. *Narrative Medicine: The Use of History and Story in the Healing Process.* Rochester, VT: Bear and Company.

Miller, P. J. 1995.*Personal Storytelling in Everyday Life.* Available at: http://books. google.com/books?hl=en&lr=&id=mR2B-FdDzDoC&oi=fnd&pg=PA17 7&dq=%22Miller%22+%22Personal+storytelling+in+everyday+life:+So cial+and+...%22+&ots=SELurFDGuE&sig=yBewRLFbk_aWoW8Me_ p3cAHZIUg.

Napoli, M. 2002. "Holistic Health Care for Native Women: An Integrated Model." *American Journal of Public Health* 92: 1573–75.

Oatley, K. 1999. "Why Fiction May Be Twice as True as Fact: Fiction as Cognitive and Emotional Simulation." *Review of General Psychology* 3: 101–17.

Omer, H. and Alon, N. 1996. "Principles of Psychotherapeutic Strategy." *Psychotherapy: Theory, Research, Practice, Training,* 26 (3): 282–89. Available at: http://content.apa.org/journals/pst.rss.

O'Nell, T. D. 1996. *Disciplined Hearts: History, Identity, and Depression in an American Indian Community.* Berkeley: University of California Press.

Pennebaker, J. W. and Seagal, J. D. 1999. *Forming a Story: The Health Benefits of Narrative.* Available at: http://www3.interscience.wiley.com/journal/31171/home; http://www3.interscience.wiley.com/journal/66000637/issue. F

Schank, R., and Abelson, R. 1995. "Knowledge and Memory: The Real Story." In *Knowledge and Memory: The Real Story,* ed. R. S. Wyer. New York: Routledge, 1995: 1–85.

Shepard, B, O'Neill, L., and Guenette, F. 2006. "Counseling with First Nations Women: Considerations of Oppression and Renewal." *International Journal for the Advancement of Counseling* 28 (3): 227–40.

Struthers, R. and Lowe, J. 2003. "Nursing in the Native American Culture and Historical Trauma." *Issues in Mental Health Nursing* 24: 257–72.

van der Kolk, B. A., and Fisler, R. 1995. "Dissociation and the Fragmentary Nature of Traumatic Memories: Overview and Exploratory Study." *Journal of Traumatic Stress* 8: 505–25.

Waldram, J. B., Herring, D. A., and Young, T. K. 2006. *Aboriginal Health in Canada: Historical, Cultural, and Epidemiological Perspectives.* 2nd. ed. Toronto, ON: University of Toronto Press.

Walters, K. L. and Simoni, J., M. 2002. "Reconceptualizing Native Women's Health: An 'Indigenist' Stress-Coping Model." *Future Health Needs of Women of Color* 92: 520–24.

Whattam, T. 2003. "Reflections on Residential Schools and our Future: 'Daylight in Our Minds'." *International Journal of Qualitative Studies in Education* 16 (3): 435–48.

Whitbeck, L. B, Adams, G. W., Hoyt, D. R., and Chen, X. 2004. "Conceptualizing and Measuring Historical Trauma among American Indian People." *American Journal of Community Psychology* 33 (3–4): 119–30.

Wheeler, S. C., Green, M. C., and Brock, T. C. 1999. "Fictional Narratives Change Beliefs: Replications of Prentice, Gerrig, and Bailis (1997) with Mixed Corroboration." *Psychon Bull Rev* 6 (1): 136–41.

Chapter 20

TRAUMATIZED BY HUMILIATION IN TIMES OF GLOBALIZATION

Transforming Humiliation into Constructive Meaning

Evelin G. Lindner

It has always been a mystery to me how men can feel themselves honored by the humiliation of their fellow beings.
—Mahatma Gandhi, 1869–1948

INTRODUCTION

This chapter is part of an anthology with Frankl's seminal work as guiding
paradigm. At 15 years old, this author read all of Frankl's early work. Born
in 1954, the author was one of the many millions of displaced families
from Central Europe who lived in Germany. As a small child, the horrors
of the Holocaust accompanied her—she had nightmares every night and
feared she would be killed immediately if found. Her family's trauma of
having lost their homeland (her parents are from Silesia) added to her deep
sense of anomie. As a so-called refugee-child, she grew up with a minus-
identity: not belonging to and feeling alienated from humanity. Her sense
of identity could be described as "here where we live is not our home,
but there is no home for us to return to. We are unwelcome guests on this
planet."

Her parents' trauma also formed the rest of their lives. Even today,
60 years later, they have not recovered. They have disengaged from the
earthly world that proved to be so hostile to them, and they pray for hours
every day—already, before death, living beyond Earth. The author's

work—dedicating her life to "never again"—is the only consolation that she can offer her parents, and she does so in Frankl's spirit.

When we study Frankl's work, we see that he succeeded in creating lifesaving meaning by widening his horizon in two ways, outward and inward. Frankl was interviewed when he was 90 years old (Scully 1995):

> If you call "religious" a man who believes in what I call a Supermeaning, a meaning so comprehensive that you can no longer grasp it, get hold of it in rational intellectual terminology, then one should feel free to call me religious, really. And actually, I have come to define religion as an expression, a manifestation, of not only man's will to meaning, but of man's longing for an ultimate meaning, that is to say a meaning that is so comprehensive that it is no longer comprehensible . . . . But it becomes a matter of believing rather than thinking, of faith rather than intellect. The positing of a supermeaning that evades mere rational grasp is one of the main tenets of logotherapy, after all. And a religious person may identify Supermeaning as something paralleling a Super being, and this Superbeing we would call God. (Scully 1995, quoted from http://print.firstthings.com/ftissues/ft9504/scully.html)

Even while suffering utter humiliation from sadistic Nazi SS guards, Frankl did not lose control of his inner life. He found hope and strength by thinking of his wife. Those who had nothing to live for were the first to die in the concentration camp. Frankl wrote, "And as we stumbled on for miles, slipping on icy spots, supporting each other time and again, dragging one another up and onward, nothing was said, but we both knew: each of us was thinking of his wife" (Frankl 1985, 56).

This chapter is dedicated to analyzing the role of humiliation for trauma and trauma recovery. It argues that humiliation is gaining significance for the field of trauma research with two processes: the coming together of humankind (a phenomenon that is part of globalization), and the progress of the human rights movement. Humiliation plays a role as soon as a disaster is perceived to be caused by human negligence or disregard (for example, by global warming, or war), and it is as relevant in all post-disaster situations, including natural disasters, when rescue efforts and rebuilding strategies are inadequate.

This chapter makes the point that learning about humiliation dynamics and how to cope with them is essential for meaning-making and resilience, and that Frankl draws the path before us. Frankl lifted his eyes to a higher order of meaning, and he turned his eyes inward, finding the image of his wife that gave him strength. This chapter attempts to achieve precisely this, the widening of the explanatory horizon for the reader, by offering a journey, a journey of reaching both more outward and more inward. It is of core importance if we want to understand the "impact of human-made disasters," as humiliation is related to intentional human interference—usually, one does not feel humiliated by an animal, an accident, or by natural disaster where no consciously intending actor can be identified.

This chapter is written with the background of the transdisciplinary work on humiliation carried out by the author of this chapter. Humiliation Studies is a very new field due to the phenomenon of humiliation itself only very recently gathering significance, in the wake of a globalizing world that is exposed to the human rights message. The study of humiliation needs to be transdisciplinary in order to be comprehensive, a fact that makes it difficult to fit into traditional research—academic disciplines usually also discipline their scholars. In her work, the author draws on political science, sociology, anthropology, history, theology, social psychology and clinical psychology (see, among others, Lindner 2006 and www. humiliationstudies.org/whoweare/evelin02.php.).

The author began building a global network entitled Human Dignity and Humiliation Studies (HumanDHS, www.humiliationstudies.org.) in 2001, subsequent to four years of doctoral research on humiliation (Lindner 2000a). In 1996, she set out to design her research project on the concept of humiliation and its role in genocide and war. German history served as a starting point. It is often assumed that the humiliation of the Germans through the Versailles Treaties after World War I was partly responsible for the Holocaust and the Second World War. From 1997–2001, she interviewed over 200 people who were either implicated in or knowledgeable about the genocides in Rwanda, Somalia, and Nazi Germany. Since 2001, she has included more cases, writing an early draft for this chapter in Japan. Her research indicates that, indeed, the dynamics of humiliation may be at the core of war, genocides, and current phenomena such as global terror.

In the following, it will be shown that the phenomenon of humiliation is currently gaining significance because it is in the process of changing: humiliation presently transmutes from being regarded as a prosocial lesson, to being deemed as an antisocial violation. Understanding the historical dimension of this change, which also deeply impacts experiences of trauma, represents the lifting of our eyes. Only by understanding the larger context can we insert humiliating experiences in constructive and meaningful ways into our larger world view. Understanding the historical dimension, however, also facilitates the inward turning of the eyes, humanizing our own inner world. Both movements are essential for meaning-making and resilience in times of crisis, particularly at the current point of historic crises.

CURRENT STATE OF THE ART WITH RESPECT TO RESEARCH ON HUMILIATION

As mentioned earlier, the phenomenon of humiliation has become visible only very recently, and only very few researchers have studied this phenomenon explicitly so far. Mostly, the phenomenon of humiliation figures implicitly in literature on violence and war. The view that humiliation may be a particularly forceful phenomenon is supported by the research of many authors (Gilligan 1996; Hale 1994; Hartling and Luchetta 1999; Klein 1991; Lewis 1971; Miller 1993; Retzinger 1991; Scheff 1990; Volkan 2004).

The notion of *oppression* is related to humiliation (Deutsch 2006), as is the concept of *domination* (Pettit 1996). There is a significant literature in philosophy on the *politics of recognition* and *resentment* (Honneth 1995; Honneth 1997; Scheler 1912). Using the examples of Ethiopia and Eritrea, Liah Greenfeld suggests that resentment plays a central role in nation building (Greenfeld 1992; Greenfeld 1996). Philosopher Avishai Margalit's call for a *Decent Society* (Margalit 1996), in which institutions no longer humiliate citizens, would mean, in practice, working for the Millennium Goals, and for building global institutions that protect the common good of humankind, institutions that free the top global level from the current might-is-right power dynamics that contravene human rights at all levels.

According to Goffman, *face* is the positive social value a person wishes to attain in a social interaction. Humiliation can be described as a loss of face; the picture one wishes to present is suddenly discredited (Goffman 1953; Goffman 1967). The relationship between *guilt, shame* and *aggression* has been addressed (Tangney et al. 1992) as has the relationship between *anger* and *aggression* (Averill 2001). The link between *humiliation* and *aggression,* however, has not received much attention among researchers. Among the few scholars addressing this topic are Mischel and De Smet (2000), who explain that *rejection-sensitive* men may get hooked on situations of debasement where they can feel humiliated. Furthermore, *malignant narcissism* has been linked to humiliation. Feelings of humiliation and shame may lead to narcissistic rage and acts of aggression meant to lessen pain and increase self-worth; international leaders, when publicly humiliated, in some cases, may instigate mass destruction and war (Steinberg 1991; Steinberg 1996). *Hazing* and *bullying* entail humiliation at their core (Olweus 1993, a pioneer in research on bullying). And at last, there is also a link between help and humiliation; help may be resented by low-status groups (Nadler 2002).

From the author's work, the word humiliation refers to three different elements of experience—the perpetrator's act, the victim's feeling, and the social process (the reader is asked to infer which element is alluded to at any given point, because otherwise language becomes too convoluted). To add to this complexity, different cultures, different groups within a culture, and different individuals within a group often disagree as to whether or not an experience is eligible to be defined as humiliation, and since all such decisions are subjective, each side of a dispute will typically insist on applying the word to its own experience and deny it to the other.

Underlying all cultural variance, we find one single core feature in all dynamics of humiliation, namely that it entails the pushing down and holding down of something or somebody (see relevant work on the embodied mind and spatial metaphors by Lakoff and Johnson 1999). When we search further, in an attempt to understand how this holding down practice may be employed, we discern that two contradictory scripts can be built around this practice and that these two scripts permeate all world cultures (if analyzed in the spirit of a Weberian *ideal-type* approach, see a good explanation of this approach in Coser 1977, 224). The author labels these two cultural definitions, which are mutually exclusive, *honor humiliation* and *dignity humiliation*.

Hitler played out the script of honor humiliation. He plunged the world into World War II, supposedly remedying the national humiliation that had been inflicted on Germany by way of the Versailles Treaties at the end of World War I with the aim to keep Germans down and discourage them from repeating aggression. Unfortunately, this strategy backfired and Hitler invited all Germans into a narrative of national humiliation, for which he offered war as remedy—and millions paid with their lives. Hitler translated feelings of humiliation into atrocious acts of humiliation and turned the cycle of humiliation into suicidal homicide, not unlike today's so-called suicide-bombers, except that Hitler sacrificed millions for his vision of redeeming honor humiliation.

The modern definition of humiliation—dignity humiliation—is very different. This contemporary definition is based on the human rights ideal of equal dignity for all. The first paragraph of Article 1 of the Universal Declaration of Human Rights (UDHR), which was adopted by the United Nations General Assembly on December 10, 1948, reads: "All human beings are born free and equal in dignity and rights." Human rights endow every single human being with an inner core of equal dignity that ought not to be held down. The human rights revolution thus turns formerly legitimate humbling of underlings into illegitimate humiliation. Feelings of humiliation among the downtrodden are the very fuel of the human rights revolution. In the world of honor, holding down underlings is no violation—it only becomes a violation in a human rights frame that prescribes equal dignity for all. In the world of honor, only the elite have the right to interpret an attempt to put them down as violation, not their underlings—in a world defined by human rights everybody has the right to protest against being held down.

Human rights introduce two transformations, (1) the dismantling of the tyrants of our world (in former times this happened frequently, however, typically with the usurpers merely transmuting into new tyrants) and (2) the dismantling, in addition, of all tyrannical top-down systems and their ways of defining human conduct, including all dominating practices that we ourselves might still employ.

Mandela—in contrast to Hitler—demonstrated how the explosiveness of feelings of humiliation can be channeled into constructive social change. Mandela attempted to bring down tyrants, dismantle a tyrannical system, and do that in dignified ways, without demonizing and humiliating his opponents. This constructive channeling is not only in line with human rights ideals; incidentally, it is also at the core of recovery from both mass and individual trauma. In Frankl's spirit, it means redeeming humiliation by ending cycles of humiliation.

The historical beginning of the transition from honor humiliation to dignity humiliation can be pinpointed quite accurately, at least in the English speaking world. According to the *Oxford English Dictionary,* the earliest recorded use of *to humiliate* meaning "to mortify or to lower or to depress the dignity or self-respect of someone" does not occur until 1757. Prior to 1757 (and still today, in some world regions), holding down a person—demeaning, denigrating, degrading her—was not necessarily regarded as illegitimate. The verbs *to humble* and *to humiliate* were used rather interchangeably. Around 250 years ago, the meanings of those two verbs separated and developed in diametrically opposed directions in the English language: *humility* remained to be seen as a virtue, while *humiliation* acquired the taste of an illicit violation.

Apart from being a complex phenomenon, with two fundamentally irreconcilable cultural definitions and scripts, humiliation has another important feature, namely that of potency. In *Making Enemies: Humiliation and International Conflict* (Lindner 2006), chapter seven is entitled "The Humiliation Addiction," explaining that feelings of humiliation can turn out to be as strong and compelling as an addiction. For drug addicts, for example, self-interest is replaced by their craving for the next fix. Likewise, people who feel humiliated may hunger for revenge and might act in ways that lead to suicide and homicide. On the other hand, Philosopher Margalit proposes that some people may become obsessively attached to feeling humiliated, also because this secures the "benefits" of the victim status and an entitlement for retaliation (Margalit 2002). Thus, trauma experts need to understand the potency of humiliation.

They need to be aware and extremely cautious when bringing human rights to the downtrodden, marginalized and underprivileged, to those who are neglected in disaster scenarios. Human rights defenders need to do more than nurture and teach a sense of violation. They have to show and embody the Mandela and Frankl way out of feelings of humiliation, because these feelings are so strong that they can lead not only to depressed apathy or noble empowerment, but also to violent backlashes.

Feeling victimized by honor humiliation can lead to Hitler-like mayhem, while feeling victimized by dignity humiliation causes even deeper wounds, since it means being excluded from the family of humankind altogether. Trauma experts and caregivers in disasters have to channel those explosive feelings into constructive advocacy of social change in the spirit of Mandela and Frankl; otherwise helpers may contribute to compounding trauma rather than alleviating it.

THE HISTORICAL TRANSITION FROM HONOR HUMILIATION TO DIGNITY HUMILIATION

Natural disasters, disasters that are not human-made, traumatize people, but they do not humiliate them. The aspect of humiliation is missing when there is no perpetrator (unless one believes in God wishing to punish, humble, and humiliate his sinful followers by sending disasters). Victimhood and trauma are less intense in natural disasters than when the same pain is flowing from fellow human beings, particularly when this happens in the framework of human rights. The reason for this is that the phenomenon of humiliation is deeply relational.

The first question asked about the 2003 blackout in North America was "Was it terrorism?" The relief was almost palpable when it became clear that there was no terrorism involved. The hardship was identical, but it was easier to bear when people knew that the inconvenience was not the result of another terrorist message of humiliation. The academic term for this phenomenon is the so-called *controllability dimension.* Research shows, that we only get angry and want to harm others, either overtly or covertly, when we believe they could have avoided hurting us (Allred 1999; Averill 1993).

Humiliation seeps in whenever we conclude that disasters are caused by human negligence (global climate change, for example, that could have been avoided with more care), or when disasters are responded to in negligent and fraudulent ways, as when some line their pockets with the funds intended for victims. In the latter case, the deepest trauma might develop post-disaster, from being defrauded in ways that remove dignity, rather than from the disaster itself. In other words, we can have trauma without humiliation, but also trauma caused by humiliation.

The point is that the weighting of human responsibility, the gauging of what can be excused and what not, is not fixed, but subject to the larger normative frame that people employ. And this frame has changed over the past millennia. In this chapter, it is argued that much of the trauma that is experienced in today's world is related to this historical shift. Merely becoming aware of this larger context can calm desperation; after all, the current human rights movement is historically very young and there is no reason to lose hope and give up supporting it.

HUMILIATION WAS ONCE SEEN AS NEGLIGIBLE PAIN, OR EVEN AS PROSOCIAL LESSON

Earlier, the historical turning point of 1757 was introduced, when the practice of holding down people moved from being recommended as prosocial to being condemned as antisocial. Let us now try to make meaning out of this transition and understand the context in which it occurred. To do that, we need to go much farther back in history. The lifting our eyes up to this larger historical context may be vital for helpers and victims.

There are people who believe that it is futile to think that humankind can be improved. Homo sapiens, they say, is hard-wired to focus on narrow self-interest, disregard others' sufferings, maim, kill, and perpetrate mayhem. However, this is a misconception. There is no archeological evidence for systematic war prior to 10,000 years ago. There is no proof of organized fighting among early hunters and gatherers (Ury 1999). "The Hobbesian view of humans in a constant state of 'Warre' is simply not supported by the archaeological record" (Haas 1998).

In other words, when we study the historic facts, we find that for millions of years, hominids evolving toward Homo sapiens roamed the globe as hunters and gatherers without engaging in systematic war. They lived in small groups and enjoyed rather egalitarian societal institutions and remarkably high quality of life.

The hunter-gatherer way of life dominated the globe until about 10,000 years ago, when it hit the wall, and experienced a turning point, akin to the one 10,000 years later, in 1757. Around 10,000 years ago, rather suddenly in terms of long-term history, hunter-gatherers no longer could merely wander off and find untouched abundance of wild food in the next valley. The reason was that other people were already there (*circumscription* is the anthropological term). Many of the easily accessible parts of planet Earth were inhabited by Homo sapiens. We could call this the first round of globalization for humankind.

William Ury, an anthropologist, and director of the Harvard University Project on Preventing War, draws up a simplified depiction of history (Ury 1999). He pulls together elements from anthropology, game theory and conflict studies to describe three major types of society: (a) simple hunter-gatherers, (b) complex agriculturists, and (c) the currently emerging knowledge society. In Ury's system, simple hunter-gatherers lived in a world of coexistence and open networks, within which conflicts were negotiated, rather than addressed by coercion. The abundance of wild food represented an *expandable pie of resources* that did not force opponents into win-lose paradigms.

10,000 years ago, when the globe filled up, and hunting and gathering turned increasingly unfeasible, humankind came up with a response, namely agriculture (*intensification* is the anthropological term). However, as Ury spells out, this response was rather problematic. No longer did abundance of wild food offer an expandable pie of resources. Land is either mine or yours and represents a *fixed pie* that pushes antagonists into win-lose situations. Complex agriculturalists therefore lived in a world of coercion, within closed hierarchical pyramids of power.

The world of honorable domination/submission, including honor humiliation, could be regarded as an adaptation to a strong security dilemma, which emanated from the fact that land became the resource of most of humankind, a resource that, by definition, is not expandable. In a world of honorable domination/submission, nobody doubts that it is God's will or nature's order that some people are born higher and ought to hold down lesser beings. From kowtowing to regular beatings and killings so as to remind underlings of their due lowly place, even the most atrocious methods are seen as honorable medicine. Victims have no right to invoke the notion of humiliation as a form of violation. Only the masters themselves, when their privileged position is questioned, can appeal to humiliation as an infringement on their honor and redeem it, by duelling. Human rights, in contrast to honorable domination/submission, represent an adaptation to new circumstances, namely to the contemporary round of globalization that, if it is guided to lead up to a globally integrated knowledge society, entails a push toward the removal of the security dilemma as defining principle.

TODAY, HUMILIATION IS REGARDED AS A VIOLATION OF HUMAN DIGNITY

Ury posits that a knowledgeable society resembles the hunter-gatherer model because the pie of resources—knowledge—appears to be infinitely expandable (there are always new ideas to be developed), leading to win-win solutions. This type of society moves away from rigid hierarchical structures toward the open network of our earliest hunter-gatherer ancestors. Negotiation and contract replace command lines, and coexistence is the primary strategy.

Under the security dilemma, the negative emotion that ruled the world was fear, fear of attack. One community feared the other, the enemy. Human rights, in contrast, invite all human beings into one single human family, where everybody enjoys equal dignity. All are neighbors, no longer we against them and friends versus enemies. Everybody is told that he or she can expect to be treated with respect. And everybody feels humiliated if this respect is failing. Thus, while the period of honor was defined by fear, collective fear of attack from out-groups, human rights introduce humiliation as defining negative emotion—feelings of humiliation as a reaction to failing to have respect for equal dignity on the part of each individual, qua being an individual, no longer qua being part of a collective.

Prior to globalization, as long as humankind lived in a fragmented world of us, the in-group, versus them, the out-groups, all were steeped in a host of malign framings and biases. People skewed reality and developed biases that favored one's self and one's in-group and disfavored others (so-called *attribution errors*). People created *moral boundaries* where individuals or groups inside the moral in-group boundary were seen as deserving of a better moral treatment than those outside this boundary (Coleman 2000; Opotow 1995).

If we turn our eyes inward, and ask where moral courage comes from, then it emanates, not least, from using our brain properly. New research on emotions indicates that our behavior is regulated by *feedback loops* that are organized hierarchically (Powers 1973; Powers 1998). Superordinate loops attend to longer-term, abstract goals. Embedded within them are subordinate loops for short-term tasks. We create or maintain destructive conflict, when we allow lower-order mechanisms to supersede higher-order mechanisms. We invite failure when we permit phylogenically more immediate and automated emotional processes to override the more abstracted regulatory ones. Long-term goals require that we refrain from jumping at them with short-term mental tools. In other words, when we look inward, into the workings of our brain, we notice that the evolution of the human brain's structure mirrors the lifting of the eyes to higher-order contexts and solutions.

HOW HUMILIATION GAINED SIGNIFICANCE
FOR RESEARCH ON TRAUMA AND COPING
WITH DISASTER

In the following, a continuum will be drawn—see Table 20.1—that maps out the transition from trauma without humiliation to trauma that is precisely traumatic because of humiliation (this section is adapted from Lindner 2001).

Humiliation may enter a relationship by chance. Rebels may kidnap victims arbitrarily and treat them in humiliating ways. The hostages will feel humiliated and develop resentment and hatred towards the kidnappers. People who formerly were not party to any cycle of humiliation may thus, inadvertently, be drawn into it. The infamous strategy of divide-and-rule instrumentalizes this dynamic.

Humiliation may also enter a relationship in a piecemeal fashion. Intimate relationships such as, marriage may develop into humiliating relationships over time (Vogel and Lazare 1990). The same dynamics may unfold at macro levels; history shows that dictators may be loved and welcomed at first, just to bring humiliation upon their followers later. Somalia enthusiastically welcomed Siad Barre in 1969. Hitler started his career as a Robin Hood figure (Lindner 2000b), poised to rescue the Germans. The Rwandan Hutu elite lifted up formerly suppressed Hutu and aimed at creating a state in which Hutu could live with dignity. Utter humiliation of neighbors and minorities, even genocide, was the result in all three cases, Somalia, Nazi Germany, and Rwanda.

Trauma might also be brought on a person intentionally, to teach this person humility, and the victim may even accept this lesson humbly. The Bible recounts how Job learned to understand that God wanted to teach him humility—the true believer learns from Job's struggle that his efforts are exemplary, namely not to reject God's strikes as gruesome humiliation but accept them as beneficial humbling. Indeed, as discussed earlier, it is typical for hierarchical honor societies, where humiliation is a routine strategy to maintain the ranking order, that masters bring trauma on people intentionally, to teach them that they are lowly or unworthy and, sometimes, people may accept this as perfectly legitimate. History books describe how duels were means to calibrate ranks in honorable ranking orders. At the micro level, breaking the will of children was recommended as child rearing method—the aim was to teach children obedience in a hierarchy (see Miller 1983).

In other cases, however, victims may react differently, and not accept that they are being rightfully humbled. A prisoner waiting for capital punishment, perhaps just too poor to pay a lawyer who could prove his innocence, may be expected to object to the views of the judge that this situation is to be described as beneficial humbling. In hierarchical societies, masters may generally believe that any abasement they inflict on underlings is good for them, while the supposed happy beneficiaries may violently object to this definition. Typically, in a democratic society that is built on human rights principles, where citizens expect to be treated with respect as equals among equals, victims subjected to trauma that aims to teach them that they are unworthy, will perceive this as an illegitimate violation.

Table 20.1 lays out a spectrum ranging from trauma that does not entail humiliation (left pole) to trauma that is traumatic precisely through the presence of humiliation (right pole). It becomes apparent that the right pole is introduced by human rights ideals that protect individual dignity and turn its violation into trauma.

If we think of possible future research, the topic of humiliation is not just a psychological issue; it is inherently transdisciplinary, transcultural, and transreligious. In many cultures and religions we find liberation branches that define humiliation as a violation of equal dignity, in contrast to more traditional branches that regard the practice of humiliating underlings as due humbling. *Ubuntu,* for example, the African philosophy and practice that is based on "I am because you are" can serve as an illustration for a liberation culture.

The more equal dignity for all becomes the guiding principle in a community, the academic community included, the more the topic of humiliation is bound to gain significance, because no longer do underlings suffer in silence. Disasters caused or compounded by human negligence and disregard are no longer lived with in quiet sufferance; on the contrary, they are deemed to be profoundly humiliating. Scholars should study these dynamics in order to help channel them in Frankl's spirit toward constructive action.

As discussed earlier, the core feature of meaning-making in Frankl's work is the widening of our horizon, both inward and outward. For the case of research on trauma, humiliation, recovery, and resilience, this means that these phenomena need to be studied in a transdisciplinary fashion, starting at the micro level, for example, in fields such as neuropsychology and psychotherapy (turning our eyes inward), while at the same time proceeding through the entire gamut of disciplines up to political science, theology, and history (turning our eyes up and outward). As we have seen, feelings of humiliation are no stand-alone phenomena, but embedded into scripts that are provided by larger cultural and religious contexts, which, in turn, are subject to long-term anthropological adaptations throughout history.

To illustrate this point, suicide bombing, motivated by humiliation, is a phenomenon worth studying by psychology as much as by political science, or theology. The current chasm between the West and the East is as much psychological as political. Disasters, natural or human-made, are embedded into these larger contexts. Whenever political will is lacking to prevent genocide (such as in Darfur), this humiliates not only its

Table 20.1
Trauma and Humiliation

| | Trauma and humiliation | | | | |
| Trauma without humiliation | Actors are involved, but not intending to humiliate me, at least not initially | | | Humiliation as core of trauma | |
No actor		←	→	An actor intends to humiliate me	
(1) A natural disaster happens to me, and I see no perpetrator	(2) An accident happens to me and the perpetrator apologizes	(3) An accident happens to me and the perpetrator treats me in a humiliating way	(4) An accident leads to a humiliating situation after some time	(6) An actor wants to teach me unworthiness in a context where this is routine behavior and everybody behaves in this way	(7) An actor wants to teach me my unworthiness in a context where this is not routine but illegitimate and violates my inner core of dignity
Earthquake, flood	A car accident; the driver apologizes	Rebels arbitrarily kidnap people	Some cases of marriage; dictators	Duels; "breaking the will" of children; torture, in an honor context	Mobbing and bullying, in a human rights context

immediate victims, but the humanity in all who have been touched by the human rights message and Frankl's work.

The Human Dignity and Humiliation Studies network has therefore three main agendas: research (transdisciplinary), education, and intervention. The members of the network combine transdisciplinarily, including bridging the gap to practice, while at the same time self-reflectively focusing on themselves and making sure that they walk their talk (turning their eyes upward and inward).

THE ROLE PLAYED BY GENDER

As long as humankind lived in a world of fragmentation between us and them, caught in the security dilemma, identity constructs such as patriotism were developed, as was the so-called gender division. Joshua Goldstein (2001) shows how war and the gender division are interlinked. The world of honor was divided into a female domestic sphere, and a male public sphere.

For centuries, domestic chastisement was an entitlement and duty for masters to carry out—a disobedient wife or child or slave had to accept being brutally punished. The pain that was inflicted was seen as prosocial pain, as a necessary lesson, necessary to achieve calm and stability in the hierarchical system.

To use the author's personal example, she grew up in a rather conservative family where a good woman is called upon to be subservient to her husband. The author struggled for years with this definition and was less than efficient in making the transition to redefining what a good woman means for her, namely a woman who deserves equal dignity to a man and to a husband. For a long while, she merely felt bad.

If we describe her identity in the world of ranked honor, to be a good woman means to be a respectful and subservient daughter and wife so as to protect the honor of her men; her worldview is to be that it is nature's order that she is born as a lesser being and that justice is being done when she is chastised in case of disobedience; she sins against her religion and her spiritual orientation when she does not know her due lowly place; for her to demonstrate leadership is to show her daughters the path of due respectful subservience. Disaster relief and development that occurs within this framing means that conflict transformation is successful when unruly females, since they are by definition underlings, are made to accept quietly and thankfully the authority of their patrons; and the term trauma, like humiliation, is a word that only the elite are entitled to invoke.

The author worked as a clinical psychologist in Egypt for seven years (1984–1991), and learned the many facets of this definition that is common in the non-Western world.

In contrast, if we translate her identity into a human rights framing, to be a good woman means to demand to be treated as equal in dignity with her brothers and her husband; her worldview is that it is nature's order that she deserves to be treated as equal in dignity with everybody else and that justice is being done when her dignity is respected; she sins against her religion and her spiritual orientation when she allows humiliation to occur, both for herself and others; for her to demonstrate leadership is to show her sons and daughters the path of respect for equal dignity for all. Disaster relief and development that occurs within this framing means that conflict transformation is successful when females are given a voice and elevated to the same level of dignity as everybody else; and the term trauma, like humiliation, is a concept that can be used to bring help to the downtrodden.

Both framings are not simply two equivalent framings. Human rights are not just a moral call; they are also very practical and advantageous. They free human abilities that were suppressed under the conditions of the security dilemma. A world of equal dignity for all is favorable for everybody, because the old division of an elite dominating inferiors handicapped all participants: subordinates were disallowed to bring their leadership into society, and superordinates had no chance to enjoy caring and nurturing. Fathers did not take pleasure in domestic life; they would not change the diapers of their babies, play with them, and see them mature. Inversely, their wives would refrain from strategic decisions and follow their husbands' guidance. Both were at a loss, both sacrificed the fulfillment that life in its entirety has to offer, in caring and in leadership. Also society at large was at a loss, because it underutilized available talents for leadership, innovative creativity, and nurturing.

To employ the metaphor of the body, men were permitted to only use their right sword arm, while their nurturing arm was bound behind their back. Correspondingly, women did not strategize and lead; they were only permitted to use their left arm for maintaining the private sphere. Human rights free both arms for everybody. This is why human rights are so humanizing—not only are they morally compelling, but also deeply useful as defining frame for structuring human life. It is not least therefore that human rights may be regarded as universal and not just as a Western scheme.

CULTURAL AND SPIRITUAL RITUALS THAT ARE EMBEDDED INTO HONOR CONTEXTS

Cultural and spiritual rituals in honor contexts are often irreconcilable with rituals that promote human rights. The author often uses the example of the Chinese tradition of foot binding to exemplify practices that underpin cultures of honor. Many rituals are fashioned upon this template of handicapping inferiors, in different cultures in various ways. In *The Chalice and the Blade: Our History, Our Future,* Riane Eisler (1987) describes how otherwise widely divergent societies, from the samurai of Japan to the Aztecs of Meso-America, were characterized by very similar hierarchies of domination and a rigidly male-dominant strong-man rule, both in the family and state. Hierarchies of domination were maintained by a high degree of institutionalized (socially accepted) violence, ranging from wife- and child-beating within the family to aggressive warfare on the larger tribal or national level, including a large range of cultural and spiritual rituals that supported what Eisler calls the dominator model (in contrast to the partnership model).

The author's doctoral research in Somalia (where almost all adult men are fierce noblemen), Rwanda and Burundi (where the Hutu majority traditionally lived under Tutsi rule), rendered rich material that illustrated this difference (Lindner 2000a, 302–4). Many expatriates related to me that they tended to prefer Somalis, "who would spit into your face if they do not agree with you," to the "soft smile where you never know where you are" in Rwanda. Proverb 2121 that I saw in *Proverbes du Rwanda* may illustrate this experience: "*Kurárama sî kó kuramukanya*": "Disdain transpires even when the rules of politeness are scrupulously observed" (Crépeau and Bizimana 1979).

In Rwanda and Burundi the author found a complex web of beliefs and rituals surrounding the notion of evil spirits. Bernd Morast (personal meeting on February 11, 1999) had collected proverbs, some from the Great Lakes region, and shared a list that he had found in the writings of Father E. Rodegem (1983): *Mpemuke ndamuke*: "It is better to betray than to die," or proverb number 395 in Rodegem, *Kmênyo agusekéra niyo akurya*: "The same teeth that smile at you will eat you," or proverb 161, *Akabanga gasumba ingabíre*: "The guarded secret is worth more than a cow received as a gift." Later the author heard about a Tutsi proverb, "Never teach a Hutu to shoot with bow and arrow, because he will kill you with it."

In Rwanda the author collected many accounts of traditions of mistrust among Hutu (from an informant with a Tutsi background): "There are Hutu names that illustrate that there must be quite a large amount of suspicion or méfiance in the Hutu population." Names may mean: "I am surrounded by hatred" ("*je suis dans la haine*"), "they will kill me" ("*ils me tuerions*"), "I am not there because they want it," or, "if they could do as they like I would not live" ("*je ne suis pas là grâce à eux*"), or "I am there only because of God." However, méfiance is perhaps not just a Hutu problem. "The Batutsi Mwamis also manipulated a complex web of spies, and thus not only maintained their power, but developed a capacity for political intrigue and paranoia that remains to this day throughout Rwandan society" (Waller and Oxfam 1996, 4).

In Burundi, the author heard from a physician (also with Tutsi background): "When I visited my grandmother in the Collines (the hills in the country side) as a child, I was told to smile to the neighbors, but not to accept even a glass of water since this could be poisoned. Everybody was seemingly very kind to visitors, but when the visitor had left, one behaved quite differently! When I worked at the hospital as a doctor, just in the beginning, and I had, say, 20 patients I was responsible for, I asked myself: This patient has tuberculosis, this patient has malaria, this patient has diabetes, and this patient has this or that. Where are the patients who have *des esprits*? I still was somewhere convinced that *des esprits* cause illness! Because this was what people in the Collines think! When somebody falls sick, then they believe that the neighbor has poisoned or bewitched the victim."

In *Proverbes du Rwanda* the author found many proverbs that illustrate these points, proverb 3785 may serve as an example: *Umwânzi akubaliliza nk'úmukûnzi*: "The enemy tries to know everything about you to better prepare his coup"; also proverb 3789, *Umwânzi ntâbà kure*: "The enemy is not far"; as well as proverb 3792, *Umwânzi ntânùká*: "One is often not aware of the enemy" (Crépau and Bizimana 1979).

CULTURAL AND SPIRITUAL RITUALS
THAT PROMOTE HUMAN RIGHTS

The author of this chapter calls on researchers and practitioners of intercultural communication to develop a new field, namely, the field of global interhuman communication (Lindner 2007). This new field would set as its task to make a triage of rituals and select those that promote human rights as templates to be used and implemented more widely. Traditions such a foot-binding or those that systematically foster mutual mistrust are not compatible with a human rights context; they have their place in cultural contexts that were adapted to conditions of the past.

As alluded to earlier, all the major religions include significant ideals of equality. Buddhism has a claim for equal dignity, as has New Testament Christianity, Islam, the Sikh faith, and so forth. However, in the past these ideals were typically pushed into the background by the overall hierarchical structures of the larger social and societal environments. Since only in the past couple of hundred years have these ideals begun to carry significant influence, new rituals have yet to be forged.

CONCLUSION

Two irreconcilable normative frames currently compete, namely norms of ranked honor versus human rights norms of equal dignity for all. From the point of view of one normative frame, the respective other normative frame seems mad or evil. For human rights defenders, people who condone the domination of lesser beings (women, for example) by higher beings (men, for example), may seem wicked. And vice versa: People who hold the opposite to be true, namely that God ordained precisely that superiors are placed above inferiors, feel that human rights poke holes into the very rock of true morality. And national elites, even those who use the terminology of human rights, for reasons of national security and national stability, in practice often side with the dominators of the world in practice by ways of double standards. The result is that all sides feel that the other side humiliates the core of their most treasured moral beliefs, and denigrates their most noble motives. All are at an impasse that traumatizes everybody.

In the eyes of its neighbors, Japan fails to apologize adequately for the atrocities they committed in the past; or Turkey is criticized for not acknowledging the Armenian genocide (Kalayjian, Jesmaridyan, and Swenson 2006). Both respond to this criticism from within a culture of national honor that equates apology with weakness. Honor societies (as defined in this chapter)—including many national leaders—believe in the validity of structuring society and relationships top-down, strong masters ruling over subservient underlings. In contrast, human rights defenders think and feel within the equal dignity framework, where relationships are structured through mutual connection and negotiation. All buzzwords—freedom, security, trauma, humiliation, resilience, healing—have diametrically opposing significations within each of those two frameworks.

This conundrum contributes to creating a world that is split into terrorists and heroes, responded to by war on terrorism on one side, and heroic resistance of freedom fighters on the other side. This split forecloses what the world needs most in order to make globalization humane and fair, including adequate responses to local and global disasters, namely cooperation and joint caring for the survival of humankind and its planet. This split represents a global disaster that calls on global society to respond. The task at hand for all citizens of the world is to turn their eyes upward in Frankl's and Mandela's spirit and work for a more meaningful global context.

The task to be tackled is the completion of the historic transition toward human rights, a transition that at present proceeds in a much too jumbled and incomplete fashion. In certain regions of this world, the suffering of people is not yet deemed to be important. When the American Embassy in Kenya was bombed in 1998, American psychiatrists flew in. Kenyan friends were thankful. However, they shared, with a certain amount of bitterness that millions of Africans live under circumstances of poverty and conflict that are more traumatizing than the bombing—trauma represents normality for them—and they all have to cope on their own. There are no helpers, care-givers, or funds available to help them, either because of disregard or lack of resources. "They are traumatized by normality and they are expected to accept the wounds of trauma quietly and refrain from crying humiliation!" (Nairobi, May 24–25, 1999, 1st Regional Meeting of the World Psychiatric Association and the Kenya Psychiatric Association).

As is widely known, not only in Africa, but all around the world, millions live in abject traumatizing poverty. And the transition toward betterment is often progressing only in a one-step-forward-two-steps-back fashion. Helpers and caregivers have a responsibility to not only focus on local disasters but must help build a *decent* global community, in the spirit of Margalit's call for a *Decent Society* (1996), within which local disasters can be embedded more efficiently. Political will, both globally and locally, has to be mobilized. This entails working for the Millennium Development Goals (MDG United Nations, 2000) and building superordinate global institutions that bring human rights to global levels, where currently might-is-right power dynamics sour all human rights efforts.

But how should a human rights worker, a helper, a trauma expert, the reader of this book, act efficiently in such a disarray? In the new world of technology, every single individual can become a Viktor Frankl or Nelson Mandela, by creating peace within and peace outside with ample expressions of forgiveness. The old order honor, a harsh adaptation to the brutal security dilemma, entailed many malign aspects. Human rights offer a much more benign moral framework. In the spirit of Logotherapy, these benign aspects can be identified and given preeminence, both to enable us to turn our eyes outward and inward. Frankl, at the age of 90, explains "Logotherapy sees the human patient in all his humanness. I step up to the core of the patient's being. And that is a being in search of meaning, a being that is transcending him, a being capable of acting in love for others. . . . You see, any human being is originally—he may forget it, or repress this—but originally he is a being reaching out for meanings to be fulfilled or persons to be loved" (Scully 1995).

REFERENCES

Allred, K.G. 1999. "Anger and Retaliation: Toward an Understanding of Impassioned Conflict in Organizations." In *Research on Negotiations in Organizations.* Vol. 7, eds. R.J. Bies, R.J. Lewicki, and B.H. Sheppard, 27–58. Greenwich, CT: JAI Press.

Averill, J.R. 1993. "Illusions of Anger." In *Aggression and Violence: Social Interactionist Perspectives,* eds. R.B. Felson and J.T. Tedeschi, 171–92. Washington, DC: American Psychological Association.

Averill, J. R. 2001. "Studies on Anger and Aggression: Implications for Theories of Emotion." In *Emotions in Social Psychology: Essential Readings,* ed. W. G. Parrott, 337–52. Philadelphia: Psychology Press.

Coleman, P. T. 2000. "Power and Conflict." In *The Handbook of Conflict Resolution: Theory and Practice,* eds. M. Deutsch and P. T. Coleman, 108–30. San Francisco: Jossey-Bass.

Coser, L. A. 1977. *Masters of Sociological Thought: Ideas in Historical and Social Context.* 2nd ed. Fort Worth, TX: Harcourt Brace Jovanovich.

Crépeau, P., and Bizimana, S. 1979. *Proverbes du Rwanda.* Turvuren, Belgium: Royal Museum of Central Africa.

Deutsch, M. 2006. "A Framework for Thinking about Oppression and its Change." *Social Justice Research* 19: 7–41.

Eisler, R. 1987. *The Chalice and the Blade: Our History, Our Future.* London: Unwin Hyman.

Frankl, V. E. 1985. *Man's Search for Meaning: An Introduction to Logotherapy.* Rev. and updated ed. New York: Washington Square Press, Simon and Schuster. Earlier title, 1959, *From Death-Camp to Existentialism.* Originally published in 1946 as *Ein Psycholog erlebt das Konzentrationslager.*

Gilligan, J. 1996. *Violence: Our Deadly Epidemic and How to Treat It.* New York: Putnam.

Goffman, E. 1953. *Stigma: Notes on the Management of Spoiled Identity.* Englewood Cliffs, NJ: Prentice-Hall.

Goffman, E. 1967. *Interaction Ritual: Essays in Face-to-Face Behavior.* Hawthorne, NY: Aldine de Gruyter.

Goldstein, J. S. 2001. *War and Gender: How Gender Shapes the War Systems and Vice Versa.* Cambridge, UK: Cambridge University Press.

Greenfeld, L. 1992. *Nationalism: Five Roads to Modernity.* Cambridge, MA: Harvard University Press.

Greenfeld, L. 1996. "Nationalism and modernity." *Social Research* 63: 3–40.

Haas, J. 1998. *Warfare and the Evolution of Culture.* Available at Santa Fe Institute Web site: http://www.santafe.edu/sfi//Working-Papers/98-10-088.pdf.

Hale, R. L. 1994. "The Role of Humiliation and Embarrassment in Serial Murder." *Psychology: A Journal of Human Behavior* 31: 17–23.

Hartling, L. M., Luchetta, T. 1999. "Humiliation: Assessing the Impact of Derision, Degradation, and Debasement." *Journal of Primary Prevention* 19: 259–78.

Honneth, A. 1995. *The Struggle for Recognition: The Moral Grammar of Social Conflicts.* Cambridge, UK: Polity Press.

Honneth, A. 1997. "Recognition and Moral Obligation." *Social Research* 64: 16–35.

Kalayjian, A. S., Jesmaridyan, S., and Swenson, E. 2006. "Adolescence in Armenia." In *Routledge International Encyclopedia of Adolescence,* ed. J. Arnett. New York: Taylor and Francis Group.

Klein, D. C. 1991. "The Humiliation Dynamic: An Overview." *The Journal of Primary Prevention.* 12 (2): 93–121.

Lakoff, G., and Johnson, M. 1999. *Philosophy in the Flesh: The Embodied Mind and its Challenge to Western Thought.* New York: Basic Books.

Lewis, H. B. 1971. *Shame and Guilt in Neurosis.* New York: International Universities Press.

Lindner, E. G. 2000(a). *The Psychology of Humiliation: Somalia, Rwanda/Burundi, and Hitler's Germany.* Unpublished doctoral dissertation, University of Oslo, Norway.

Lindner, E. G. 2000(b). "Were Hitler and Siad Barre "Robin Hoods" Who Felt Humiliated by Their Own Followers?" (Part I). *Medlemsblad for Norske Leger Mot Atomvåpen, Med Bidrag Fra Psykologer for Fred* 3: 20–25.

Lindner, E. G. 2001. "Humiliation—Trauma that Has Been Overlooked: An Analysis Based on Fieldwork in Germany, Rwanda/Burundi, and Somalia." *Traumatology* 7 (1): 43–68.

Lindner, E. G. 2006. *Making Enemies: Humiliation and International Conflict.* Westport, CT: Greenwood/Praeger Security International.

Lindner, E. G. 2007. "Avoiding Humiliation: From Intercultural Communication to Global Interhuman Communication." *Journal of Intercultural Communication* 10: 21–38.

Margalit, A. 1996. *The Decent Society.* Cambridge, MA: Harvard University Press.

Margalit, A. 2002. *The Ethics of Memory.* Cambridge, MA: Harvard University Press.

Miller, A. 1983. *For Your Own Good: Hidden Cruelty in Child-Rearing and the Roots of Violence.* London: Virago Press.

Miller, W. I. 1993. *Humiliation and Other Essays on Honor, Social Discomfort, and Violence.* Ithaca, NY: Cornell University Press.

Mischel, W., and De Smet, A. L. 2000. "Self-Regulation in the Service of Conflict Resolution." In *The Handbook of Conflict Resolution: Theory and Practice,* ed. M. Deutsch, 256–75). San Francisco: Jossey-Bass.

Nadler, A. 2002. "Inter-Group Helping Relations as Power Relations: Maintaining or Challenging Social Dominance between Groups through Helping." *Journal of Social Issues* 58: 487–502.

Olweus, D. Å. 1993. *Bullying at School: What We Know and What We Can Do.* Oxford: Blackwell.

Opotow, S. 1995. "Drawing the Line: Social Categorization, Moral Exclusion, and the scope of justice." In *Cooperation, Conflict, and Justice: Essays Inspired by the Work of Morton Deutsch,* eds. B. B. Bunker and J. Z. Rubin, 347–69. New York: Russell Sage Foundation.

Pettit, P. 1996. "Freedom as Antipower." *Ethics* 106: 576–604.

Powers, W. T. 1973. *Behavior: The Control of Perception.* Chicago: Aldine.

Powers, W. T. 1998. *Making Sense of Behavior: The Meaning of Control.* New Canaan, CT: Benchmark.

Retzinger, S. M. 1991. *Violent Emotions: Shame and Rage in Marital Quarrels.* Newbury Park, CA: Sage.

Rodegem, Father E. 1983. *Paroles de sagesse au Burundi.* Leuven, Belgium: Peeters.

Scheff, T.J. 1990. *Bloody Revenge: Emotions, Nationalism and War.* Chicago: University of Chicago Press.

Scheler, M. 1912. *Über Ressentiment und moralisches: Werturteil.* Leipzig: Engelmann.

Scully, M. 1995. *Viktor Frankl at Ninety: An Interview.* Available at: http://www. firstthings.com/ftissues/ft9504/scully.html.

Steinberg, B.S. 1991. "Shame and Humiliation in the Cuban Missile Crisis: A Psychoanalytic Perspective. *Political Psychology* 12: 653–90.

Steinberg, B.S. 1996. *Shame and Humiliation: Presidential Decision Making on Vietnam.* Montreal: McGill-Queen's.

Tangney, J.P., Wagner, P., Fletcher, C., and Gramzow, R. 1992. "Shamed into Anger? The Relation of Shame and Guilt to Anger and Self-Reported Aggression." *Journal of Personality and Social Psychology* 62: 669–75.

United Nations 2000. Millennium Development Goals.

Ury, W. 1999. *Getting to Peace: Transforming Conflict at Home, at Work, and in the World.* New York: Viking.

Vogel, W., and Lazare, A. 1990. "The Unforgivable Humiliation: A Dilemma in Couples' Treatment." *Contemporary Family Therapy* 12: 139–51.

Volkan, V.D. 2004. *Blind Trust: Large Groups and their Leaders in Times of Crisis and Terror.* Charlottesville, VA: Pitchstone.

Waller, D., and Oxfam 1996. *Rwanda: Which Way now? An Oxfam Country Profile.* Oxford, U.K.: Oxfam.

Chapter 21

GYPSIES AS VICTIMS OF NAZI PERSECUTION

Historical, Sociocultural, and Coping Perspectives

Andrea Zielke-Nadkarni

To remain silent is forbidden, to speak out is impossible.
—Elie Wiesel, as cited by Strauss 2000, 11

Sinti dwell here in the midst of us Germans. We need them very much. . . . They can be of help to us by chipping away at the bastions of our orderly society. . . . Something of their way of life may well rub off on us, adding a bit of color. After so many losses, they would be to our gain.
—Günter Grass 1988

INTRODUCTION

In Germany today, most people believe that Holocaust survivors either emigrated immediately after the war or have all passed away. However, there are more than approximately 100,000 Holocaust survivors who still reside in Germany. These individuals were prosecuted by the Nazis either because they were Jews, Jehovah's Witnesses, Communists, homosexuals, social outcasts, or gypsies.

The Sinti tribe is the oldest gypsy tribe in Germany. They fled from slavery 700 years ago and settled in Western Europe, where they traditionally worked as musicians, blacksmiths, and traders. The Roma tribe is regarded as the largest ethnic minority group in central and Eastern Europe.

They immigrated to central Europe during the 19th and 20th centuries in several waves.

However, gypsies in general are a minority group who have suffered from poverty, limited educational opportunities, and discrimination. Several European studies report that gypsies have a particularly poor health status, including high maternal death rate, low immunization levels, poor access to health services, and the poorest life expectancy in Europe (Gleeson 2008; Lynch 2006; Papadopoulos and Lay 2007; Parry et al. 2007). The problems most societies have with gypsies are expressed in terms of oppressive legislation as well as racism, socioeconomic deprivation, unemployment, and illiteracy (Papadopoulos and Lay 2007).

This chapter focuses on the traumatic events gypsies have experienced throughout history, especially in Nazi Germany; concomitantly, it focuses on their coping strategies and on the way they are still struggling with social acceptance.

METHOD AND ETHICAL ASPECTS

The target group of this project was elderly individuals who had experienced Nazi prosecution, and included members of the Sinti and Roma tribes. Semi-structured ethnographic interviews (Spradley 1979) were conducted to investigate their sociocultural background and its impact on their present life and health care needs. With their permission, interviews were audiotaped, anonymized and transcribed verbatim. Each participant had the right to refuse to answer questions or to withdraw from the study entirely, at any time. In order to avoid the participant's fear of self-disclosure, several visits were scheduled, during which the goals of the project were explained in detail. In fact, the interviews were only possible because the Holocaust victims had already received substantial support from the interviewer, who was then working for the *Federation for Information & Advice for Victims of Nazi Prosecution* (Bundesverband Information & Beratung fuer NS-Verfolgte) and had been supporting them in their fight for compensation. It was the recurring presence of the interviewer over several years which allowed her to ask such difficult questions. This long-term relationship also provided a guarantee that the interviewer would use sensitivity, protective strategies, and compassion as well as respect.

As a result of the prosecution and because the pain of confronting the trauma of the holocaust is so great, there were only two elderly Sintessa participants, Rosa M and Josefa O, as well as Josefa's son Adam (both from families who had been supported by the *Federation*) who were willing to testify and share their stories. Therefore, in order to substantiate our findings we looked to other sources of information. As there are only a few (historical) sources written by gypsies themselves, (Yoors 1989; (original: 1967); Genner 1979; Fonseca 1996; Hohmann 1981, 1982) research on gypsies depends greatly on oral testimonies.

DEFINITIONS

Because of the many tribes and cultures found within various European countries, gypsies cannot be regarded as a united sociocultural group. While many of the names they have been called are derogatory, the term gypsy (in German, Zigeuner) is used by some as a generic term to refer to all the different tribes (e.g. by Yoors[1] or Fonseca, 1996). The English phrase, to gyp, which means to swindle or cheat, originates from the word gypsy (Lewy 2001, 27). Other terms used by nongypsies such as *cigan*, *Tsigan* or *cygani* are accepted because the gypsies do not feel shamed by them and do not expect that a new name will change the way they are viewed by others (Fonseca 1996, 308). The term Rom means human being and today, Rom is used as a generic term for all gypsies by the gypsies themselves. However, the gypsies differentiate among three main groups of Roma: the Kaldera (from the countries of the lower Danube), the Gitanos or Kale/Calé (from Spain, Portugal, North Africa, and the South of France), and the Manush/Sinti (from Central Europe) (Samer 2008). As a result, any differentiation made between Roma and Sinti is regarded as a tautology.

THE HISTORY OF THE GYPSIES

Quotations from our interviews as well as other (oral) sources are employed to illustrate the personal experience of survivors and to connect them with the historical facts.

Origin and Migration to and within Europe until the 1930s

The Northern Indian tribes of the Luri and Dom are believed to have left their country of origin (India) sometime in the 10th century and to have reached the Balkans during the 13th century, from where they spread out all over Europe (Fonseca 1996, 129). The area from where they came is the place of origin of the Aryans.

Gypsies are believed to have first immigrated to German-speaking lands around 1410. Although initially they were well received, by 1450 gypsies were no longer welcome and in many cases were expelled. This was followed by discriminating legislative measures: in 1498 gypsies were outlawed by the Reichstag in Freiburg. From then on, members of the community who committed crimes against gypsies were not subjected to punishment. Between 1497 and 1774 in the area of the German Reich, which consisted of many small principalities, a total of 146 edicts were issued against the gypsies. However, there were some princes who supplied them with passports. Yet, the gypsies were not just discriminated against in this manner. The growing power of the trade guilds led to a monopoly of the handicraft trades and, as a consequence, the gypsies were no longer permitted to continue their trades. At the same time, they were also prohibited from camping inside the cities. Thus, they were left with only dishonorable occupations such as tinkering, music-making, and working as entertainers. The general population believed that gypsies had magical powers, which gave them another source of income (i.e., as fortune-tellers) as well as a certain level of protection. However, none of these occupations could provide a sufficient income, so gypsies were virtually forced into poaching, stealing, and swindling the nongypsy population. They were also forced to move around constantly. The destructive effects of the Thirty Years War (1618–1648) on the population, as well as on agriculture and the production of wares and trade, led to a further deterioration in their position. From the middle of the 18th century, the Roma were prosecuted by the so-called Gypsy News Service. They were discriminated against by extremely strict legislation that prohibited them from speaking their own language, promoting enforced marriages with nongypsies, and laying down a legal basis for removing their children from them (Lewy 2001, 14).

The beginning of industrialism brought about a temporary improvement in the lives of gypsies, as they were able to find employment as unskilled workers on farms (Soest 1979, 24). After 1900, more and more gypsies moved to the big cities, where they lived in large gypsy settlements (e.g., Hamburg, Frankfort, and Berlin). These settlements were created due to the need to have a permanent residence in order to obtain a license to trade goods (Soest 1979, 30). Also, during the second half of the 19th century, more gypsies migrated from the Balkan States and Hungary to Central Europe. During this period, laws were issued all over Europe against gypsies and other nomadic peoples. This was done in an attempt to control them and place limitations on the issuing of business licenses (Lewy 2001, 17). As there were so many regulations, the nomadic way of life almost inevitably led to violations of these regulations (Lewy 2001, 21).

In 1899, a special Gypsy Police Department was founded in Munich, which in 1929 became known as the Central Office for the Struggle against the Gypsies in the German Reich (Zentralstelle zur Zigeunerbeka-empfung im Deutschen Reich) (Soest 1979, 30). The goals of this office were to prevent crime, restrict traveling, and control epidemics (Schmidt 2007, 163).

In response to the growing suppression in the 19th century, gypsies began to use more than one name. This tactic was used if they were arrested by the police, fled from detention or deserted the army (Lewy 2001, 29). As the result of the ministerial decree of September 3, 1927, the Gypsy Police Department registered the fingerprints, photographs, and other particulars of all gypsies.

Even the fingerprints of babies and small children were taken: 6-year-old gypsy children, like criminals, became a motif of the police photographer (Hohmann 1980, 28).

Persecution under the Nazi Regime

In the early 1930s, the gypsies began to be deported to so-called gypsy-camps. In some cities, like Cologne, Frankfort, Gelsenkirchen and Dusseldorf, the authorities erected camps that had barbed-wire fences and housed an average of 400 people. The gypsies were subsequently forced to engage in hard labor.

Regina L: *For a time I attended a music school, I wanted to become a musician. But I could not stay there for very long. Most of my knowledge I learnt from my brothers, without notes, just by hearing. I have no professional training . . . we were not allowed to go to school any longer, that was prohibited* (Strauss 2000, 83).

From 1936, the Sinti and Roma like the Jews, were prohibited from marrying anyone with German blood, in accordance to the laws of the protection of the blood (*Blutschutz*) and healthy heritage (*Erbgesundheitsgesetz*). According to Doering (1967, 193) the following phases of prosecution were described:

Spring 1938 to October 1939: Heinrich Himmler, chief of the German police, wanted a fundamental regulation for the gypsies within the German Reich. Therefore, research was prepared with the aim of categorizing the gypsies as racially pure or half-castes. The ethnologist Robert Ritter (1938, 425) (who termed the gypsies *Untermenschen*, which means subhumans) and his team (in particular Eva Justin) carried out this research. For this purpose, they measured the noses, eyes, and mouths of as many gypsies as they could, taking particular note of the color of their hair and eyes as well as the pattern of their fingerprints. In order to get the gypsies to consent to this, they used various means. If two of a person's four grand-parents were gypsies, they were regarded as partially gypsy, which made him/her a candidate for the camps (Fonseca 1996, 349). Ritter regarded the gypsies as primitive, with no potential for cultural development. His goal was to prove that criminal and antisocial behaviors are hereditary. Conse-quently, antisocial behavior was construed to be proof of a hereditary dis-ease which, in turn, was used to justify imprisonment and extermination. It was Ritter who invented the term "camouflaged mental deficiency" for children who were particularly self-confident, cheeky, and quick-witted. This allowed him to diagnose almost anyone as having a mental deficiency (Lewy 2001, 77). By 1939, Ritter's research institute had collected data on more than 20,000 gypsies (Lewy 2001, 84).

October 1939 to summer 1940: From October 17, 1939, gypsies were no longer allowed to travel within the Reich. The plan was to deport them to parts of Poland that had not been incorporated into the Reich. In May 1940, systematic deportation had begun—disguised under the term the re-settlement of the gypsies (Strauss 2000, 9).

Summer 1940 to fall 1942: Gypsies from Burgenland and East Prus-sia were placed in camps during 1941 and 1942. In the fall of 1941, mass murders began in the occupied territories of the Soviet Union. From 1942 onwards, gypsies were dismissed from the Wehrmacht (the German army during the Nazi time) and in every respect were afforded the same legal status as the Jews. Some tried to flee and many of those who succeeded survived in the woods:

> Rosa M (then a child) recalls that her parents had to hide: *They ran away to the woods and lived off the land, on potatoes and things like that. Some-times they were taken in by farmers for a short while. There they did a bit of work for a few days or so, and were given a bit to eat . . . Sometimes, the farmers let them spend the night in the stables . . . they had to be on the move all the time* (Hilgendorff 2009a, 66).

Rosa M is a Sintessa who came to Germany from Czechoslovakia when she was almost 20 years old. She married and raised her children in Ger-many. Today, she is close to 65 years old and feels that in her old age both her awareness of discrimination and her fears are increasing.

Josefa O, also a Sintessa, has been living in Germany since the end of the 1940s. She was born in Prague in 1941 and as a child lived in hid-ing with her parents. Josefa and her family had to flee permanently from persecution. In 1938, after an international agreement had been disregarded, Czechoslovakia, Bohemia, and Moravia became protectorates of the German Reich. The Sinti had been living there for centuries, particularly on the Bohemian border, and in 1939 they were the first to be affected by the compulsory measures. Traveling around in wagons was forbidden and a nomadic existence could lead to imprisonment. Therefore, many of the Sinti people were faced with a hopeless situation as communities often refused to allow them to settle down. In 1940, the gypsy-camps, work camps for Sinti and Roma, were erected in Lety and Hodonin. Although initially only men were placed there under detention, later, whole families were forced into these camps. Josefa O's family, like many others, went into hiding to escape this fate. Her parents tried to find a safe place in Hungary and Austria, and hid in forests. But at some point they were discovered, arrested by the Gestapo and forced to work for the local farmers. After the war they never received any compensation money, as they had not been registered as forced labor.

Her son adds what he heard from his grandmother about the hardship of a life of hiding deep inside the woods, things his mother finds too hard to say:

Adam O: *In order to survive . . . when it is snowing . . . they made themselves shoes from cow-pats and they wrapped big leaves around that, or rags. And then they went into the woods, pine forests, which are dense. There they first of all, cleared some open space, lit a fire, and then extinguished the fire so that the earth was warm* (Hilgendorff 2009b, 151).

Fall 1942 to April 1943: In accordance to the 1938 Decree of the Struggle against the Gypsy Plague (*Bekaempfung der Zigeunerplage*) all gypsies who were not imprisoned were to be sterilized. In many European countries in the 1920s and 30s, compulsory sterilization was done on people with severe hereditary diseases (Lewy 2001, 75). In the United States between 1907 and 1931, more than 12,000 people had been sterilized (Haller 1963). In Germany, by comparison, there were as many as 43,775 sterilizations per year (Bock 1986). Although compulsory sterilization was strictly prohibited by law, at the beginning of the mass deportations, many gypsies were given the choice of either being sterilized and remaining free or being separated from their families and put into camps. As word had already spread about the camps, many gypsies opted for sterilization in an attempt to avoid extermination. Gypsies, who were considered to be social outcasts, were forced to have abortions or be sterilized (Hohmann 1980, 44). All in all, by 1945 between 290,000 and 300,000 gypsies had been sterilized by the Nazis (Lewy 2001, 75).

Below are a few examples of the unbelievable atrocities that the gypsies were subjected to: Adam O recalls that his parents told him that in the camps some gypsies pretended not to be gypsy, for good reasons, as the supervisor of the camp was always looking for tall and blond people who then had to beat up their own people, and do all kinds of other atrocities.

Josefa O: *If one of them ran away, all of the others had to stand outside in the court until this one had been found or killed in winter, naked.*

Adam O: *This caused the cancer in my father's bones; his bone consumption came from the concentration camp. He hurt his leg and then this inflammation developed.*

Josefa O: *My husband had to work in a quarry. As a child, he hurt himself there with the stones. Later it became a big hole that never closed. He had several operations, but the bone continued to be inflamed. Then the bone would be scraped—until the next inflammation.*

Adam O: *But also his psyche: he used to wake up in the night, screaming. He heard small children stamping their feet and he would wake up sweating. . . .* (Hilgendorff 2009b, 149).

Everyone had to do hard labor for 14 hours a day, while receiving hardly anything to eat. After only a few weeks, the Roma and Sinti were dying from malnutrition, illness and exhaustion. Thousands were ill-treated, beaten or shot by the SS guards. More than half of the gypsies were deported to Poland and did not survive the camps. Others became the victims of medical experiments by SS doctors. In the concentration camps, experiments with castration and sterilization took place in order to test new, faster procedures. Individuals were sterilized without anesthesia, which resulted in many deaths. In Auschwitz, 8-year-old Sinti girls had their uteruses and tubes filled with a contrast medium or were sterilized through injections into their uterus. Moreover, the Roma and Sinti were specifically abused for research by the German doctor Josef Mengele, who experimented without anesthesia, in order to compare twins' sensitivity to pain. Young Sinti girls and boys were artificially contaminated with pathogens or given blood transfusions, as Mengele wanted to study the twins' blood serum. On his orders, approximately 40 pairs of twins were deliberately put to death and dissected for the specific purpose of removing their organs.

April 1943 to September 1944: In August, those gypsies who were no longer able to work were gassed in Auschwitz-Birkenau. The Sinti and Roma were also exterminated in those parts of Europe which had been occupied by the national socialists for the purpose of ethnic cleansing. An estimated 500,000 gypsies died in the concentration camps at Dachau,

Buchenwald, Bergen-Belsen, Sachsenhausen, Ravensbrueck, Treblinka and Auschwitz-Birkenau. Hundreds of thousands were murdered, along with Jews, in massacres and mass shootings in Poland, the Ukraine, Lithuania, and Estonia as well as in the Caucasus, the Crimea, and the Carpathian Mountains. Many also died in mobile gas chambers.

The Situation since 1945

At the end of World War II, the number of Roma and Sinti in Germany was about 5,000–10,000. The survivors of the camps were traumatized, without means of subsistence, and demoralized. Many of the older gypsies who had served as models of proper behavior were no longer alive and compulsory sterilizations had lowered the self-esteem of others, as social status depends on fertility and child-bearing capability (Lewy 2001, 331). During the Holocaust, many of their leaders had been killed, tribal structures had been destroyed, and their norms and values had been weakened (Soest 1979, 51). In addition, many of them were provisionally housed in displaced persons camps or had to return to the communal gypsy-camps from which they had been deported. Others were able to obtain horses and start their travels again (Lewy 2001, 331). However, due to industrialization, more and more gypsies lost their traditional sources of income and had to resort to government aid (Soest 1979, 51). Soon, the old accusations (e.g., antisocial, criminal, thieves, beggars, swindlers) could once more be heard. Officers from criminal investigation departments complained about the gypsies again.

> Adam O remembers that the police sometimes came to their caravan site when he was a child and everyone was frightened: *Police, police, you must, you must. . . . Then the men hid us children away. Such things happened. But the worst is that they still happen today . . . that there are still such people* (Hilgendorff 2009b, 158).

Although the Allied Control Council had decreed in June 1946 that gypsies were protected by the military government and could not be subjected to special measures of control on the grounds of their race, the Bavarian government issued a new Vagrant Regulation in October 1953 which was based on the 1929 law for the "Combat of Gypsies, vagrants and people unwilling to work." Only with the changes in the political climate of the 1960s were many of these regulations abolished.

However, most of the gypsies were, as a result of a verdict of the German Federal Supreme Court of Justice in 1956, excluded from compensation payments. This downgraded the Roma and Sinti to the status of third-class victims because the judges did not acknowledge the racial nature of their persecution. This decision was only revoked in 1963 when the same court admitted to the racial motivation of the persecution. However, getting compensation remained extremely difficult, due to the illiteracy of many gypsies, their fear of authorities, and their reluctance to be exposed yet again to persecution. Many of the doctors who had to write references on the health of gypsy applicants were prejudiced and crafted their references in such a way as to exclude their clients from compensation (Lewy 2001, 355).

The absence of compensation together with a lack of any official remembrance resembles a kind of embezzlement genocide. It was only when the Society for Endangered Peoples started a public civil rights' campaign for these people in Germany (in March 1979), that public debate changed direction (Lewy 2001, 357).

At the beginning of the 1970s, the gypsies started to organize a Civil Rights' Movement. During the First Romani World Congress in 1971 both national and international Equal Rights Groups were founded. In 1971, the Central Committee of the Sinti in Western Germany was established, which now calls itself the Association of German Sinti. In 1982, a number of gypsy organizations came together under the umbrella of the Central Council of German Sinti and Roma, which is financially supported by the government. The Civil Rights Movement achieved the erection of several memorial monuments (e.g., in Buchenwald and Ravensbrueck) as well as a documentary and cultural center in Heidelberg, where conferences are held and research on the history and culture of the gypsies is published. Since 1993, Gypsies have the right to vote in the United Nations, instead of the merely symbolic consultative status (Fonseca 1996, 394).

By the end of the 1970s, most gypsies had permanently settled down and only a few continued to travel. Josefa O is one of the Sinti whose family continued to travel around Germany in a caravan. She never went to school and she is proud of the independent and self-reliant life which they led when they could sell carpets, table cloths and leather goods. They moved from house to house and as time went by even had regular customers. If there was an emergency situation Josefa O could go to these Germans who had been her customers for about 30 years and they would help her.

Josefa O: *For a long time I sold things to these people. I never cheated anyone. That way I was able to come back and sell some other things again later. . . . It was nice. . . . If you can earn a bit of money everything is fine. . . . But now . . . the way things are here, they are very bad, especially with the authorities. There are some decent people, but others . . . oh dear, horrible, horrible* (Hilgendorff 2009b, 153).

At some point, Josefa O's business license was confiscated; she lost her livelihood as a tradeswoman and had to apply for government aid. For many years, she fought to get it back, but succeeded only when she was 62 years old and then it was too late to resume her old way of life.

During the last 20 years, many of the refugees from Eastern Europe seeking asylum in Germany have been gypsies. To this day, the offices for non-residents, as well as the asylum authorities, consistently refuse to acknowledge the right of non-German Roma and Sinti to remain in the country, although as a group they are still being persecuted. As only 4 percent of all asylum seekers are granted asylum in Germany, the gypsies too are generally denied. When their applications are finally turned down, families are often split up and deported to different countries.

There still remains resentment in Germany toward Roma and Sinti and there are, though rare, acts of violence against them. Rosa M experienced several such incidences from the authorities, in shops, from some doctors and in everyday situations:

> *For example on one occasion several of us went into a cafe. They told us to leave and that we would not be served. . . . Another incidence happened to my mother and me in the street, some young people passed us by and said, just like that, out of the blue: "Hitler must have forgotten to gas you." They were 16, 17 years old, girls and boys* (Hilgendorff 2009a, 69).

Although the authorities are well aware that especially older Sinti mostly cannot read or write they ask them to fill in application forms themselves:

> Rosa M: *And they treat us differently. They send us from one place to another. . . . Instead of saying politely: 'Could you wait a moment, please' they just wave us away with their hands. . . . If we complain to the manager he believes his member of staff rather than us. So, I've given up complaining* (Hilgendorff 2009a, 70).

Coping Strategies of the Gypsies

The above account of the history of the gypsies demonstrates their need for coping strategies to enable them to survive the discrimination against their lifestyle. Not surprisingly, in our work the following, two taxonomies emerged: (a) watching over and guarding against the gadje (nongypsies are called gadje) (also identified by Bodner and Leininger 1992) with the subcategories of language as a means of protection and exclusion, and family as source of strength and meaning-making, and (b) self-reliance and staying in control (identified by Van Cleemput et al. 2007) with the subcategories of maintaining moral codes, norms, values, and attitudes, and their wariness of doctors, nurses and researchers.

LANGUAGE AS A MEANS OF PROTECTION AND EXCLUSION FROM THE GADJE

The gypsies' special way of concealing their means of communication should be regarded as a strategy of caution. Originally, Romani, the Indo-European language spoken by the Roma and Sinti, was a North Indian dialect that can be traced back to Sanskrit. It is regarded as one of the oldest languages in the world (Schmidt 2007, 48). It was spoken by the Luri and Dom, who were probably either expelled from India or enslaved in the 10th century A.D. (Schmidt 2007, 159; Soest 1979, 21).

Until the end of the 20th century, Romani was only an oral language, as the gypsies wanted to keep it secret to protect themselves. Today, various written versions exist and the linguistic commission of the International Romani Union has suggested that an international standard based on the Kaldera-variation (Vlax), be recognized (Samer 2008). As it was kept a secret, many people believed that Romani is not a language, but a thieves' argot. Yoors describes the power of the Romani language using an imaginary tale of the Roma:

> The old Bidshika once told us the fairytale of the moon, who was pulled down to the earth merely by the power, the weight and the magic of Romani.—It seemed to me that it might be true (Yoors 1989, 45).

Due to the lack of written testimonies, norms and values of the culture are passed on orally, colored by the imagination and the tales of Romani.

> Josefa O: As a child I listened to[what] all my parents and other relations told us. They lit a fire and then sat down outside and everybody told their story (Hilgendorff 2009b, 149).

Like many gypsies of their generation, neither Josefa O nor Rosa M learned to read or write. Their knowledge and abilities are based on their experience and on the oral tradition (Hilgendorff 2009a, 2009b).

Due to their travels and the influence of other languages, gypsies have synonyms for many words and secondary meanings which are not easily discerned (Fonseca 1996, 23).

Nongypsies who want to learn the language may still be misled in order to preserve its secret nature. In Europe alone, there are more than 60 Romani dialects. They have changed over time and new words were brought in or had to be created. By keeping their language clandestine, the Roma and Sinti were and are able to communicate without witnesses, to veil their history, values, and traditions and to protect themselves in dangerous situations.

Family as Source of Strength and Meaning-Making

Within the traditional social organization, the extended family, the tséra, is the smallest social unit of the Roma and Sinti, followed by the vitsa or clan (which consists of several extended families). The clans in turn make up a variety of tribes (e.g. the Kaldera or Lowara). There is also the kumpania, a socioeconomic union of members from different vitsi (Koenig 1989, 36). A special unit of the Sinti is called the hermanation (brotherhood) which has as its social characteristic "cohesion based on the sense of duty between members of a group of kinsfolk," "a community united by close ties of blood, common past and common future" (Weitzel as cited by Koenig 1989, 36).

Depending on how threatening or relaxed the environment was/is at any time, traveling families journeyed together or split up (Yoors 1989; Koenig 1989). When walking into towns, gypsies usually enter in a group.

> Josefa O: *We were always together as a big family. If my father noticed that I was not there or had been elsewhere for one or two days, I had to come back* (Hilgendorff 2009b, 152).

Thus, their appearance in a group and their nomadic lifestyle, in combination with social isolation, served as a refuge from outside hostility. This lifestyle left first the clan and later (after the Holocaust) the extended family, as the main source of support. Josefa O stressed the support of her family: "My parents used to take all my burdens just as I take those of my children" (Hilgendorff 2009b 152). Within the family, mutual support and help are a self-evident part of the feeling of belonging together. The social bonding amongst tribe members was and is to this day strengthened by the traditional norms and values.

Outside the family and between the tribes, ethnic solidarity is the key principle which ensures assistance amongst the gypsy people and keeps hostilities between tribes at bay (Koenig 1989, 35). Yoors (1989, 133) describes a certain aspect of the protective system the gypsies developed: while traveling they left messages for each other made of the local materials (wood, stone, etc.) indicating "don't stop here," "police and population hostile" or "get a move on and catch up with caravans ahead." To avoid any trace of them, the meaning of the signs was kept secret. Another means of protecting tribal members was the strategy of exchanging people between clans:

Each member of the Gypsy family is linked up with some real or imaginary
cousin in some other Gypsy community, who, when a member of a particu-
lar camp has committed some offence, proceeds to change place with his
relative. This movement may go on for some considerable time with the
result that it becomes difficult for the police to trace the particular offender
(Yoors 1989, 37).

SELF-RELIANCE AND STAYING IN CONTROL

Maintaining Moral Codes, Norms, Values, and Attitudes

Moral codes, norms and values are binding links within a culture. Purity
and impurity rules are a means to that end in many cultures and they can
also be found in specific forms amongst the gypsies (see also: Bodner and
Leininger 1992).

The following are examples of the differentiation between pure (*ujo* in
Romani) and impure (*mahrime*): plates are not washed in the same bowl
as clothes, there are strict rules for physical hygiene (which is the basis for
ritual cleanliness). Drinking water is kept separated from water used for
other purposes. Traditionally, toilets (as impure items) were disapproved
of inside the house. While the inside of the caravan is kept clean, in the
past the camp sites outside were often very dirty (Lewy 2001, 32; Yoors
1989, 147). The reason for this is that other people's garbage is considered
unclean and touching it causes ritual impurity (Fonseca 1996, 144). Certain jobs, such as cleaning toilets, were also taboo, which helped certain
diseases to spread (Soest 1979, 58).

Reid and Taylor (2007) state with regard to the Republic of Ireland,
that for many gypsy husbands, participation in matters of pregnancy and
birth is unacceptable. Doctors, midwives, and nurses are regarded as ritu-
ally impure, which is why close contact with them is avoided (Sobeck
1972, 4). Women giving birth are isolated from their families and are only
fully received back into the community after six weeks. During this period, sexual intercourse is forbidden. The woman is to rest and breast-feed
her baby while older women of the family look after her. The baby, too, is
considered impure during this time (Soest 1979, 58). However, later on, it
is adored and even thought to provide purity (Fonseca 1996, 64).

In addition, the Sinti were/are not allowed to eat horse meat or to have
contact with people who kill horses or process their meat (Soest 1979, 58).

There are strict traditional hierarchies of age and sex (Vivian and Dundes
2004).

Men (including married men) engage in multiple relationships outside the
family and have much more relationship power and control than women.

Women are expected to keep their virginity before marriage and then to
practice sexual exclusivity restricted to their husbands (Kelly et al. 2004).

Traditionally, women were allowed to wear only dresses and skirts, a
rule which today is observed less strictly. Men must not touch the clothes
of a menstruating woman, as she and anything she touches are impure
(Soest 1979, 58).

In the past, infringements of rules and norms could lead to physical
mutilation or even death. The exclusion from the clan or the tribe was at
the discretion of the speaker or the kris (court) and is still a type of punishment today.

Many gypsies live their lives under the sacred canopy of a mixture of
animism, ancestral cult, superstition, and a partial adoption of the religion
of the society they live (Fonseca 1996, 70). Therefore, gypsies traditionally do not get married in church, but have their own familial ceremony
(Fonseca 1996, 323).

For hygienic reasons, the belongings of deceased family members, with
the exception of few souvenirs, used to be burned. After a death, around
which there are many rites, the Sinti are not allowed to drink any alcohol
or participate in festivities for one year (Soest 1979, 58).

All such norms and values, which safeguard the bond between the members, can form a strong barrier against intruders.

Their Wariness of Doctors, Nurses, and Researchers

One of the frequently-expressed consequences of prosecution is a fear
of doctors, nurses or anyone who is in the position to question them. This
is because such people often trigger memories of horror stories from relatives or friends. Rosa M had difficulty talking about the suffering of her
extended family, of whom many lost their lives:

Children of my aunts, children pulled away which was horrible. They were
exposed to a number of different experiments. . . . Many of them are still
alive. . . . For example, out of six or seven heads of one family only one came
out again. All stayed inside, either gassed or shot. That was horrible. . . .
Some carry a lot of damages as a result, e.g. diseases in winter . . . Some had
nervous illnesses. After all that (Hilgendorff 2009a, 67).

Geiges and Wette (in: Koenig 1989, 10) quote a Sinto and former victim
of persecution:

They are again doing research on us and because we have been registered
with the authorities, we feel insecure. Our people are once more afraid and
think that things will start again like they did at the time when Mr. Ritter

came and measured our ears, mouth and nose and the result will be that we
end up in a camp. This is what our people are saying.

For years, Rosa M has been suffering from diffuse pain, but all her visits
to doctors were no help. She feels unwell with the doctors, who do not
seem to take her seriously. She feels that they want to get rid of her. This
is what she explains:

Sometimes the pains are stronger sometimes they are less. The doctors say
that it is my nerves. And then they send me elsewhere, where they give me
one medicine and then another medicine. And if I do not ask for certain
examinations myself, not every doctor will do them. . . . By 'my nerves' they
mean that it is something to do with my life. They think the reason is my
divorce, but I don't think it is that (Hilgendorff 2009a, 65).

The trauma left severe psychological problems which may be expressed
somatically.

Josefa O, like Rosa M, has been suffering from pain in her joints for
years. The doctors she consulted with all have different theories. Two said
that she has osteoporosis, one said that she had nothing although she is
constantly in pain. The doctors then suggested therapies which she finds
incomprehensible:

Now, listen to that! I now have to take 4 tablets in 4 weeks, one per week.
But I have to take it standing up, without eating anything beforehand. I don't
know why. And afterwards? How long am I supposed to . . . I said to her (the
doctor, ZN) if I don't have this osteoporosis now, do I have to continue with
those tablets? Yes, you have to continue (Hilgendorff 2009b, 155).

A particularly hurtful form of rejection by nurses was experienced by
Rosa M, when her sister lay dying in a hospital and Rosa M was not told
that she was about to die:

They sent me home, they said: 'You have to go!' We stayed till 10 in the
evening. In the night I cooked a soup for my sister. When I arrived back, she
was already dead. Neither the nurse nor the doctors had told us she was
dying, and in this situation they sent us home . . . my sister died all alone.
This was because we are Sinti (Hilgendorff 2009a, 70).

Their endurance of poverty, illness and disease, as well as discrimination, has resulted in an attitude which borders on fatalism. Endurance here
contains the notion of the normalization and acceptance of these hardships, which has become a way of coping. Several sources describe the

adaptability of gypsies as one of their successful coping strategies (Hohmann 1980; Fonseca, 1996; Van Cleemput et al. 2007).

As Josefa O puts it:

> *Yes, it is a hard life. But it is always a question of how you take it. Sometimes you despair, that's true, because we have to cope with too many things. But you have to find a way along which you can walk, and then you can go on* (Hilgendorff 2009b, 152).

Another, extreme example, was given by Adam O (see p. 389), who described how his grandparents had made shoes for themselves and their children out of cow-pats and leaves, when they were hiding in the woods.

DISCUSSION AND CONCLUSION

A critical look at the gypsies' life situation makes it very clear that their coping strategies have developed largely as a reaction to their hostile environment. However, many of these coping strategies have both positive and negative components. For instance, most older gypsies never learned to read and write and the more recent generations did not have much success in school as their parents were constantly moving them around. Also, while speaking Romani strengthens the gypsy's sense of identity, it alienates them from the rest of the host society. The gypsies compensate for the aforementioned disadvantages by normalizing their situation. Although this may help keep their spirits up, it does not solve any of their problems.

Adhering to their traditional moral codes, norms, and values helps to maintain their identity. This is the most effective strategy in safeguarding their self-image while, at the same time, it can lead to intergenerational frictions as younger members become more integrated into society.

Their wariness of doctors, nurses, and researchers is effective as a means to control and protect; however, it can lead to poor health. In addition, having the family/clan as the sole source of support can be helpful in some situations and insufficient in others.

Therefore, to ameliorate the gypsies' situation, the general public needs to become more aware of their history, culture, and sufferings in order to combat widespread discrimination. At the same time, the various helping professions must be trained to deal effectively with their gypsy clientele, by rendering services which are nonoppressive and by working with them on their own terms. Family and the community-based health care services can improve the acceptability and effectiveness of providers. Appropriate health services, however, are impossible without a serious attempt to identify and integrate gypsies' cultural beliefs, values, and attitudes towards their own health and illness.

REFERENCES

Bock, G. 1986. *Zwangssterilisation im Nationalsozialismus Studien zur Rassenpolitik und Frauenpolitik.* Opladen: Westdeutscher Verlag.

Bodner, A., and Leiniger, M. 1992. "Transcultural Nursing Care Values, Beliefs, and Practices of American (USA) Gypsies." *Journal of Transcultural Nursing* 4n (1): 17–28.

Bundesministerium des Innern, ed. 2004. *Zweiter Bericht der Bundesrepublik Deutschland gemaess Artikel 25 Abs. 2 des Rahmenuebereinkommens des Europarats zum Schutz nationaler Minderheiten.* Berlin.

Doering, H. J. 1967. "Die Zigeuner im Nationalsozialistischen Staat." *Kriminologische Schriftenreihe aus der Deutschen Kriminologischen Gesellschaft.* Hamburg, Bd. 12.

Fonseca, I. 1996. *"Begrabt mich aufrecht." Auf den Spuren der Zigeuner.* München: Kindler.

Genner, M. 1979. *Eine Gegengeschichte des Altertums nach den Legenden der Zigeuner.* Bd.1. München: Spartakus.

Gleeson, P. 2008. "Changing Times." *Nursing in the Community* 9 (1): 8–9.

Grass, G. 1988. Speech delivered on Loss in Munich.

Haller, M. H. 1963. *Eugenics: Hereditarian Attitudes in American Thought.* New Brunswick, NJ: Rutgers University Press.

Hilgendorff, C. 2009(a). *"Man fühlt sich irgendwo doch ein bisschen fremd hier, fremd und verlassen—Begegnung mit Rosa M."* In *Man sieht nur, was man weiss,* eds.A. Zielke-Nadkarni, C. Hilgendorff, S. Schlegel, M. Poser, 64–72. *NS-Verfolgte im Alter.* Frankfurt/Main: Mabuse.

Hilgendorff, C. 2009(b). *"Man muss einen Weg finden, wo man laufen kann, dann geht es weiter—Begegnung mit Josefa O. und ihrem Sohn Adam O."* In *Man sieht nur, was man weisz. NS-Verfolgte im Alter.* Frankfurt/Main: Mabuse, eds. A. Zielke-Nadkarni, C. Hilgendorff, S. Schlegel, M. Poser, 149–58. Frankfurt: Mabuse.

Hohmann, J. S. 1980. *Zigeuner und Zigeunerwissenschaft: ein Beitrag zur Grundlagenforschung und Dokumentation des Voelkermords im Dritten Reich.* Marburg: Guttandin und Hoppe.

Hohmann, J. S. 1981. *Geschichte der Zigeunerverfolgung in Deutschland.* ed., M. Frankf. New York: Greenwood.

Hohmann, J. S. (1982). *Zehn in der Nacht sind neun. Geschichte und Geschichten der Zigeuner.* Darmstadt Neuwied: Luchterhand.

Kelly, J. A.,. Amirkhanian, Y. A., Kabachieva, E., Csepe, P., Seal, D. W., Antonova, R., Mihaylov, A., and Gyukits, G. 2004. "Gender Roles and HIV Sexual Risk Vulnerability of Roma (Gypsies) Men and Women in Bulgaria and Hungary: An Ethnographic Study." *AIDS Care* 16 (2): 231–45.

Koenig, U. 1989. *Sinti und Roma unter dem Nationalsozialismus: Verfolgung und Widerstand.* Bochum: Studienverlag Dr. N. Brockmeyer.

Lagrene, I. G., and Lagrene, R. 2000. "Erinnerung tut weh." In *Weggekommen.* ed. D. Strauss, 15–25. Muenchen: Philo.

Lewy, G. 2001. *Rueckkehr nicht erwuenscht. Die Verfolgung der Zigeuner im Dritten Reich.* München Berlin: Propyläen.

Lynch, E. 2006. "Travelers' Tales." *Nursing Standard* 20 (41): 20–21.

Matl, W. September 5, 1997. Ein Albtraum von reinen Schweden. *Die Zeit* (September 5): 13–15.

Papadopoulos, I., and Lay, M.2007. "The Health Promotion Needs and Preferences of Gypsy Travelers in Wales." *Diversity in Health and Social Care* 4 (3): 167–76.

Parry, G., Van Cleemput, P., Peters, J., Walters, S., Thomas, K., and Cooper, C. 2007. "Health Status of Gypsies and Travelers in England." *Journal of Epidemiology and Community Health* 61 (3): 198–204.

Reid, B., and Taylor J. 2007. "A Feminist Exploration of Traveler Women's Experience of Maternity Care in the Republic of Ireland." *Midwifery* 23 (3): 248–59.

Ritter, R. 1938. "Zur Frage der Rassenbiologie und Rassenpsychologie der Zigeuner in Deutschland." *Reichsgesundheitsblatt, Berlin* 13 (22): 425.

Ritter, R. 1940. "Die Bestandsaufnahme der Zigeuner und Zigeunermischlinge in Deutschland." *Der öffentliche Gesundheitsdienst* 6/B: 477–89.

Samer, H. 2008. *Geschichte und Politik. Von 1945 bis zur Gegenwart. Emanzipation: International.* Available at: http://ling.kfunigraz.ac.at/~rombase/cgi bin/art.cgi?src=data/hist/current/self-inter.de.xml.

Schmidt, H. G. 2007. *Die Zigeuner kommen.* Wien: Pictus.

Sobeck, S. 1972. Zur Entwicklungsgeschichte des neuen Zigeuner-Wohnwagenprojektes Koeln-Tenhoven, Fortuinweg. Koeln.

Soest, von G. 1979. *Zigeuner zwischen Verfolgung und Integration. Geschichte, Lebensbedingungen und Eingliederungsversuche.* Weinheim Basel: Beltz.

Spradley, J. P. 1979. "The Ethnographic Interview." Fort Worth: Harcourt Brace Jovanovich College Publishers.

Strauss, D., ed. 2000. *Weggekommen.* Muenchen: Philo.

Van Cleemput, P., Parry, G., Thomas, K., Peters, J., and Cooper, C. 2007. "Health-Related Beliefs and Experiences of Gypsies and Travelers: A Qualitative Study." *Epidemiology and Community Health* 61 (3): 205–10.

Vivian, C., and Dundes, L. 2004. "The Crossroads of Culture and Health among the Roma." *Journal of Nursing Scholarship* 36 (1): 86–91.

Vossen, R. 1983. *Zigeuner. Roma, Sinti, Gitanos, Gypsies. Zwischen Verfolgung und Romantisierung.* Frankfurt (Main): Ullstein.

Weitershagen, P. 1980. "Meine Zigeunerklasse in Koeln." In: *Zigeuner und Zigeunerwissenschaft: ein Beitrag zur Grundlagenforschung und Dokumentation des Voelkermords im Dritten Reich,* ed. J. S. Hohmann, 155 ff. Marburg: Guttandin und Hoppe.

Yoors, J. 1989. *Das wunderbare Volk. Meine Jahre mit den Zigeunern.* München: dtv.

Zielke-Nadkarni, A., Hilgendorff, C., Schlegel, S., and Poser, M. 2009. *Man sieht nur, was man weiss. NS-Verfolgte im Alter.* Frankfurt/Main: Mabuse.

NOTE

1. Yoors is not a gypsy by origin, but lived with a Roma family from the Lowara tribe for many years. He was recognized as one of them and even given a gypsy name.

Chapter 22

UNDER THREAT FROM HIV/AIDS

Burial Societies in Limpopo Province, South Africa

Beverly L. Peters

We are all affected by the AIDS pandemic. But more than others, this epidemic carries the face of women. For it is women who bear the most significant burden of HIV/AIDS. As daughters, mothers, sisters and grandmothers, every day they experience and live out the reality of this epidemic.

—Nelson Mandela

INTRODUCTION

Belief in the life hereafter is an essential part of the spirituality of the Venda people, who live in South Africa's Limpopo Province. VhaVenda that subscribe to Christian and ancestral belief systems, or a combination of both, use funerals to grieve and pay respect, and to signify and celebrate that the deceased is embarking on the journey to the afterlife. Given the importance placed on paying respect and journeying to the afterlife, funerals have become elaborate affairs in Venda villages, where literally hundreds of people come together to cry, laugh, and share stories and food.

Burial societies, or informal associations whose membership comprises households, help to organize and pay for the elaborate funerals in Venda society. Members of burial societies pull their funds and donate labor to help prepare for funerals, while providing emotional support to the bereaved. Several different kinds of burial societies, which villagers refer to as the village, community, family, and church societies, collect funds and offer labor to support funerals. This is particularly important in Venda society, where villages subsist to a large extent on remittances, government pensions, and informal employment. However, over the course of the past decade, as death rates have increased in the Limpopo Province, largely as a result of HIV/AIDS, burial societies have been forced to change the level of support they are able to give to bereaved families.

This case study uses ethnographic methods to investigate the effects of increased death rates and high HIV/AIDS prevalence rates have on burial societies and funeral customs in the Venda villages of Tshivhulani and Lukalo. The research will show the importance villagers place on funeral rites, in addition to the ways that they use burial societies to prepare for funerals. The study will also show that high HIV/AIDS prevalence rates and the duration from infection to death threaten the ability of burial societies to cover the costs of funerals. As a result, villagers are starting to change the operations of burial societies, and by extension what is a culturally acceptable funeral, to reflect increasing death rates and decreasing rural incomes.

METHODOLOGY AND FIELDSITES

This study used a census, semi-structured interview schedule, participant observation, and ethnographic and focus group interviews to investigate the operations of the four different kinds of burial societies found in Tshivulani and Lukalo.[1] The census and schedule sampled 55 households in Tshivhulani and 55 households in Lukalo using nonprobability representative sampling, a common anthropological technique that samples different categories of the population for in-depth ethnographic analysis (Bernard 2001). These categories included men and women of all ages, employment status, and education and income levels, in addition to those who follow Christian and traditional religious beliefs, or both. The sample population included female- and male-headed households, state pensioner households, and households with and without children and grandchildren.

Tshivhulani and Lukalo represent the two different types of villages which exist in the Venda region of the Limpopo Province. Villages such as Tshivhulani have access to a greater amount of income given the proximity of the employment centers in the region, and as a result are largely able to sustain themselves without migrant labor. In contrast, villages such as Lukalo largely rely on pensions and remittances to sustain households. Without pensions and remittances, many households in Lukalo would not have enough resources to survive. Villagers in Tshivulani and Lukalo share the same religious beliefs, including beliefs in God and the ancestors, and have the same funeral practices. However, those in Lukalo have

less of the influence of city life and modernization than those in Tshivhulani. For example, attendance in traditional female puberty rites is higher
in Lukalo than it is in Tshivhulani; and the use of *muti,* or what Westerners might refer to as witchcraft, is more common in Lukalo than it is in
Tshivhulani.

The researcher administered the semi-structured interview schedule
to the female manager in the household, whether she was the mother or
grandmother. The female manager generally is the person who belongs to
burial societies on behalf of the household, and takes the responsibility to
make financial contributions and attend burial society meetings. Knowing
that the research was on burial societies, men in many of the households
deferred answering questions to female managers within the household.
The researcher carried out ethnographic interviews with men, in order to
collect data on male perceptions and participation in burial societies.

The researcher collected data on the effects of HIV/AIDS on the burial
societies using mainly ethnographic and focus group interviews. Participant observation of burial society meetings and at funerals provided additional data on burial society operations and HIV/AIDS. Interviews were
also conducted with Care Group Members and health officials working in
Tshivhulani and Lukalo.[2]

Limitations in the data are related to the lack of available population
statistics and current HIV/AIDS rates in the Limpopo Province. Official
population data for small villages in the province are suspect at best, given
that such statistics tend to be aggregated within districts. Critics have also
argued that available census data is not accurate, given mobility rates and
inadequate training of census-takers. Although HIV/AIDS infection rates
for the Limpopo Province are available, reliable statistical rates for individual villages are not, as villagers and local health officials tend not to
collect data on infection rates or attribute deaths to HIV/AIDS (Barnett
and Whiteside 2002). As a result, data on HIV/AIDS rates and cases in the
two villages under study is anecdotal at best.

Discussing issues of HIV/AIDS with villagers is additionally difficult
given the stigma against the virus and those who are living with or who
have died as a result of it. Villagers often speak of HIV/AIDS in esoteric
terms, referring to the virus as the thief in the night, yet are unwilling to
discuss it openly. This limitation is offset to a certain degree given the
amount of time spent conducting research and the integration of the researcher into the research sites.

Tshivhulani

Tshivhulani is a peri-urban village located off a tarred road less than five
kilometers from Thohoyandou, one of two major governmental, financial,

and commercial centers of the Venda region. The village subsists to a large extent on government pensions and formal and informal employment in Thohoyandou. According to the headman, there are 700 homesteads in the village, each with four to five members. If these data are accurate, Tshivhulani's population numbers between 2800 and 3500.[3]

Due to the location of the village, its residents have easy access to the formal and informal employment and financial centers in Thohoyandou, as well as access to hospitals, schools, and public transportation facilities. The majority of residents in Tshivhulani have water taps and pit toilets on their property. To those villagers who can afford it, electricity is available in the village, and a number of villagers have electric lights, refrigerators, stoves, and televisions in their homes. Most villagers in Tshivhulani engage in rainfed agriculture and some are also involved in small-scale irrigated agriculture. The majority of the sample population attends Christian churches, and holds traditional beliefs in the ancestors.

Lukalo

Lukalo, a rural village located more than 35 kilometers from Thohoyandou, borders the Kruger National Park, the largest national park and malarial zone in South Africa. Lukalo is reachable only by a dirt road which is often impassable during the summer rains; public transportation to and from Thohoyandou is quite unreliable. Given its location and unreliable public transportation, villagers in Lukalo do not enjoy easy access to the government, financial, and commercial amenities in Thohoyandou. The village subsists to a large extent on remittances, government pensions, and informal labor. According to the village headman, there are 370 households in Lukalo, totaling a population of 2500, or 6 or 7 people per household.[4]

The Department of Water Affairs has equipped Lukalo with two boreholes; while the boreholes may be close to some households, a number of villagers must walk from 1 to 3 kilometers to fetch water from the nearest pump. Some villagers have pit toilets on their property, and electricity is slowly becoming available in the region. The success of rainfed agriculture is limited in Lukalo, as the village is located in a dry area. Villagers attempt rainfed agriculture, and oftentimes carry water from the borehole or a local creek to irrigate their crops. As is the case in Tshivhulani, the majority of the population attends Christian churches and holds beliefs in the ancestors.

HIV/AIDS in Tshivhulani and Lukalo

The Limpopo Province, where upwards of 21 percent of the population is HIV positive, has one of the highest poverty rates and fastest growing

HIV rates in South Africa (Avert 2008). In villages such as Tshivhulani and Lukalo, HIV/AIDS-affected households often experience decreased agricultural production, income, and savings ability as a result of the infection of one or more household members. It is not uncommon in villages such as Tshivhulani and Lukalo for affected households to take out small loans from village moneylenders while using all available savings to care for those living with HIV/AIDS. This diversion of income leaves less money for other household expenses such as food and education. One teenage female caregiver whose parents have both fallen ill in Tshivhulani claims:

> There is no money at home. My father and mother spent all of the money on medicines because there is no medical aid [health insurance]. My uncles send some money to pay my brother and sister's [primary] school fees. I want to study at the technical college but I must stay here and look after my parents.

Costs to HIV/AIDS-infected households can be characterized in various stages related to different stages of the virus, and increase dramatically over the course of infection. During the asymptomatic stage, which can last up to 10 years, healthcare costs are low. It is only during the stages in which the virus starts to manifest itself, generally the early stage, that opportunistic infections increase doctor and hospital visits. During this stage households additionally suffer from lost income as affected members are often too sick to engage in formal or informal employment. Opportunity costs of lost income dramatically increase, as do the costs of treatment during the bedridden stage, whether a patient is cared for at home or in a hospital; as infections become extremely frequent, medical care is required usually on a constant basis, and patients as well as caregivers lose income as they are no longer able to work. The cost of death not only includes funeral and burial costs, but often results in care for orphans. Economic recovery and coping mechanisms after death depend on household assets and the social safety nets available (Barnett and Whiteside 2002).

In one not uncommon case in Lukalo, Johannes was working in Johannesburg for a number of years as a security guard in a local chain store when he contracted HIV/AIDS.[5] He carried HIV back with him to Lukalo when he visited during the Christmas holidays, and infected his wife, who became pregnant. Upon his returning to his place of employment in Johannesburg, Johannes fell ill with opportunistic infections a number of times, and missed a great deal of work. He carried health insurance with his employer, and was able to get treatment for his infections, but not antiretroviral drugs because they were not part of his health insurance plan. Antiretroviral drugs were also not available in government-run clinics. Once he contracted tuberculosis, Johannes was absent from work for weeks at a time, and unfortunately lost his job and his health insurance as a result.

Johannes returned to Lukalo to continue his treatment for tuberculosis from a government-run clinic. His pregnant wife, Miriam, took care of Johannes and their three children. After depleting their savings on living expenses, Miriam went to work selling vegetables and Johannes took out small loans from village moneylenders to pay expenses such as school fees. The couple also decided to take their eldest daughter out of school to help care for Johannes while Miriam was working during the day.

Without antiretroviral drugs and given the household's poor nutritional levels, Johannes died about a year after returning to Lukalo. His wife, who was also HIV positive, had already given birth to a baby girl, who became infected with the virus during birth and died shortly thereafter. Miriam is now ill, and although her eldest daughter is taking care of her, the household has no savings, and will soon be led by a teenage girl who was not able to complete her education.

The household had been forced to drop its burial society membership as a result of loss of income, and therefore could not rely on its membership to help prepare for the funerals. Extended family living in Johannesburg paid for Johannes' funeral, and that of his daughter before him. Both funerals celebrated the lives of the deceased, and the death of the two was attributed simply to a long illness.

DEATH, RELIGIOUS BELIEFS, AND FUNERALS IN VENDA SOCIETY

During South Africa's colonial and apartheid periods, missionaries lived in the Venda region and converted upwards of 80 percent of the local population to Christianity. Today, 84 percent of the households under study in Tshivhulani and Lukalo identify themselves as Christian, and attend churches including the Zion Christian Church (ZCC), the Apostle Church, the Assembly of God, the Church of God in Sabath, the Christian Centre, the Swiss Faith Mission, the Dutch Reformed Church, the Baptist Church, the Lutheran Church, and the Catholic Church. Villagers go to church services, which can last from two to six hours, every Sunday, and celebrate Christian holidays including Easter and Christmas.

Conversion to Christianity was successful in the villages for two reasons. First, as was the case in other regions in South Africa and Africa, conversion to Christianity granted converts access to education, healthcare, and employment in the colonial economy. Once they were members of a local church, villagers enjoyed access to local schools and hospitals for Christians, and were more employable in the urban centers (which was an important factor given forced taxation of local populations). Second, the traditional religious beliefs held by villagers in Tshivhulani and Lukalo were very similar to those held by the missionaries and Christian churches, and as a result, conversion, at least nominally, was not that much of a stretch for the VhaVenda. Both the missionaries and the VhaVenda believed in one benevolent God, which the VhaVenda called Mwali, in divine control over all life, and in the afterlife. In addition, many VhaVenda likely understood their own traditional religious beliefs in Christianity's terms, as can be seen today. Currently, many in the villages compare their ancestors to the Christian saints, and even refer to Jesus as the chief ancestor.

Today, this study showed that many villagers in Tshivhulani and most in Lukalo mix Christianity with traditional or customary Venda beliefs in the ancestors. To believers, after a person dies his or her soul has the potential to enter the realm of the ancestors and essentially to live on earth unseen by humans. About a year after a person dies, his or her family will perform a death ceremony, and brew beer to honor the deceased. Sometimes villagers will reenact some of the deceased's favorite things to do, such as dance or ride a bicycle, at the ceremony. On one level, the death ceremony is held to announce or welcome the deceased's soul to the realm of the ancestors, where the soul will live with the other ancestors (and for Christians with Jesus Christ and the ancestors) for eternity. On another level, the death ceremony is a healing mechanism for villagers, who come together a year after the death to celebrate the deceased's life and the soul's entrance to heaven.

To villagers, the cause of death does not impact the deceased's ability to enter the Christian or ancestral afterlife, or their funerals or death ceremonies. This is also the case with HIV/AIDS, although villagers tend not to attribute death to the virus, but to other illnesses such as tuberculosis, or simply as a long illness. In the times before colonialism and amongst some elders still today, it was believed that all death was unnatural, and caused by events such as another's ill-feelings toward the deceased or an unhappy ancestor. After a death the bereaved would go to a traditional doctor, referred to as a witchdoctor in Western terms, to learn what was at fault for the death. The family would thereafter brew beer and ask their ancestors for protection against additional deaths.

Given the belief in the Christian and/or ancestral afterlife, the VhaVenda also place a great deal of importance on burial and funeral rites. Where relatives, friends, and neighbors attend funerals to provide respect and support to the bereaved family, it is equally important that the family provide a culturally appropriate funeral to celebrate the deceased's life and afterlife. Ndou (1993, 55) writes:

The burial rites play a significant role in Venda culture as it is a pointer to the new world of the living dead. Burial services will act as [a] springboard to the VhaVenda concept of life hereafter. Although the manner in which these burial services are performed may differ from area and among different clans, the underlying purpose and belief is more or less the same. The burial rites make it quite vivid that the bereaved believe strongly and convincingly that the dead is only making a way or taking a journey to his final destiny, the new world only known to the deceased.

As a means to grieve and a celebration of the deceased's life and the journey to the afterlife, funerals are important cultural affairs in Venda society. Hundreds of friends, neighbors, and extended family attend funerals to pay respect to the deceased and lend support to the bereaved family.

The bereaved generally hold their funerals over weekends, perhaps a week or more after a death, to ensure enough time to make arrangements and travel plans for guests, who often come hundreds of miles to attend. Christian and traditional funerals consist of a Saturday service, which includes sermons, prayers, speeches honoring the deceased, and burial. In Christian funerals, a priest or pastor will officiate and lead prayers for the deceased and family. In families who are not Christian, a Chief or other elder will likely officiate over the funeral, oftentimes recounting or even acting out stories of the deceased. Funerals also include Saturday and Sunday feasts, which oftentimes require slaughtering a bull and several chickens for the guests. For example, in one not uncommon case in Tshivhulani, more than a thousand people attended the funeral of a local journalist who died suddenly. The family rented tents and erected temporary shelter for the guests, slaughtered two cows and multiple chickens, and spent more than a week preparing for the funeral feast.

The expenses associated with death are quite prohibitive in the villages, and include the financial costs of the burial and funeral, in addition to the labor required to prepare for the funeral feast. Villagers usually hire the funeral services of undertakers rather than prepare the body and grave themselves, as was the traditional practice about 50 years ago. Undertakers collect the body after death and store it until it is put on display at the funeral, provide a coffin, and dig the grave in an area demarcated by the village headman. Such services, including the coffin and grave marker, cost hundreds of dollars.

However, the funeral feast is often more expensive than the actual burial; bereaved families feed hundreds of friends, neighbors, and extended family over the course of the funeral. Women spend upwards of a week preparing food for the feast. For example, in the village of Lukalo, a bereaved household that had lost its male head, and only income earner, catered for more than 500 funeral guests, slaughtering a bull and a goat for the feast. Such costs are quite formidable for a population existing to a large extent on informal employment, remittances from migrant labor, and government pensions. As a result, most households join burial societies, which help to provide assistance for culturally acceptable funerals.

HISTORY OF BURIAL SOCIETIES
IN SOUTH AFRICA

Historically, burial societies played different roles among the European, people of mixed descent, and African populations of South Africa. At the turn of the 18th century, many poor whites, particularly Afrikaners, belonged to self–help groups known as sick and burial societies that were not necessarily connected to the church (Laidler and Gelfan 1971). These societies provided funds to pay for burial and funerals, and oftentimes provided funds and employment opportunities for bereaved families. Societies such as the European Sick and Burial Society, founded in Cape Town in 1796, had 150 members, most of whom were poor Afrikaners.

The Christian missionaries started sick and burial societies in Cape Town in the 19th century to cater for people of mixed descent. These societies provided resources to member households to cover doctor and funeral costs, welfare funds, and self–help opportunities (Iliffe 1992).

The first formal, institutionalized burial society for Africans was founded near Johannesburg in 1932 (Iliffe 1992). Restrictions on the African population during colonialism, and later during apartheid, probably prevented the establishment of formal burial societies such as those of the white and mixed descent population. However, informal burial societies were likely in operation amongst the African population long before the 1930s, as workers and neighbors collected funds to help pay for funeral and burial costs of their colleagues in the cities.

The spread of informal burial societies in the African population can be linked to the operation of the colonial and apartheid economies. Under white rule in South Africa, Africans were forced to migrate to the urban areas and mining centers to find work. There they formed burial societies as community support mechanisms and to help pay for the costs of funerals (Delius 1993). Living away from home for weeks or months at a time, migrant workers from the same villages formed burial societies to provide for their burial in the event of a sudden death, which was unfortunately common, given the working conditions in the mining industry. The burial society would make arrangements for the burial and funeral for its members, including transportation of the body back to the home villages. Burial societies were also ways for people from the same villages to remain in touch with each other and with their extended families at home. Members would get together to reconnect with other villagers and discuss issues of importance to the village. For example, members of the BaPedi population that migrated to work in the Sekhukhuneland mines formed burial societies that paid for funeral services and transportation of a corpse to the rural areas for a culturally acceptable burial. The Pedi burial societies also served as a means of communication between the urban populations, the rural homesteads, and the rural chieftaincy. As such, "[b]urial societies also provided a context in which the affairs of home could be mulled over and discussed in minute detail, and a channel of communication between migrants and chiefs" (Delius 1993, 149).

BURIAL SOCIETIES IN TSHIVULANI
AND LUKALO

Members in 84 percent of the sample households in Tshivulani and Lukalo belong to a burial society. The popularity of burial societies among the sample population can be linked to the importance of funerals and the cost of funeral services in the two villages. The number of people involved in burial societies is in part indicative of the importance of burial and funeral rites in modern Venda society, and the financial cost and amount of labor required to prepare for a culturally acceptable funeral.

Burial society membership in Venda society ensures that a family is able to afford and prepare for a culturally-acceptable funeral, while giving social and emotional support to the bereaved. Generally burial societies in Tshivhulani and Lukalo adopt names to describe the group's purpose or character. Common names of burial societies show their support function, and include "come together," "help one another," or "makes us happy."

Burial societies thus perform three practical functions. First, they provide a lump sum of cash that the member household can use to pay costs related to the funeral and burial. Second, the financial payout that a bereaved household receives also provides cash to offset, albeit temporarily, any income shortfall resulting from the death of a family member. Third, burial society members often help the bereaved household prepare for the upcoming funeral, by helping to cook food and prepare for houseguests. Nheria, a widow who is a member of a burial society in Tshivhulani, explains:

> When my husband died, the burial society paid for the funeral and prepared the food for the feast. Our household could not afford to have a proper funeral otherwise. The money from the burial society also paid the school fees for the children for the next term. I was lucky to have money for the school fees before I started growing and selling vegetables in town.

Each burial society retains its own guidelines as to contributions and methods of disbursement. An elected body usually governs the operations of the burial society, overseeing contributions and benefits, and carrying out the mandate of the burial society's constitution, as written by the members. Contributions to burial societies are made either on a monthly or per funeral basis, depending on the constitution of the burial society. If the burial society operates on a monthly contribution schedule, members will meet once a month to collect monies for deposit into the society's bank account. Upon the death of a burial society member or eligible relatives, a pre-set sum is paid to the member or member household. If a burial society collects money on a per funeral basis, members will either submit contributions to the bereaved themselves or to an elected committee who oversees this process, once an eligible death has occurred in the household.

Burial societies in Tshivhulani and Lukalo tend to form among neighbor, kinship, or community lines, and include the village, family, community, and church burial societies.

- *Village burial societies:* The most popular burial society in Tshivhulani and Lukalo is the village burial society which, extending membership eligibility to every household in the village, collects contributions of 50 cents to $1 for every funeral.

- *Family burial societies:* The next most popular burial society is the family burial society, which extends membership eligibility to all family members, and thus includes member households from all over the country. Members in family burial societies contribute either on a monthly or on a per funeral basis.

- *Community burial societies:* Membership in community burial societies is based on a selective group of peers living in Tshivhulani or Lukalo, and most often includes friends, neighbors, and coworkers. Members make predictable monthly contributions of $10–20 at a meeting, which often becomes a social affair, held at one of the member's homesteads.

- *Church burial societies:* Church burial societies draw their membership from members of certain churches in the villages, and are often part of a larger church hierarchy. For this reason, membership and payment processes tend to be strictly monitored, as are the $1 per funeral payments of members.

Members join burial societies on a household basis; generally one member of the household, either a man or woman, will join a burial society in order to provide coverage for the entire household. Contributions are made on a household basis, regardless of the number of people covered under the membership. In other words, a household whose coverage includes four members would pay the same household contribution than another household whose coverage includes ten members, since membership is on a household-unit basis. Should certain members of the household—generally the wife, husband, parents, parents–in–law, children, and grandchildren—pass away, the burial society will provide a cash sum to pay for the funeral and temporarily offset income shortfalls, and help the family of the deceased prepare for the funeral and feast. According to a female subsistence farmer member who belongs to a burial society in Tshivhulani:

> The benefits of the burial society are there. The benefit is that the burial society buys the coffin and the food and gives you cash. The society also prepares food for the guests. The weakness is that it is difficult to find US$1 to give to the burial society when someone dies.

Once news of a death spreads to the hierarchy of the burial society, the elected committee of the chairperson, treasurer, and secretary meet to arrange for the transfer of monies from various households or the society's bank account to the burial society member or bereaved household. The member or beneficiary uses the money to cover the costs of the funeral and burial, or to cover other household costs, as she or he sees fit. Usually members of the burial society will arrive at the house of the deceased soon after the death to offer respect and support, and start preparing food for the friends, neighbors, and extended family that will attend the funeral.

TRANSPARENCY AND RECIPROCITY

The smooth day-to-day operation of burial societies in Tshivhulani and Lukalo depends on two related factors, namely transparency and reciprocity (Ardener and Burman 1996; Coate and Ravallion 1993; Morduch 1999; Ntombi 2001; Ntombi 2003). Ensuring transparency, burial society members usually make contributions in full view of the community or burial society. For example, one community burial society in Tshivhulani holds monthly meetings where members make their individual contributions of US$10 after the secretary calls their names. All members of the burial society thus view the contribution process. After all collections are made, the secretary and treasurer count the funds in full view of the burial society. At least three members of the burial society travel together to the bank in Thohoyandou to deposit the funds thereafter. According to one community burial society member, a female pensioner in Lukalo:

> Since we make contributions in front of everyone, it is impossible to cheat. This burial society has a lunch every month where you must go to contribute your US$10. You must contribute to the burial society in this way in front of everyone. Everybody knows that everybody else contributes.

Members make financial and labor contributions to bereaved households on the basis of reciprocity, or the assumption that society members in these households will in turn contribute in the case of death in other households belonging to the burial society. The literature calls this an "enforcement capacity," and in Tshivhulani and Lukalo reciprocity is related to reputation and peer pressure. While members make contributions to support other bereaved members financially and emotionally, they are also pressured into making contributions to protect their reputation in the villages. For example, when a death occurs among members of a church burial society in Tshivhulani or Lukalo, male members will slaughter a cow and female members will prepare the meat for the feast. In return members expect that should a death occur in one of their households, the favor will be returned and the burial society will arrive at the bereaved household to cook for those who attend the funeral.

In the majority of cases in Tshivhulani and Lukalo, transparency and reciprocity remain intact, and burial societies continue to operate under their intended guidelines and purposes. However, transparency and reciprocity occasionally break down. If membership in burial societies becomes quite large and record-keeping cumbersome, contributions are not as transparent, and can affect reciprocity. In the case of the village and church burial societies, which have hundreds of member households, clerks, secretaries, and treasurers find difficulty in recording contributions. Members may not feel as compelled to contribute to a large burial society if record keeping is problematic and peer pressure does not ensure reciprocity, especially in cases in which members do not have extra money to give to the burial society. One member of a community burial society in Lukalo maintains:

> This is why I am no longer a member of the village burial society. Someone dies and then the households do not pay. I joined a small community society with some pensioners who all get the state pension. They all have money to give every month to the burial society.

Reciprocity could also break down if members migrate to urban areas to work. When a member of a burial society migrates to an urban area, the other members of the burial society may not be able to pressure the absent member to make payments, and it may not be as important to the member to maintain his reputation in the village, especially if the absent member is not planning on living in the village again. In such a case, the burial society will likely revoke the membership of the absent member, canceling any future benefits, without compensation for any contributions that she or he has made to the burial society. In one instance in Tshivhulani, a member of a community burial society migrated with her husband to Johannesburg to find work, not making arrangements to make her contributions to the burial society. After three months, the burial society revoked her membership and kept her previous contributions, among much discussion and in great disappointment. Although the absent member visits Tshivhilani, she has no plans to return there to live.

Case Study of Mulalo Community Burial Society

Ntendeni, a teacher in a local school, is the chairperson of a burial society called *Mulalo* in Tshivhulani. *Mulalo* means patience in TshiVenda, and represents the mindset of the society's middle-aged all-female members. The Mulalo burial society collects a relatively large monthly sum from its members, $10. The Mulalo Burial Society has been in existence since January 1993, when a group of 25 friends, neighbors, and family members established the burial society and wrote the association's constitution. Ntendeni explains the membership and operations of the Mulalo Burial Society:

> There are officers in the burial society. We have the chairperson, the secretary, the treasurer, the deputy-chair, and the deputy-treasurer. The chair makes sure everyone is happy, that there are no complaints. The secretary writes down the names of the people when they give the money. And the treasurer counts the money and together with the secretary goes to the bank in Thohoyandou to deposit the money. The bank account is in Thohoyandou, in the name of the burial society. The secretary and treasurer travel every month to deposit the money there in an account.

The Mulalo Burial Society's constitution stipulates guidelines for contributions and benefits. For a monthly contribution of $10, members or their households receive $300 upon the death of the member or her husband, and $200 upon the death of another eligible family member such as a child. Mulalo holds its meetings once a month on a Sunday at one of the member's households. The hosting member prepares tea, soda, and cookies for the other members to share. After discussing the burial society's business, members often turn to socializing and dancing.

Mashudu, the treasurer, argues that members of the Mulalo Burial Society are seldom delinquent in payments. Members of the burial society are friends, neighbors, relatives, and coworkers living in the same village who feel a certain amount of peer pressure to attend meetings and make payments; nonattendance or nonpayment may mean that the member is ostracized from the burial society and perhaps the community.

In the past, the burial society forced two members to withdraw due to lack of payment; and three members withdrew themselves when they joined their family burial society and left the Mulalo Burial Society. A decision to expel a member is not made lightly, and usually is discussed at length by burial society members during their monthly meetings. For example, during one monthly meeting, the burial society discussed the nonattendance of a continually delinquent member. The member, named Gundo, had not attended a meeting for 3 months. One of Gundo's neighbors (a woman whose husband was working in Johannesburg), explained that Gundo had moved to Johannesburg to be with her husband and had not sent word nor money back to the burial society. Ntendeni assigned the member to get in touch with Gundo (perhaps through her husband) to warn her that she would lose her benefits and former contributions if she did not come to the next meeting and bring her outstanding contributions.

During that same meeting, members discussed the death of a Mulalo Burial Society household member: the mother-in-law of one of the members had passed away during the week. Ntendeni announced that the funeral would be held on the following Saturday at the bereaved member's house, where the mother-in-law lived. Ntendeni announced that people would be needed to cook for the funeral from the Friday to Saturday night and perhaps Sunday morning. Ntendeni requested members to make arrangements to come to prepare for the funeral. Members gave sympathies for the loss individually, after the end of the formal meeting.

Membership in societies such as the Mulalo Burial Society provides for support and camaraderie, both in times of grief and in times of plenty. Burial society meetings usually start with a Christian prayer in TshiVenda to bless the burial society, its members, and their families. Members tend to share the same faith and oftentimes belong to the same church or pay respect to the same ancestors. Burial society meetings also include a venue to discuss village affairs, offer advice and support to fellow members, and celebrate Venda culture. Meetings usually include a great deal of traditional singing and dancing.

Grace, the member of Mulalo Burial Society who hosted the above meeting at her house, explained that many of the women belong to the society for entertainment. She argued that it was part of rural life to have burial society parties with your friends and neighbors. Grace looked forward to hosting the burial society function that Sunday, and had spent extra time cleaning her courtyard and borrowing mats and cups for everyone to use. She claimed that the party is not very expensive, as she just served tea and a few biscuits to the members. She argued that the expense was worth the entertainment that members get each month.

One of Grace's neighbors, a government worker named Mudalo, explains that the burial society plays a more important role in her life:

418 MASS TRAUMA AND EMOTIONAL HEALING

> Things do not change in the rural areas. Especially since so many men are leaving for Johannesburg anyway. So we women are left in the village and we cope. We come together and support one another. That is why the societies are named certain things, like "come together." So when someone dies, then we have the burial society to cope, to pay for the funeral and to cook for the guests. We can no longer rely on our husbands to pay for these things.

Although meetings and procedures of societies vary from burial society to burial society, the operations of the Mulalo Burial Society are illustrative of those of other burial societies in Tshivhulani and Lukalo. Contributions are made in a transparent manner, in front of the entire burial society, and members assume reciprocity in their contributions. All of the members of the burial society see that everyone has paid her money. The deposit of the money into a formal financial institution is also transparent; the treasurer and the secretary travel to the urban area to deposit the money and show the dated deposit slip as proof that the money went into the society's banking account.

The Mulalo Burial Society, like other community burial societies, restricts its membership to women. More than 75 percent of the community burial societies under study restrict their membership to women. Men are not allowed to join the Mulalo Burial Society, as men do not hold up to the dual nature of the contribution. Members of the Mulalo Burial Society are required to make a monthly financial contribution and are additionally required to cook for the funeral guests. Cooking in the villages is among the duties assigned to women in the gender division of labor; men are not responsible for cooking nor do they cook when they belong to burial societies. Members of burial societies such as the Mulalo Burial Society recognize that men will not contribute to the task of cooking, and as such allow only female members to join.

HIV/AIDS AND BURIAL SOCIETIES

Burial societies such as Mulalo Burial Society and others in Tshivhulani and Lukalo operate best when risk is private and idiosyncratic, and thus can be shared among members. Members can pool their funds and labor to support other members when individual death is natural or accidental. Burial societies do not operate as seamlessly when risk is shared, for example, in times of drought or disease, when entire villages and income levels are affected. In other words, since burial societies depend solely on the income of their members, decreases in income across all members inevitably affect society operations.

HIV/AIDS potentially presents a very difficult challenge for burial societies, given the nature of infection and the resulting very common household income loss. When one household is affected by HIV/AIDS and drops its burial society membership, as was the case of Johannes and Miriam in Lukalo, the burial society can absorb the loss and will likely attract another member to fill the position. However, if a substantial number of households either drop their burial society membership or draw on the funds of the burial society simultaneously, the associations may not be able to provide adequate financial or labor support to members.

Despite the continued importance of funerals and the positive role that burial societies play in supporting bereaved families financially and emotionally, the nature of HIV/AIDS and the risk that it poses to families and communities threatens to change both cultural norms and the operations of burial societies in villages such as Tshivhulani and Lukalo. Making burial society payments and redistributing funds from an unaffected to an affected household upon bereavement has become a difficult endeavor for many households in the villages, as family incomes have decreased due to death or been diverted to pay for treatment of opportunistic infections.

Until now, the importance placed on a culturally acceptable funeral has in effect protected the primary function of burial societies in Tshivhulani and Lukalo; that is, providing funeral coverage, often at the expense of their very important secondary function, offsetting income shortfalls. In other words, in the face of decreased benefits, bereaved members choose to spend their association benefits not on living expenses, but rather on burials and funerals. A member of a community burial society in Lukalo claims:

> The burial society now only gives enough money for the burial and the funeral. There is no money for other necessities. This makes things difficult.

Where burial societies are only now recording increases in death rates, members do anticipate that death rates will increase in the coming years due to HIV/AIDS. With a perception of increasing death rates, members of burial societies have begun to discuss and institute changes in the operations of the associations in order that they are able to continue and provide support to bereaved households. These changes, as proposed by village, family, community, and church burial societies in Tshivhulani and Lukalo include decreases in donation and benefit amounts, changes in membership by household, and changes in possible benefactors.

One coping mechanism is decreasing donation and/or benefit amounts. Decreases in the donation and/or in benefits would allow for a greater number of donations to be made to an increasing number of bereaved families. One family burial society in Lukalo, for instance, has halved its monthly household contribution requirement and its bereavement benefit. Without large payouts, an already cash-strapped household may use all of its available resources to provide a culturally acceptable funeral, including taking out loans from village moneylenders, or it may not be able to provide such a funeral at all. As seen in the case of a community burial society in Lu-kalo, as noted above, decreases in benefit amounts also threaten the ability of burial society members to use funds to offset income shortfalls.

A second coping mechanism includes changing the nature of the house-hold donation. Extended household membership in burial societies in Tshivhulani and Lukalo is cultural in nature. Often a very large extended household is covered by one donation, regardless of the number of people living in the household. One coping mechanism to raise funds would be to charge each nuclear family within the extended household its own con-tribution to the burial society, or to charge for each person covered by the burial society. This is contradictory to the communal nature of many of the burial societies, who tend to view life communally rather than indi-vidually. This would also render record-keeping quite cumbersome, and could be nearly impossible in the larger associations such as the village and church burial societies.

A third coping mechanism includes changing benefactor eligibility. Changing the lists of eligible benefactors could limit stress on finances of the burial societies. Burial societies could limit eligibility to immedi-ate family, or base eligibility on contributions, as discussed above. Burial societies in Tshivhulani adopted such a strategy years ago, when an out-break of malaria caused many grandchildren to pass away. Burial societies decided at that time either to limit or eliminate the bereavement benefit for grandchildren.

CONCLUSION

As death rates increase resulting from HIV/AIDS, declining incomes and stress on available burial society funds may eventually affect culturally ac-ceptable funeral practices. The conceptualization of what is a decent burial could change in the process, albeit over time, and only when increases in death rates and incomes decline enough to affect the everyday operations of households and burial societies. Research from other regional countries, such as Botswana, has shown that local chiefs are calling for a halt to lav-ish spending at funerals, and insisting that burial society funds rather be spent on orphans and household expenses (Ntombi 2001). However, this has yet to happen in Tshivhulani or Lukalo, given the cultural importance placed on funerals.

To a large degree, burial societies are no longer able to provide income to offset shortfalls, and are adopting coping mechanisms to ensure their very survival in the face of increasing death rates. This in and of itself could influence changes in the perceptions of culturally acceptable funer-als and in the operations of burial societies. Whereas the operations of burial societies and the culture of what constitutes a decent burial may change over time in VhaVenda society, villagers realize that they may not be able to afford to save and invest in education or in income-generating and other activities if most of their available household savings is spent on healthcare and burial and funeral services.

What is likely not to change as a result of HIV/AIDS is the social and emotional support that burial societies offer member households. As burial societies adopt mechanisms to cope with increasing death rates and decreasing household incomes, the associations continue to provide labor to prepare for funerals, and a network of support that members can rely upon during a time of bereavement. Changes in donations, benefits, and membership simply allows burial societies to survive, and their members to continue providing support, to the bereaved.

REFERENCES

Ardener, Shirley, and Burman, Sandra, eds. 2006. *Money-Go-Rounds: The Importance of Rotating Savings and Credit Associations for Women.* Oxford: Berg.

Avert, *South Africa: AIDS Statistics.* 2008. West Sussex, UK: Avert. Available at: http://www.avert.org/safricastats.htm.

Barnett, Tony, and Whiteside, Alan. 2002. *AIDS in the Twenty-First Century: Disease and Globalization.* London: Macmillan.

Bernard, H. Russell. 2001. *Research Methods in Anthropology: Qualitative and Quantitative Approaches.* 3rd ed. Lanham, MD: Rowman and Littlefield.

Chadford, Kathryn. 1995. *South African Management Principles within Stokvels.* MA dissertation, Business Administration, University of Witwatersrand.

Coate, Stephen, and Ravallion, Martin. 1993. "Reciprocity without Commitment: Characterization and Performance of Risk Sharing Arrangements." *Journal of Development Economics* 40 (1): 1–24.

Dandala, H., and Moraka, K. 1990. *Masingcwabisane, a Re Bolokaneng: A Book on the Burial Societies.* Johannesburg: Stokaville.

Delius, Peter. 1989. "Sebatakgomo, Immigrant Organization, the ANC and the Sekhukhuneland Revolt." *Journal of Southern African Studies* 15(4): 581–615.

Dhemba, J., Gumbo, P., and Nyamusara, J. 2002. "Zunde ra Mambo and Burial Societies." *Journal of Social Development in Africa* 17 (2): 132–53.

Ferreira, Monica. 1983. *Burial Aid Societies and Elderly Coloreds in Rural Areas: Some Sociological Comments on the Dynamics of Consumer Exploitation within a Culture of Poverty.* Pretoria: Human Sciences Research Council.

Iliffe, John. 1992. *The African Poor.* Cambridge, UK: Cambridge University Press.

Laidler, Percy War, and Gelfand, Michael. 1971. *South Africa: Its Medical History: 1652–1898.* Cape Town: Struik.

Morduch, Jonathan. 1999. "The Microfinance Promise." *Journal of Economic Literature* 37 (4): 1569–1614.

Ndou, Rufus Muthuphei. 1993. *The Vhavenda Concept of Life Hereafter: A Comparison Between the Traditional Venda Religion and the Christian Tradition.* MA Dissertation, Biblical and Religious Studies, University of Venda.

Ntombi, Ngwenya Barbara. 2001. "Evading Household Indebtedness Through Participation in Group Solidarity: Coping Strategies in Contemporary Botswana." *Eastern Africa Social Science Research Review* 20 (2): 1–30.

Ntombi, Ngwenya Barbara. 2002. "Gender, Dress and Self-Empowerment: Women and Burial Societies in Botswana." *African Sociological Review* 6 (2): 1–27.

Ntombi, Ngwenya Barbara. 2003. "Redefining Kin and Family Relations: Burial Societies and Emergency Relief in Botswana." *Journal of Social Development in Africa* 18 (1): 85–110.

Pankhurst, Alula, and Haile, Damen. 2000. "The Iddir in Ethiopia: Historical Development, Social Function, and Potential Role in HIV/AIDS Prevention and Control Northeast." *African Studies* 7 (2): 35–56.

Peters, Beverly. 1999. *Savings and Credit Societies in the Rural Areas of South Africa: Gender and Socio–Economic Dynamics in two VhaVenda Villages.* Pittsburgh, PA: Graduate School of Public and International Affairs, PhD dissertation.

Ross, Robert. 1999. *A Concise History of South Africa.* New York: Cambridge University Press.

Stanford, Mindy. 1991-92. "Stokvels: People's Ways and Means." *New Ground Summer:* 34–37.

United Nations Integrated Regional Information Networks. January 13, 2004. *Ethiopia: Traditional Burial Societies to Help People Living with HIV/AIDS.* New York: IRIN.

NOTES

1. Background research for this project was carried out as part of the author's PhD dissertation with the Graduate School of Public and International Affairs at the University of Pittsburgh.

2. Run from local hospitals, Care Groups are voluntary associations that educate people in villages about nutrition, healthcare, and sanitation.

3. This data corresponds with that collected in the census and semi-structured interview schedule in the village. Accurate government statistics, often aggregated to include urban centers, are not currently available for Tshivhulani.

4. This date corresponds to that collected in the census and semi-structured interview schedule in the village. Accurate government statistics are not currently available for Lukalo.

5. The researcher learned of the case from a neighbor who was a healthcare provider, and was willing to discuss HIV/AIDS openly with villagers and outsiders alike.

Chapter 23

THE CAMBODIAN REFUGEE EXPERIENCE

An Integrative Model of Trauma and Recovery

Carl F. Auerbach and
Edith Shiro-Gelrud

Character cannot be developed in ease and quiet. Only through experience of trial and suffering can the soul be strengthened, vision cleared, ambition inspired, and success achieved.
—Hellen Keller

ABSTRACT

This paper presents a model of trauma and recovery that integrates disparate ideas about the process into a unified whole. The process of trauma and recovery is divided into four stages: traumatization, safety, reprocessing and rebuilding, and integration. Within each stage are three dimensions of experience: strength/self, connection/other, and philosophy. Therefore, the 4 stages each with 3 dimensions yield 12 experiences that can be useful for describing the overall process. In this paper we utilize this model with a Cambodian refugee from the Pol Pot regime, and offer recommendations for working with other traumatized groups.

INTRODUCTION

It often seems as though there are many different approaches to trauma and recovery. The purpose of this paper is not to produce yet another one. Instead, our goal is to present a conceptual model that integrates various theories and perspectives on trauma and recovery. We intend to describe a psychological and experiential model that exists in the process of trauma and recovery, a structure that readers can use to organize the information and ideas they already have.

This paper is organized into several sections. In the first, we present a general model for trauma and recovery. Then, we apply the model to a Cambodian refugee from the Khmer Rouge regime. Lastly, we discuss the clinical implications of our model.

Defining Trauma

The word trauma is derived from the Greek word for wound or injury. According to the *Oxford English Dictionary,* a trauma is a "psychic injury, especially one caused by emotional shock, the memory of which is repressed and remains unhealed." Siegel (2003) conceptualizes trauma as "directly impairing the core integrative capacity of the mind" (31). This is because traumatic events produce intense emotions that "interfere with the integration of overwhelming physical experience" (van der Kolk 2003, 174).

The Basic Ideas of the Model

The model in Table 23.1 incorporates five basic ideas. Because these ideas are interrelated, fully understanding any one of them requires understanding all of them. As we develop the model, therefore, we will explain each idea in terms of the others. We state these ideas briefly below, and will more fully develop them in subsequent sections.

Table 23.1
A Conceptual Model of Trauma and Recovery: Stages and Dimensions

Stages/ dimensions	Traumatization	Safety	Reprocessing and rebuilding	Integration
Strength/self	Vulnerability	Protection	Support	Hardiness/ resilience
Connection/ other	Isolation	Care	Validation	Belonging/ community
Philosophy of life	Overwhelmed/ disorganized	Acknowledgment	Perspective	Meaning/ purpose

Note. The columns indicate the stages of the process, and the rows indicate the dimensions present throughout the stages. The cells indicate the experiences and dynamics of each dimension for each stage.

Shattering of the Assumptive World: Traumatic events shatter people's assumptive world. This shattering is described in column 1 of Table 23.1, entitled Traumatization.

Stages of Recovery: Recovery from trauma involves reconstructing the shattered assumptive world. The reconstruction process occurs in three psychologically meaningful stages: (a) Safety, (b) Reprocessing and Rebuilding, and (c) Integration. These stages are described in columns 2, 3, and 4 of Table 23.1.

Dimensions: People's experience of themselves and the world can be organized in terms of three basic dimensions: Strength/Self, Connection/Other, and Philosophy of Life. These dimensions are described in rows 1, 2, and 3 of Table 23.1.

Experiences: The dimensions are experienced differently in each stage of trauma and recovery. Combining the four stages of trauma and recovery, with the three dimension at each stage yields twelve characteristic experiences associated with the trauma and recovery process, ranging from *VULNERABILITY* (the absence of strength during the traumatization stage) to *PURPOSE/MEANING* (the presence of philosophy of life during the integration stage). These characteristic experiences are described in the twelve cells of Table 23.1.

Dynamics: Each stage involves a characteristic dynamic or pattern of relationship between the traumatized person and his/her therapist.

We use the word therapist to refer to the person or people who facilitate the process of recovery, whether or not they are officially a mental health professional. This is important to note as the process of healing and recovery depends on the relationship between the traumatized person and the other, whether or not they are a mental health professional.

CASE MATERIAL

We will apply this model to Mr. X, a Cambodian refugee, whose narrative will be used to illustrate our premises. For our purposes, we are interested in Mr. X's experiences during the period of Cambodian history ranging from 1975 to 1979. (For more details see Shiro-Gelrud 2001.)

Cambodia is a small and peaceful country in Southeast Asia that is sandwiched between Thailand, Laos, and Vietnam. However, in 1975, just after the end of the Vietnam war, it was taken over by the Khmer Rouge, a radical Maoist group led by Pol Pot. The goal of the Khmer Rouge was to convert Cambodia into a communist agrarian society, replacing the traditional Cambodian social structures with new ones consistent with their ideology. Instituting a poorly planned agricultural program, they moved a large number of city dwellers to the country side, and forced them to do farm labor on harshly regimented agricultural collectives.

In order to prevent subversive foreign influence, the Khmer Rouge executed members of potential opposition groups, including government officials, Buddhist monks, and military leaders. When the much anticipated increases in rice production did not come to fruition, more enemies of the revolution were executed. Many who were not killed, died of disease and starvation in areas of the Cambodian countryside known as the killing fields. During the Pol Pot regime, it is estimated that between one and three million of the 7 million inhabitants of Cambodia died in the killing fields.

The killing only ended in 1979, when the Vietnamese government invaded Cambodia and overthrew the Khmer Rouge. The Cambodian tragedy did more than just kill individuals; it destroyed the very fabric of Cambodian life and society. Many Cambodians became refugees, fleeing first to Thailand and then to other countries, including the United States, Canada, France, and Australia (Kinzie, Boehlein, and Sack 1998).

Mr. X was one of these refugees. At the time of our interview on January 24, 2001, Mr. X was 58 years old. He exhibited a peaceful demeanor, and appeared younger than his chronological age. He is married to a Cambodian woman with whom he has six children. He speaks three languages: Khmer, French, and English.

Before the Khmer Rouge takeover, Mr. X worked for the Cambodian air force in Phnom Peng, where he lived with his wife and family. He continued his work during the Khmer Rouge period, although his family was moved to the country side where he was not allowed to communicate with them. In 1979 Mr. X fled Cambodia to a refugee camp in Thailand, and from there came to the United States. Presently, he is a leader of the Cambodian community in the Bronx, New York, where he is in charge of the Buddhist temple.

Explication of the Model

We now turn to a detailed development of our model, in which we elaborate its five basic ideas, and apply them to Mr. X.

Shattering of the Assumptive World

Our model postulates that trauma shatters an individual's assumptive world. The assumptive world is a construct that was first proposed by Parkes (1971), who said that "The assumptive world is the only world we know, and it includes everything we know or think we know. It includes our interpretation of the past and our expectations of the future, our plans and our prejudices. Any or all of these may need to change as a result of changes in our life space." According to Janoff-Bulman (1992), traumatic events disrupt previously stable assumptions, and thus shatter the pretraumatic assumptive world. Mr. X's assumptive world was shattered by the Khmer Rouge. He states:

> When the (Vietnam) war started everybody wanted peace . . . at the end of April 17, 1975, (when the Khmer Rouge took over Phnom Pehn) we thought the end of the war will bring peace to us but everything changed overnight. Khmer Rouge came and the 'killing fields' started. . . . The nightmare for the people.

When Mr. X said that "the end of the war will bring peace to us," he is referring to his pretraumatic assumptions, and when he said that "everything changed overnight" he is describing how these assumptions were disrupted and shattered. Similarly, when he calls the killing fields "the nightmare for the people," he is referring to a disruption of ordinary and predictable reality.

DIMENSIONS

In our model, trauma and recovery experience is organized around three basic dimensions: Strength/Self, Connection/Other, and Philosophy of Life. Each of these dimensions characterizes the person's perception of self, the world, and the relationship between them. The perception of the self and the perception of the world can be positive or negative. Traumatization drives the person to the negative poles of each dimension. Recovery requires returning to the positive poles.

Our dimensions are based on Tedeschi and Calhoun's (1995) theory of post-traumatic growth. They propose that post-traumatic growth occurs in three areas (1) self-perception (particularly with regard to strength), (2) interpersonal relations, and (3) philosophy of life. Our concept of positive and negative poles is based on Janoff-Bulman's proposal that trauma shatters three fundamental assumptions about the self and the world: (1) the world is benevolent, (2) the world is meaningful, and (3) the self is worthy.

Janoff-Bulman offers us the positive pole of these assumptions; our model makes the negative pole explicit.

We examine how these dimensions in combination with the four stages produce the twelve characteristic experiences of trauma and recovery. We will first consider the traumatization stage (column 1 of Table 23.1).

Strength/Self describes the person's relation to the powerful forces of the world. It encompasses two factors: the world's disposition towards the person, and the person's ability to survive these powerful forces. Each factor has a positive and a negative pole. The powerful forces may be benevolent or malevolent, that is positively or negatively disposed towards the person. Similarly, the person may be strong or weak, that is, capable or not capable of surviving the world's power.

To make this concrete, let us consider the strength dimension for Mr. X during the traumatization stage. Mr. X reported that:

> Cambodians themselves were treated like enemies . . . I worked hard during the Khmer Rouge, but I got starvation. We had no food, nothing, no food, and no medication for when I got sick. I was scared that some day they were going to take me away to kill me . . . I saw other people that were taken away to be "re-educated" but they never returned home . . . People got killed because they talked too much, people got killed because they found out from other people. They would trick you, they would test you to see if you would talk . . . The way you shut up your mouth was the way you survived during the Khmer Rouge.

Here Mr. X's describes the world as malevolent. The Khmer Rouge were likely to take him away and kill him. Also, his fellow Cambodians were likely to give him up to the Khmer Rouge.

Mr. X describes himself as weak. He reports that he had no food, no medication, and no defenses to guard him. His one method of self protection was to keep his mouth shut.

We use the term *VULNERABILITY* to describe the experience of a weak self in a malevolent world. In Table 23.1, vulnerability appears in column 1 (stage of Traumatization), row 1 (dimension of Strength/Self).

Connection/Other describes the person's relationship to the interpersonal world. It encompasses two factors: other people's attitude toward the self, and the person's own self-perception. Each factor has a positive and a negative pole: other people may be either caring or indifferent, and the person may feel either connected or isolated.

During the traumatization stage, Mr. X describes his experience regarding connection by stating:

> My family stayed in the countryside while I was working in the capital. We could not communicate. The government controlled everything. They cut

communication . . . During the war I didn't talk. The way you shut your mouth was the way you survived during the Khmer Rouge . . . the more you voiced your opinion the more trouble you had.

Mr. X describes how the Khmer Rouge was indifferent towards him—they severed communication between him and his family. In addition, he felt isolated—he didn't talk during the war.

We use the term *ISOLATION* to describe a person in an indifferent world (Table 23.1, column 1, row 2).

Philosophy of Life describes how the person, as an active agent, relates to the deeper order/structure of the world. It encompasses two factors: the person's belief that there is a deep order/structure to the world, and the person's belief that they can make use of this order/structure. As with the other dimensions, each factor has a positive and a negative pole. At the positive pole, the world is orderly and the person is active; at the negative pole the world is chaotic and the person is passive and/or immobilized.

The following quotation illustrates how the philosophy dimension was experienced by Mr. X:

We saw people getting killed, but we didn't care, because we had to move someplace else, move away. Go with the flow . . . . I could not decide anything about my life.

Mr. X describes a chaotic world—he was always being moved around, with no order and for no reason. He describes himself as being passive—he could not decide anything about his life.

We use the term *OVERWHELMED/DISORGANIZATION* to describe the experience of a passive self in a chaotic world (Table 23.1, column 1, row 3).

We now turn to the stages of recovery. The stages that we propose are based on Judith Herman's stages of recovery (Herman 1992).

FIRST STAGE: SAFETY

Traumatization shatters the assumptive world, leaving the person vulnerable, isolated, and overwhelmed. Therefore, the task of the therapist during the safety stage is to offer the person a safe place to retreat to.

The safety stage, as well as the other stages, has its own dynamic and requires specific psychological work on the part of the therapist. During the safety stage, the therapist must provide the person with a positive alternative to the traumatic world. Next, the person must take in and use the positive world provided by the therapist. In this section, we examine how the therapist, or the therapeutic environment, can provide a positive influence on the strength, self, and philosophy dimensions.

Protection: the provision of strength during the safety stage. Traumatization leaves a person vulnerable, a weakened self in a malevolent world. During the safety stage, the therapist must provide a positive alternative to the malevolent world, a benevolent world that shelters the person until he/she can regain his/her strength.

The refugee camp to which Mr. X fled following his escape from Cambodia provided him with such a world. He explained:

> I started feeling better when I was in the (refugee) camp. In 1979, in the border between Cambodia and Thailand, I escaped, went to the camp, got food, got shelter.

During his traumatization, Mr. X was at the mercy of the Khmer Rouge. The refugee camps which offered him food and shelter also provided a benevolent alternative to his previously malevolent world. Thus, the refugee camp environment fostered strength that he did not possess before.

We use the term *PROTECTION* to describe the experience of a benevolent alternative to a malevolent world (Table 23.1, column 2, row 1).

Care: The provision of connection during the safety stage. Traumatization leaves the person isolated and faced with an indifferent world. During the safety stage, the therapist must provide a positive alternative to the indifferent world.

The refugee camp provided this for Mr. X.

> In 1979, in (the refugee camp), we saw the Red Cross, we saw the light of hope . . . we saw the Red Cross members, the medical teams from around the world, people from the U.N. . . . Until there was an official camp built in the border they didn't want people to know what had happened. Only after the Red Cross created an official camp outside Thailand the people learned more about the process.

Before Mr. X's arrived at the refugee camp, the world was indifferent to Mr. X; however in the refugee camp, the Red Cross and the associated medical teams provided him with care. Offering Mr. X a positive alternative to the indifferent world of the Khmer Rouge, the refugee camp provide him with the interpersonal connection and care that he needed to recover.

We use the term *CARE* to describe provision of a positive alternative to traumatic indifference (Table 23.1, column 2, row 2).

Acknowledgement: The provision of philosophy during the safety stage. Traumatization overwhelms a person, leaving him/her as a passive self in a chaotic world. During the safety stage the therapist must provide a positive alternative to the chaotic world by acknowledging the suffering the person has experienced. In so doing, the therapist provides a structured world in which effective action is an alternative to passivity.

The refugee camp provided this for Mr. X.

> I saw the Red Cross. I went there and spoke to the people and I asked them if they need help because I spoke French and English. I came out and showed my identity. I saw the sign of the Red Cross and I knew . . . I met with the Red Cross team and the medical team. That's when I stopped and understood my life to the life I had to change into . . . I (became) a leader.

During Mr. X's traumatization by the Khmer Rouge, his environment was chaotic; nothing made sense and no effective action was possible. All he could do was hide. However, in the refugee camp, the Red Cross and associated medical teams acknowledged his experience and provided him with a positive alternative to the chaos—a structured environment in which Mr. X could be effective. And he was effective; Mr. X came out and became a leader.

We use the term *ACKNOWLEDGMENT* to describe provision of a positive alternative to traumatic chaos (Table 23.1, column 2, row 3).

SECOND STAGE: REPROCESSING AND REBUILDING

When people are traumatized, they experience both the self and the world as negative. In the safety stage, the therapist provides a positive alternative to the negative world. In the reprocessing and rebuilding stage, the therapist shifts the focus from the world to the self and provides a positive alternative to the traumatized negative self. The therapist does this by providing an alternative narrative account of the traumatic experience, and helping the person experience himself positively within this narrative framework. In this way, the therapist offers the person a potentially new experience within a relationship that allows the person to process the traumatic event and begin to rebuild his life.

The dynamics of this stage are different from the dynamics of the safety stage. During the safety stage, the therapist provided a safe environment which the person made use of. The dynamics of the reprocessing and rebuilding stage are more collaborative in nature. At this stage, the therapist provides a narrative rather than an environment. In addition, the person does not simply accept the narrative; rather the person and the therapist actively collaborate in using the narrative to rebuild the person's self perception.

Support: The collaborative construction of strength during the reprocessing and rebuilding stage. During traumatization, the person experiences the world as malevolent and the self as too weak to cope with it. In the safety stage the therapist provides a benevolent alternative to the malevolent world. Now, in the reprocessing and rebuilding state, the therapist provides a narrative that can be used collaboratively with the client to construct a strengthened self.

An American social worker provided such an alternative self narrative for Mr. X.

> I got help from an American social worker in 1983 . . . I taught the social worker a lot about this culture and she taught me a lot about the American culture and society. She is the one who ran from place to place, made the phone calls to the city, to the state, to Washington DC, everything to help me.

During his traumatization, Mr. X experienced himself as too weak to cope with the malevolent world of the Khmer Rouge. During the safety stage the refugee camp provided the protection that made up for this perceived lack of strength. Next, during the reprocessing and rebuilding stage, Mr. X. and the American social worker collaboratively constructed a strong self. The American social worker helped Mr. X in two primary ways. First, she taught him about American culture and provided him with a narrative map of the culture and his place within it. Second, she helped Mr. X rebuild his life by making various phone calls on his behalf. Their relationship became a place in which Mr. X could develop a new understanding of the world around him.

We use the term *SUPPORT* to describe a provision of a narrative alternative to the weak and traumatized self, a narrative within which a strong self can be collaboratively constructed (Table 23.1, column 3, row 1).

Validation: the collaborative construction of connection during the reprocessing and rebuilding stage. During traumatization, the person experiences the world as indifferent and the self as isolated. In the safety stage, the therapist provides a positive, caring alternative to an indifferent world. In the reprocessing and rebuilding stage, the therapist focuses on the self, providing a narrative and a relationship that allows for a reconstruction of a connected self.

Mr. X's relationship with the American social worker provided him with such an alternative narrative.

> The changes from my experience in the war are different than from what happened after the war. Now I know that psychology calls it being "traumatized."

During his traumatization Mr. X experienced himself as isolated and in the indifferent world of the Khmer Rouge. During the safety stage, the refugee camp that Mr. X fled to provided him with care and a positive alternative to the indifference of the Khmer Rouge. Afterwards, during the reprocessing and rebuilding stage the American social worker provided him with an alternative narrative. When she told Mr. X that he was traumatized, she offered him a framework to help him and others understand his experience. This framework also allowed Mr. X to connect his experience to the common human experience.

We use the term *VALIDATION* to describe the provision of a narrative alternative to the traumatized, isolated self (Table 23.1, column 3, row 2).

Perspective: The collaborative construction of philosophy during the reprocessing and rebuilding stage. During traumatization, the person experiences the world as chaotic, and the self as passive. In the safety stage, the therapist provides acknowledgement as well as a structured alternative to the chaotic, traumatizing world. In the reprocessing and rebuilding stage, the therapist focuses on the self and provides a narrative within which an active self can be collaboratively reconstructed.

Mr. X explained:

> When we got out from the smoke of war we thought: why did it happen like that? How come we don't live in peace without fighting but killing each other. Later on we learned that war is not one sided, they have to have political pressure from everywhere to bring to the war. What I learned is that the war doesn't bring complete peace. You can make peace without war, because democracy in Cambodia had to be implemented. War destroys life, war destroys mentalities because people cannot go to school to be educated and learn. And there is no trust.

From his experience in the United States, Mr. X learned that the chaos of war was not a constant; instead, it only characterized life under specific circumstances, circumstances that can change. He came to understand that the war had a destructive effect on himself and his fellow Cambodians; however, when the war was over, democracy could be implemented and the devastation could be improved. This new narrative offers Mr. X an alternative way of viewing himself by replacing his former passive self with an active new self.

We use the term *PERSPECTIVE* to describe the provision of a narrative alternative to the traumatized, paralyzed self (Table 23.1, column 3, row 3).

THIRD STAGE: INTEGRATION

The integration stage follows naturally from the stages that precede it. During the final integration stage, the person integrates positive experiences into a new way of *being* in the world.

The dynamics of the integration stage are different from the other stages. During the safety stage, the therapist does the bulk of the psychological work. While in the reprocessing and rebuilding stage, the client and therapist collaborate, each doing an equal amount of psychological work. With respect to the final integration stage, the client does the majority of the work while the therapist approvingly mirrors the client's efforts.

Hardiness/Resilience: the consolidation of strength during the integration stage. During traumatization, the person experiences the world as malevolent, and the self as too weak to cope with it. In the safety stage, the therapist provides a positive, benevolent alternative to the malevolent world. During the reprocessing and rebuilding stage the client and the therapist collaboratively construct a new, strengthened self. Next, in the integration stage the client must integrate what he/she has accomplished in previous stages into a new way of being in the world. Mr. X describes this experience:

> After the war I learned from experience of the war, because the experience is in my mind. I am still the same, I am still smiling, talking. But mentally I don't feel the same, I changed, I am more stable. There is no desire that can bring me to possess something I don't need. Let's say, when I came to the USA I expected that USA will provide me with new home, new car, whatever I needed, but I think that now I realize I have to get by without this bothering me.

When Mr. X said that he does not feel the same "mentally," he is describing a new way of being in the world. He has become stable, self-sufficient and capable of living without the material possessions he once required. This new sense of stability is a result of his integrating and consolidating prior experiences.

We use the term *HARDINESS/RESILIENCE* to describe consolidating prior experiences into a new sense of being (Table 23.1, column 4, row 1). Hardiness is the precise opposite of the traumatic experience of a weak self in a malevolent world.

Community/Belonging: the consolidation of connection during the integration stage. During traumatization, the person experiences the world as indifferent, and the self as isolated. In the safety stage the therapist provides a positive, caring alternative to the indifferent world. In the reprocessing and rebuilding stage the client and the therapist collaboratively construct a new, connected self. In the integration stage the client incorporates all of this into his own way of being in the world. Mr. X describes this:

> I don't consider myself as high-ranking people. I don't limit myself to anybody. I see everybody as the same thing. I don't use categories. I never think

I have to be on top of somebody . . . But I make what I learned from the Buddhist way to get calmed, to get support in the community.

Mr. X is describing a new sense of being in the world. His new a sense is more connected than before his traumatic experience with the Khmer Rouge. He now thinks of himself and everyone else as equally valuable members of humanity. In addition, he implicitly reports a new sense of being part of a larger Buddhist and Cambodian community.

We use the term *BELONGING/COMMUNITY* to describe consolidating prior experience into a new and larger sense of connection and community (Table 23.1, column 4, row 2). Belonging is the precise opposite of the traumatic experience of an isolated self in an indifferent world.

Meaning/Purpose: the consolidation of philosophy during the integration stage. During traumatization, the person experiences the world as chaotic, and the self as passive. In the safety stage the therapist provides a positive structured alternative to the chaotic world. In the reprocessing and rebuilding stage the client and therapist collaboratively construct a new, active self. As with the other issues, the client must incorporate all of this into his own way of being in the world. In the following quote Mr. X describes his own experience:

> I need to help people. The Buddhist temple is the place where I meet people and help people . . . Buddhism is not learned by word of mouth but by action . . . Every year we [Cambodian Buddhists] celebrate at the Buddhist temple . . . I am among them, the support to organize, to make things happen. What I want is to carry on the traditional way of the Cambodian, ongoing and ongoing.

Mr. X describes a new sense of being in the world, an experience of helping others by carrying on the traditional Cambodian way of life.

We use the term *PURPOSE/MEANING* to describe the process of integrating and consolidating previous experiences into meaningful direction in life (Table 23.1, column 4, row 3). Purpose is the precise opposite of the traumatic experience of a passive self in a chaotic world.

SUMMARY AND IMPLICATIONS

At the beginning of this paper, we promised to present a framework to organize what is already known about trauma. We conclude by discussing the extent to which our model delivers on this promise, considering both general treatment strategies and specific treatment stages.

First, with regards to general treatment strategies, our model offers a comprehensive map of the treatment process that can be adapted to suit the particular individual. It can also be used multiculturally, to place culturally specific experiences within a general context. Thus, an Israeli may feel threatened by a suicide bomber, and a Turkish citizen may feel endangered following a massive earthquake. However, both are dealing with the dimension of safety.

The model also applies to issues of voice. Trauma often leaves people without a voice, bereft of a way to describe what they have experienced. By utilizing the client's specific experience within the model, the therapist can help the patient find the words needed to clarify their experience and communicate it to others.

Yet this model must be used with some caution. Recovery only takes place in the context of a relationship, and the model is a tool for building a relationship. It is not a substitute for one. With this in mind, the model is a very useful tool. It affords the therapist a broad and general sense of the client's experience so that a relationship can develop. Again, it is important to note that that the therapist need not be a certified mental health professional. Anyone who interacts with the traumatized person in a therapeutic role can make use of this model.

Although we have presented the stages of trauma and recovery sequentially, we do not mean to imply that the person goes through these stages in a linear fashion. Rather, there is an inevitable back-and-forth movement in the process. For example, a client may seek out safety, reprocess, seek out safety again, and reprocess yet again. It is helpful for both the therapist and the client to understand this, in order to minimize discouragement and frustration.

We now turn to specific applications of our model. To begin, we acknowledge that our model does not include novel components. Trauma workers already know that trauma shatters the assumptive world. They are also familiar with the different treatment stages and understand the different dimensions of traumatization (although our particular formulation of these dimensions is somewhat new). Our contribution has been to put these disparate pieces of knowledge together into a unified and comprehensive model. In particular, our model describes stages in the shattering and reconstruction of the assumptive world, and the dimensions of experience that occur during each of these stages.

This allows us to suggest specific treatment recommendations for each stage. We begin with the traumatization stage. Our model postulates that trauma shatters the assumptive world, a postulate that corresponds to the client's subjective experience. After a traumatic situation is experienced, people often report that neither they nor the world that they live in will ever be the same. We recommend that therapists accept this report at face value, and use the model's framework to explore the specific ways in which everything has changed for the person.

With respect to the safety stage, our model is consistent with the common practice of providing a safe space for the traumatized person. It also reinforces the importance of acknowledging the legitimacy of the client's safety needs. However, we offer a detailed analysis of the components of safety, namely protection, care, and acknowledgment.

All trauma therapists recognize the importance of providing care and protection to their clients. To this we add the importance of acknowledgment, of explicitly recognizing the emotional reality of the client's suffering. Faced with psychological distress, many therapists feel inclined to take immediate action. In our opinion, acknowledgment of suffering, even though it does not immediately remedy the situation, is serving a very important purpose.

In the reprocessing and rebuilding stage, our model suggests offering clients our own provisional narratives which they can borrow and use as they see fit. It also suggests helping clients use their own cultural narratives to rebuild shattered assumptions. Spiritual and religious beliefs are particularly useful in this stage. Often, clients can synthesize their own narrative with their therapist's narratives, blending the pretraumatic self with the self that experienced the trauma.

This blending occurs during the integration stage, during which people alter their view of self, society, and life more generally. A new identity emerges. Although this work must ultimately be done by the client, our model informs the therapist of the work and how to facilitate it. It is during the integration stage that post-traumatic growth can occur (Tedeschi and Calhoun 1998).

Finally, we recommend that the possibility of integration be incorporated as part of trauma therapy. At the start of therapy, traumatized persons often express their wish that the traumatic event had never taken place. We suggest that the therapist acknowledge this wish. However, we also suggest that at some later point in the therapy, that the therapist says something more: that the traumatic event did happen and that the client cannot go back and alter the past. In addition, the therapist should state that the client's only real choice is to make something positive out of an otherwise terrible event. By saying this, the therapist suggests the possibility of transforming a negative, destructive past and offers the client hope for a positive, constructive future.

Having developed our model, we will now examine its implications for the broader issues of this volume: meaning-making, rituals, resilience, and forgiveness. Our discussion will make use of material from Shiro's dissertation (Shiro 2001).

We begin with resilience, as all of the refugees were highly resilient people, having survived the massive traumas of starvation, disease, days and nights working in the fields under constant threat of torture or death. The sources of their resilience may be found in their reports of *HARDINESS/RESILIENCE* during the integration phase. Mr. X, as we have seen, relied on Buddhism to give him strength. Another refugee drew on family, stating that "with support from family members . . . you can be strong . . . (and) if you are strong you can work things out. These results are consistent with the importance of family and religion in Asian culture (Kinzie, Boehlein, and Sack 1998).

Rituals embedded in cultural practice also contribute to resilience, as is shown in the refugees' reports of *COMMUNITY/belonging* in the integration phase. Mr. X used "what I learned from the Buddhist way to get calmed." Another refugee drew on the cultural norm of polite behavior, stating "I say to myself to stay in the polite way . . . politeness brings smiles to everybody and everybody smiles back at you . . . that is what happiness means to me."

Meaning-making allows people to survive when experiencing trauma (Frankl 2004), and to survive and grow after trauma (Kalayjian 2002; Park and Ai 2006). This became apparent in the reports of *MEANING/PURPOSE* during the integration phase. We have already described how Mr. X used cultural narratives of the life of Buddha to make meaning in his own life. Another refugee used his family as a meaning making resource, stating "My mother taught me how to conduct life, and how to choose good friends."

Although none of the refugees studied explicitly made mention of forgiveness, forgiveness was implicit in their narratives. Forgiveness has two components: (1) letting go of negative feelings towards the transgressor, and (2) developing positive feelings towards the transgressor (Worthington & Wade 1999). All of our participants, by virtue of their growth and resilience, were able to put their angry feelings behind them, to go on and build new meaningful lives, although most of them did not cultivate or desire positive feelings towards the Khmer Rouge. This suggests that forgiveness after trauma is at least partly facilitated by integration of the traumatic experience.

REFERENCES

Frankl, V. 2004. *Man's Search for Meaning: An Introduction to Logotherapy.* New York: Random House.

Herman, J. L. 1992. *Trauma and Recovery.* New York: Basic Books.

Janoff-Bulman, R. 1992. *Shattered Assumptions: Towards a New Psychology of Trauma.* New York: The Free Press.

Kalayjian, A. S. 2002. "Biopsychosocial and Spiritual Treatment of Trauma." In *Comprehensive Handbook of Psychotherapy: Interpersonal/Humanistic/ Existential,* ed. F. N. Kaslow, 615–37. Hoboken, NJ: John Wiley.

Kinzie, J. D., Boehlein, J., and Sack, W. H. 1998. "The Effects of Massive Trauma on Cambodian Parents and Children." In *International Handbook of Multigenerational Legacies of Trauma,* ed. Y. Danieli, 211–24. New York: Springer.

Oxford English Dictionary (2002). London: Oxford University Press.

Park, C. L., and Ai, A. L. 2008. "Meaning-Making and Growth: New Directions for Research on Survivors of Trauma." *Journal of Loss and Trauma* 11: 389–406.

Parkes, C. M. 1971. "Psycho-Social Transition: A Field of Study." *Social Science and Medicine* 5: 101–15.

Shiro-Gelrud, E. 2001. *Resiliency and Post-Traumatic Growth: The Transforming Power of Trauma in Cambodian Refugees.* Unpublished doctoral dissertation: Yeshiva University.

Siegel, D. J. 2003. "An Interpersonal Neurobiology of Psychotherapy: The Developing Mind and the Resolution of Trauma." In *Healing Trauma: Attachment, Body, and Brain,* eds. M. F. Solomon and D. J. Siegel, 1–56. New York: Norton.

Tedeschi, R., and Calhoun, L. 1995. *Trauma and Transformation: Growing in the Aftermath of Suffering.* Thousand Oaks, CA: Sage Publications.

van der Kolk, B. A. 2003. "Post-Traumatic Stress Disorder and the Nature of Trauma." In *Healing Trauma: Attachment, Body, and Brain,* 168–95. New York: W. W. Norton.

Worthington, E. L., Wade, N. G. 1999. "The Social Psychology of Unforgiveness and Forgiveness and Implications for Clinical Practice." *Journal of Social and Clinical Psychology* 18: 385–418.

AUTHOR'S NOTE

We thank Dr. Jack Saul, PhD, Dr. Ken Hardy, PhD, and Dr. Roni Berger, PhD, for their kind review of the manuscript and useful feedback. We also want to thank the Cambodian refugee families who kindly volunteered to participate in the study.

Correspondence should be addressed and sent to the authors at the following address:

Carl Auerbach, PhD, Ferkauf Graduate School of Professional Psychology
1300 Morris Park Avenue, Bronx, NY, 10461
Phone: (718) 430-3953
Fax: (718) 430-3960
E-mail: cauerbac@gmail.com

Or

Edith Shiro-Gelrud, PsyD
21200 N. E. 38 Ave, Miami, FL, 33180
Phone: (917) 723-8474
E-mail: eshiro11@yahoo.com

INDEX

Aboriginal communities. *See* Intergenerational trauma among aboriginal communities in Canada; Native Americans

Acceptance, 82, 163–65, 204–5

Accurate empathy, 142

Aceh, Indonesia, 151–53, 161–62, 165–66, 168–69, 172–74, 175. *See also* Spiritually Directed Therapy Protocol

Acknowledgment, 164, 430–31

Adam O (son of gypsy survivor), 384, 389, 390, 391, 399

Adinkra symbols, 239–40

Adolescents: Armenian earthquake survivors, 9–11; gender issues in coping strategies, 119; mental health therapy after earthquakes, 5; Turkey earthquake survivors, 3

Adults: assessment after Armenian earthquake, 11; misconceptions concerning treatment of traumatized children, 38–39

African American liberation flag, 241

African Americans: ancestral connections and familial association, 233–38; arts, 244–45; families, 319, 345; freedom symbols, 241; language, 241–42; legislation regarding, 231; music, 244; naming practices, 238–39; religion and spirituality, 246–47; rituals, 236; symbols, 240–41

Africentric programs, 243

Alabama, African American naming practices in, 238–39

Alcoholics Anonymous, 118

Allegany Reservation, flooding of, 219–21

Ambivalent style of attachment, 345–46, 351

American Psychiatric Association (APA), 161, 214, 230, 316–17

American Red Cross, 28, 96

American University of Armenia, 18

Ancestors: African American remembrance of, 237–38; in Japanese rituals, 46

Anger, and post-traumatic slave syndrome, 232–33, 239–42

Annual ceremonies, as Japanese ritual, 48, 50

ABOUT THE EDITORS

ANI KALAYJIAN, EdD, DDL, RN-BC, BCETS, DSc (Hon), is a professor of psychology at Fordham University and teaches many relevant courses such as Health Psychology, Abnormal Psychology, and Practicum in Psychology. She is also President of the Association for Trauma Outreach and Prevention (ATOP) and the Armenian American Society for Studies on Stress and Genocide. She has developed, managed, and delivered Mental Health Outreach Programs around the globe, more specifically in: Armenia, the United States, Bosnia, Dominican Republic, Japan, Mexico, Lebanon, Palestine, Pakistan, Sierra Leone, and Turkey. Kalayjian has lectured and conducted workshops nationally and internationally on this topic, and the seven-step Biopsychosocial and Eco–Spiritual Model of treatment post disasters.

Kalayjian is also involved in related topics of trauma, genocide, stress, and humanitarian intervention in the wake of several disasters. Kalayjian has been involved at the UN since 1990, where she works with several departments focusing on human rights, refugees, women, and mental health. She is the author of *Disaster and Mass Trauma: Global Perspectives in Post Disaster Mental Health Management* (1995, Vista Publishing), and the chief editor for *Forgiveness & Reconciliation: Psychological Pathways for Conflict Transformation and Peace Building* (2009, Springer Publishing). She has published more than 30 chapters and articles in refereed journals around the world. Her articles and lectures have been published in

Armenian, Greek, Japanese, Russian, Spanish, Singhalese, Tamil, Turkish, and Urdu. She has been invited to share her expertise on TV nationally and internationally: CNN, CNBC, NBC, MSNBC, CBS, FOX, NY 1, Armenian TV, Turkish CNN, TRT (Turkish Radio and TV), and many others.

DOMINIQUE EUGENE MA, LMFT, RPT-S, NTP, was born in Haiti, raised in New Jersey, and obtained her Bachelors of Arts in Psychology from Seton Hall University and her Masters of Arts in Counseling Psychology from New York University. Currently residing in Los Angeles County, California, Dominique is a Licensed Marriage and Family Therapist, holds Certificate in Nutritional Therapy Practitioner and Alternative Nutrition, and is a Registered Play Therapist and Supervisor. She is the Clinical Site Manager for the San Fernando Valley office of Pacific Asian Counseling Services, a Non-Profit Organization, holds private practice at Magnolia Counseling, and lectures at National University.

Outside of her practice, she is involved with disaster mental health outreach. She volunteers with the American Red Cross, and has participated in disaster relief work nationally and internationally. Prior to residing in Los Angeles, Dominique lived in Japan working as an Assistant Language Instructor for the Japanese Exchange Teaching Program (JET) and National Coordinator with the Association for Japanese Exchange Teaching (AJET) Peer Support Group, as she pursued her interests in cultural and health psychology. Dominique holds membership in several national and international organizations of mental health and nutrition. She has written several articles, including: "Benefits of Raw Honey," "Sri Lanka Relief Work," "Haitian Mental Health," and "Cultural Adjustment in Japan." She has presented at several play therapy workshops and been a guest speaker at several universities and colleges covering topics related to play therapy and community mental health.

ABOUT THE CONTRIBUTORS

CHRIS ABERSON, PhD, is currently Associate Professor of Psychology at Humboldt State University. He earned his PhD at the Claremont Graduate University in 1999 with a concentration in Social and Quantitative Psychology. His research interests include prejudice, racism, and affirmative action as well as interactive tutorials for teaching core statistical concepts. His work has appeared (or is forthcoming) in outlets such as *Personality and Social Psychology Review, Group Processes and Intergroup Relations, Social Justice Review, Journal of Applied Psychology, Cultural Diversity and Ethnic Minority Psychology,* and *Teaching of Psychology.*

ELISABETH ARMAN, MA, Psychologist, volunteer recovery worker for Peduli Aceh, faculty, Department of Psychology, Universitas Katolik Atma Jaya, Jakarta, Indonesia, acted as translator at the SEFA Training in Aceh in 2006.

CARL F. AUERBACH, PhD, is Professor of Psychology at the Ferkauf Graduate School of Psychology of Yeshiva University. At the University he is the director of the International Center for Trauma Studies and Treatment, and has set up a think tank on Cultural Trauma which coordinates work of the center and the Institute for Public Health Sciences. He received his BA in Physics from Reed College in 1963 and his PhD in Psychology from the University of Pennsylvania in 1968.

He is the codirector, with Dr. Louise Silverstein, of the Yeshiva University Fatherhood Project, a long-term qualitative research study of the cultural evolution of American fatherhood, and he and Dr. Silverstein have published extensively in this area. Their writing includes a book on qualitative research methodology, which is published by New York University Press. Their joint work on fatherhood has received awards from the Association of Women in Psychology and Division 51 of the American Psychological Association.

Over the past five years he and his research students have been applying the qualitative research methods developed in the fatherhood project to the qualitative study of trauma and traumatized populations. The major focus of the work is on the traumatic disruption of identity, and the processes by which identity is reconstructed. This work has been published in professional journals and presented at meetings of the Society for Traumatic Stress. His qualitative research methodology was the subject of a featured article in *Stresspoints,* the bulletin of the Society for Traumatic Stress.

SCOTT CARLIN, PhD, for the past 15 years, has worked on a variety of projects advocating sustainable development principles on Long Island. Dr. Carlin is an Associate Professor at the C.W. Post Campus of Long Island University. He is also a senior editor with climatecaucus.net, an outgrowth of a 2007 United Nations conference on Climate Change. Dr. Carlin earned his PhD in Geography from Clark University in 1995.

ALYSSA CHEADLE is a senior at Luther College graduating with an interdisciplinary major with emphases in psychology, religion, and health. She attends Harvard Divinity School studying religion and the social sciences.

ELAINE CONGRESS is Professor and Associate Dean at Fordham University Graduate School of Social Service in New York City. At the UN she serves as a representative for International Federation of Social Workers (IFSW) and also on the International Ethics Committee for IFSW. She is recording secretary for the Executive Committee of the UN Decade for Indigenous People and also a member of the NGO Committee on Migration. She has presented with Dr. Weaver at several UN Forums and other international conferences on indigenous peoples and climate change, women, and social justice issues.

In addition to multiple presentations at the UN and other international and national venues, Dr. Congress has written extensively on cultural diversity, as well as social work ethics. Her last book, *Social Work with*

Immigrants and Refugees: Legal Issues, Clinical Skills, and Advocacy, focuses on legal, policy, and practice issues in professional work with immigrants and refugees. Dr. Congress developed the culturagram, a family assessment tool for understanding families from different cultural and ethnic backgrounds.

Dr. Congress has a BA in American Civilization from Brown University, an MAT in English from Yale University, a MA in Psychology from New School of Social Research, MSSW in Social Work from Columbia University, and a DSW from City University of New York.

JOY ANGELA DEGRUY, (pronounced De-Grew), holds a Bachelor of Science degree in Communications, a master's degree in Social Work (MSW), a master's degree in Psychology, and a PhD in Social Work Research. She currently serves as an Assistant Professor of Research at Portland State University and is a member of the International faculty for London's Department of Health. With over 20 years of practical experience as a professional in the field of social work, she gives practical insight into various cultural and ethnic groups that form the basis of contemporary American society. Dr. DeGruy's workshops also go far beyond the topic of cultural sensitivity and diversity; she provides specialized work in areas of mental health and ecological resilience. Her clients have included academic institutions such as Oxford University, Harvard University, Columbia University, Fisk University, Smith College, Morehouse College and the University of Chicago, to name a few. She has also presented to federal and state agencies such as the Federal Bureau of Investigation (FBI), probation and parole agencies, the Juvenile Justice Judges Association, and police departments. She has worked with major corporations and companies such as Nordstrom's and Nike, the NBA Rookies Camp, and with the G-CAPP program based in Atlanta, Georgia.

CHRISTINA DI LIBERTO has a BA in Psychology with a minor in music from Muhlenberg College. She has been working with Dr. Kalayjian for a year and a half researching the generational transmission of trauma, global policies regarding gun control, and emotional healing. She has co-authored with Dr. Kalayjian two publications in the International Bulletin of Psychology. Christina recently earned a Certificate in Digital Media from Bloomfield College and anticipates graduate studies in social work.

ELEANOR DONOVAN is a research and editorial assistant for the Association for Trauma Outreach and Prevention. She holds a BA in Comparative Sociology from the University of Puget Sound and is a graduate of World Learning's School for International Training. Her research and fieldwork has focused on reparative justice and healing in Malawi and South Africa, and religion, media, and youth in the Pacific Northwest.

JENNY DOUGHERTY, PhD, LPC, RPT, is an Assistant Professor of Counseling and Development in the Department of Family Sciences at Texas Woman's University. Dr. Dougherty specializes in working with children, families and groups. She is a Licensed Professional Counselor in Texas and a Registered Play Therapist.

MERRY EVENSON has been an Associate Professor and Coordinator of the Counseling and Development Department of Family Sciences, Texas Woman's University (Denton, Texas), for over 25 years. Since 1980 she has had a private practice in Denton, Texas, where she specializes in working with women, couples, families, and individuals. Evenson is a licensed Professional Counselor, and Licensed Marriage and Family Therapist Clinical Member—American Association for Marital and Family Therapists.

She has some background in working Critical Incidence Stress De-Briefing with various managed care companies for the past five years. She has worked, and continues to work, as a contract worker on a 30 + hours per week basis since September 2005 as a Stress Manager at FEMA in Denton, Texas through Federal Occupational Health. Evenson is at a call center working posttrauma with telephone workers receiving calls for aid from Hurricanes Katrina and Rita victims needing Federal Emergency Management assistance. She helps with employee stress, employee self-care and fatigue, and assists with calls involving suicide threats and bomb or other types of threats. She has worked there on an ongoing basis since the disaster.

Evenson took four graduate students in Counseling and two students who have already graduated to Sri Lanka for three weeks in 2005 to work on training the helpers in some basic counseling skills for working with the people of Sri Lanka post-tsunami. They also conducted group counseling with many of the helpers.

HAROLD FINKLEMAN, communications specialist, former broadcast journalist and international correspondent, lecturer and consultant on communication psychology, joined the team in Aceh and cofacilitated men's groups with Dr. Hedva at the SEFA Training in Aceh in 2006.

SIMON GAUTHIER is a student at Université du Québec à Chicoutimi (UQAC) in the Human Science department (master in social work). Before that, he completed a license in psychology. His dissertation is about the resilience of young adult victims of negligence during their adolescence. Presently, he is a research assistant for two different projects: the impacts of telephone helpline counseling service and the impacts of disaster on the health of psychosocial worker.

BETH HEDVA, PhD, RMFT, DABPS, DAPA, Chair of Continuing Education for the International Council of Psychologists, is an internationally recognized authority in the field of change. Currently living in Calgary, Canada, Dr. Hedva is the Canadian Chair, Association of Trauma Outreach and Prevention, and Director of Training and Counseling Services for Finkleman Communications, Ltd. Her disaster response work began in 1989, while she was living and working in the San Francisco Bay area when the 6.9 Loma Prieta earthquake hit; followed by the 1991 Oakland Hills firestorm, in which she was also evacuated from her home. Listed in the *World Who's Who of Women* a year later, and subsequently nominated to the first *Who's Who in Medicine and Healthcare,* Dr. Hedva has made her reputation by blending spirituality with contemporary psychology, and has trained helping professionals in medical schools and universities across Canada and internationally in the Spiritually Directed Therapy Protocol for emotional healing and renewal.

ELISSA JACOBS received her undergraduate degree in Human Development from Cornell University and completed her Master's in Psychology from Columbia University. Elissa is a third generation Holocaust survivor who currently serves as the Research Coordinator for Meaningfulworld. In addition, Elissa is one of the founders of Reaching Out Against Eating Disorders, a nonprofit that provides support services to individuals struggling with eating disorders. Elissa will be starting her doctorate in Psychology Fall 2009 at St. John's University.

MICHELLE KIM, PhD, is the Chair of the Eco-Spirituality Working Group within the NGO committee for Spirituality, Values and Global Concerns at the United Nations, representing Franciscans International. She is also an adjunct professor at the Westchester Community College, the State University of New York. She holds a PhD in Religious Studies from Fordham University, New York, in 2007. She also holds a PhD in Computer Science from Polytechnic University of New York in 1987. She worked at the IBM T. J. Watson Research Center from 1981–2005 as a research staff member manager, and held the IBM Fellow Emeritus title until 2007.

SEHOON KIM received his MA degree from the Department of Counseling and Clinical Psychology at Teachers College, Columbia University.

He is currently an MPH candidate in the Department of Health Promotion and Behavior at the University of Georgia. His research interests include mental health, international health, social determinants of health, work-site health promotion, and eHealth promotion/communication. He was a research intern for Meaningfulworld.com and the Association for Trauma Outreach & Prevention in 2005–2006.

CHRISTINE KOPPERUD received her BA in psychology from the University of Saskatchewan and is currently pursuing her PhD in psychology. She worked with Dr. Mehl-Madrona as an undergraduate honors student in the area of aboriginal intergenerational trauma.

JUDY KURIANSKY, PhD, is a licensed clinical psychologist and adjunct faculty in the Department of Clinical Psychology at Columbia University Teachers College and the Department of Psychiatry at Columbia University College of Physicians and Surgeons. A UN representative for the International Association of Applied Psychology and the World Council for Psychotherapy, she has led workshops on peace, crisis counseling and her unique development of East/West therapy around the world, from Buenos Aires to Sagar, India, Singapore, Prague, Jerusalem, Dubai, and Tehran, Iran. Trained by the Red Cross and featured in their post-9/11 campaign, she has done disaster relief after 9/11 at Ground Zero and the Family Assistance Center, and around the world. She is a feature columnist for national and international print media, including the *New York Daily News* Web site, Singapore *Straits Times,* and the *South China Morning Post.*

Her work has been featured in the *New York Times, International Herald Tribune,* and on CBS News, CNN, and China's CCTV. She is the author of many scholarly papers in professional journals and of many books including *The Complete Idiot's Guide to a Healthy Relationship,* and has contributed chapters to *Access: A Disaster Preparedness Manual* and Praeger's *Handbook of International Disaster Psychology.* Her latest book is *Terror in the HolyLand: Inside the Anguish of the Israeli-Palestinian Conflict.*

EVELIN G. LINDNER, PhD, is a social scientist with an interdisciplinary orientation. She holds two PhDs, one in social medicine and another in social psychology. In 1996, she designed a research project on the concept of humiliation and its role in genocide and war.

From 1997–2001, Lindner carried out this research, interviewing over 200 people who were either implicated in or knowledgeable about the genocides in Rwanda, Somalia, and Nazi Germany. Her book *Making Enemies: Humiliation and International Conflict* was published by Praeger/

Greenwood in 2006. Lindner is currently establishing Human Dignity and Humiliation Studies (Human DHS) as an international platform for further work on dignity and humiliation. All students are invited to contribute with reflections and research.

Lindner designs her life as a global citizen in order to be able to build Human DHS globally. She declines offers for full professor positions, because she does not wish to be tied to one place. However, she regularly teaches as a senior lecturer and guest professor at universities in Norway (University of Oslo, and Norwegian University of Science and Technology (NTNU) in Trondheim), and is affiliated to the Maison des Sciences de l'Homme in Paris, while teaching as visiting guest professor wherever her paths leads her, for example, among others, the United States (Columbia University, New York), Japan (International Christian University, and Rikkyo University, Tokyo), Israel (Hebrew University, Jerusalem), Australia (Queensland University), or Costa Rica (United Nations-mandated University for Peace).

FREDERIC LUSKIN is Director of the Stanford Forgiveness Projects and a Senior consultant in Health Promotion at Stanford University. Dr. Luskin has written two best-selling books on forgiveness education: *Forgive for Good: A Proven Prescription for Health and Happiness* and *Forgive for Love: The Missing Ingredient for a Healthy and Lasting Relationship.*

DANIELLE MALTAIS has a PhD in Applied Human Science, is a professor at Université du Québec à Chicoutimi, in the Human Science department (social work) since 1994. During the past 10 years, their researches have focused on the impact of natural disaster on the health of people, workers, and rural communities and the links between environment and psychological health of the elderly. She wrote five French books and many scientific articles in the field of impacts of disaster on individuals, professionals, and volunteer workers. The last book (2005) included information about the role of the social worker during disaster and the impacts of disaster on the health of children and the elderly. Recently, she received grants to study the long-term impacts of the 1996 Saguenay floods.

LEWIS MEHL-MADRONA, MD, PhD, MPhil, is Director of the Psychopharmacology Program at Argosy University, Hawai'i, where he is also Associate Professor of Psychology. He is an adjunct professor of anthropology at Johnson State College in Vermont and is Education Director for the Coyote Institute for Studies of Change and Transformation, also in Vermont, USA. He is the author of *Coyote Medicine, Coyote Healing,*

Coyote Wisdom, Narrative Medicine, and *Narrative Psychiatry: Healing Mind and Brain in a Social World.* Lewis is a graduate of Stanford University School of Medicine, the Psychological Studies Institute in Palo Alto, and Massey University in Palmerston North, New Zealand. He is American board certified in family medicine and in psychiatry.

NICOLE MOORE graduated Fordham University with a double major in Women Studies and History. Her interest in women and mental health led her to start the Women Studies Major at Fordham. Nicole recognized the need to provide women's mental health support in countries around the world. This led her to receive her master's in Counseling Psychology at Fordham. To provide the best support in counseling, she specialized in multicultural counseling in trauma.

Her travels have led her to work in Sri Lanka with the tsunami survivors, and Pakistan with the earthquake survivors.

Nicole believes that the most important aspect of her work is educating and empowering the individual and community to continue the mental health work after any organization, institute, or non-government organization moves on. She actively follows human rights issues in the United States, Asia, and Africa.

BEVERLY MUSGRAVE, PhD, is a professor at Fordham University, in the Graduate School of Religion and Religious Education, Bronx, New York. She is a Mental Health Counselor, Pastoral Counselor in private practice in New York City. Dr. Musgrave is coeditor and author of the book *The Theological and Psychological Dimensions of Loss, Illness & Death,* Paulist Press, in press. She is also the coeditor and author of the book *Partners in Healing: Bringing Compassion to People with Illness & Loss,* Paulist Press, 2003. Dr. Musgrave has presented in Ireland, India, Canada, and the United States on psychological and spiritual issues. She is also a trained Spiritual Director.

GUERDA NICOLAS, PhD, who is originally from Haiti, obtained her doctoral degree in clinical psychology from Boston University. She completed her predoctoral training at Columbia University Medical Center and her postdoctoral training at the New York State Psychiatric Institute/ Columbia University, Department of Child Psychiatry. She is a licensed psychologist and focused her practice in the area of children, family, and community well-being. Prior to coming to University of Miami, she held faculty positions at Boston College, Department of Counseling, Developmental and Educational Psychology, as well as the College of Saint Elizabeth in New Jersey.

As a multicultural (Haitian American) and multilingual psychologist (Spanish, French, and Haitian Creole), her research is reflective of her background and interests.

Her current research projects focus on developing culturally effective mental health intervention for people of color, with a specific focus on immigrant children, adolescents, and families. In addition, she conducts research on social support networks of the Caribbean population with a specific focus on Haitians, spirituality and adolescents, and social support and mental health of blacks. She has published many articles and book chapters and delivered numerous invited presentations at national and international conferences in the areas of women's issues, depression and cultural interventions, social support networks of ethnic minorities, and spirituality. She is a member of the Caribbean Studies Association and the Haitian Studies Association. Starting in January 2009 she is president of the Haitian Studies Association.

AKIKO J. OHNOGI, PsyD, is a clinical psychologist in private practice in Tokyo, Japan, and adjunct faculty at the International Christian University psychology graduate school and California School of Professional Psychology, Japan campus. Dr. Ohnogi was one of 17 volunteers chosen to provide mental health support using play to Sri Lankan orphans after the 2004 Sumatra Rim tsunami. She has conducted workshops for mental health and health care providers in Niigata for supporting children affected by the 2004 Chuuetsu earthquake series. An article titled "Play Based Psychological Interventions with Traumatized Children: Work with Tsunami Orphaned Sri Lankan Children" is currently in print in the *International Journal of Counseling and Psychotherapy.* Other publications include "International Handbook of Play Therapy" and "Understanding and Dealing with Children who have Difficulty Staying Still," both in *Child Study,* the parenting advise column "Shinro Shingaku Tsushin" in *Shinken-Zemi Benesse,* as well as *Play Therapy with Very Young Children* and *Making Safe Space in Play with Children* both in print. An online interview by the *Japan Times* regarding the support efforts in Sri Lanka can be found at http://www.japantimes.co.jp/cgi-bin/getarticle.pl5?fl20050212a1.htm.

BINDIA PATEL graduated from Fordham University in 2009 with a bachelor's degree in psychology and economics. Her areas of interest include industrial/organizational psychology, social psychology, and resiliency. Currently, she is planning to pursue a dual master's degree in industrial/organizational psychology and human resource management. She currently holds membership in Psi Chi and the American Psychological Association.

NANCY PEDDLE is the former Executive Director of the International Society for the Prevention of Child Abuse and Neglect and the founder and current director of the Lemon Aid Fund, established to make a difference in the lives of people who have been affected by war and other extreme difficulties.

BEVERLY L. PETERS, PhD, currently works at George Mason's Institute for Conflict Analysis and Resolution on the institute's International Criminal Court Project.

Peters has consulted with a number of organizations in southern Africa on matters of continuing education, education and training, political risk, community development, and program monitoring and evaluation. She has designed and conducted workshops for researchers, local government officials, and training specialists. She also has five years experience developing study abroad programs in southern Africa.

Peters is a research fellow with the South African Institute of International Affairs in Johannesburg, South Africa, and an adjunct professor at Georgetown, George Washington, James Madison, and American Universities.

Beverly has appeared as a political analyst on the South African Broadcasting Corporation, South African Business News, and E-TV News (Johannesburg). She has been a guest analyst on numerous radio broadcasts including the Voice of America, the Kojo Nnamdi Show, Radio France International, the Sydney Morning News, and various South African news broadcasts such as Cape Talk, High Veld Radio, and the South African Broadcasting Corporation news radio. In addition to publishing newspaper articles, she has also been quoted in the *New York Times, Economist,* and the *Boston Globe.*

ELIZABETH PIERRE is a candidate for a Master's in Counseling Psychology at Boston College. Prior to attending Boston College, Ms. Pierre served an associate pastor at a small church in Massachusetts. Her work with congregants is what ignited her desire to pursue a degree in counseling. Since attending Boston College, Ms. Pierre's research interests are the role of spirituality/ religion in counseling. and multicultural issues within the counseling field. Currently, Ms. Pierre is a part of the Institute for the Promotion of Race and Culture team that assists with the annual conference Diversity Challenge, and also serves on the committee as supervisor for mentors for the mentoring program, Project Success.

ARTEMIS PIPINELLI, PhD, is a professional psychotherapist, gerontologist, researcher, and international psychologist. She has over 15 years experience in working with the aging population, couples, children and families. Dr. Pipinelli is the recipient of PSI CHI /National Convention Research Award for dissertation research titled "Psychological Variables and Depression among Nursing Home and Adult Caring Facility Residents," New Orleans, 2006. Dr. Pipinelli holds a Doctor of Philosophy degree in Clinical Psychology from Walden University, Minneapolis, MN, where she graduated in 2005. She holds a Master of Art degree in Psychology from New School University, in 1994 and a Master's degree in Drama Therapy from New York University, in 1990. Dr. Pipinelli has received training in family and couples therapy at the Post Graduate Center for Mental Health, New York, from 2001 to 2002. She has received training in cognitive behavior therapy at Albert Einstein College of Medicine, New York, April 2000.

Dr. Pipinelli has received training in group psychotherapy and psychodrama, 585 hours at the Psychodrama Center of New York from 1989 to 1999. She has received training in group psychotherapy at the Training Institute of Mental Health. Dr. Pipinelli has received one year training in sex therapy and couples therapy from 1997 to 1998 at the Fogel Foundation, Human Sexuality Institute, in Washington, DC. Since 1996, Dr. Pipinelli has presented at multiple Drama therapy and Psychology and Gerontological conferences on ageing, Human Trafficking, and Forgiveness and Greek and Armenian Genocide and Gendercide. In the last year she has presented her research in collaboration with well-known trauma expert Dr. Ani Kalayjian. Dr. Pipinelli is a member of the APA (American Psychological Association) Div 52, International Psychology Liaison, and a Treasurer-elect of DOWI (Division of women's issues) NYSPA (New York State Psychological Association). Dr. Pipinelli has presented her research papers and conducted workshops nationally and internationally.

KATE RICHMOND, PhD is currently a visiting Assistant Professor at Muhlenberg College and has a private practice in Philadelphia, Pennsylvania. Richmond has consulted with several agencies, governments, and clinics in various countries (Peru, Spain, the United States, Cambodia, and Canada) in the area of political and domestic violence. She has developed protocols for assessment and intervention and has worked with agencies to implement psychoeducation workshops with a specific emphasis on cultural sensitive programming.

Richmond received a presidential certificate of recognition from the American Psychological Association's Division 52: International Psychology, which honored her two-year tenure as the Early Career Representative to the Executive Board. She currently serves on the Executive Board for Division 35: Society for the Psychology of Women, is a liaison for the

Association of Women in Psychology, and is a consultant to the International Association for Applied Psychology.

Richmond has served as an adjunct professor at Nova Southeastern University and at the University of Pennsylvania; in 2003 she received the award for excellence in teaching. Richmond has over 20 refereed publications and presentations, and she has presented empirical work at international conferences in Singapore, Peru, Beijing, and Greece.

BILLIE SCHWARTZ is a mental health clinician working in research with Dr. Guerda Nicolas at the University of Miami. She received her master's degree from Boston College, conducting work and research primarily with children and families of ethnic minorities and immigrant populations in the greater Boston area. She is originally from Miami, Florida

ANTHONY SELLU is a sophomore at Luther College majoring in physics. He is a native of Sierra Leone and lived through the civil war in that country. He hopes to some day use his skills to bring peace and prosperity to developing countries.

YUKI SHIGEMOTO received his BA in social work in 2007 from the Rikkyo University in Japan. He is currently pursuing his master's degree in clinical psychology from Penn State, Harrisburg. His research interests includes post-traumatic growth after adversity, and he has presented at several national meetings. He has graduated and received a certificate in Post Disaster Humanitarian Outreach by the Association for Trauma Outreach and Prevention of Meaningfulworld. He is a member of the American Psychological Association's International Division, and presented a poster at the Annual Convention in Toronto, 2009. He has been inspired by the climate in California after he visited in 2007, and since then he wishes to take a vacation there.

EDITH SHIRO-GELRUD, PsyD is a clinical psychologist. She graduated from Yeshiva University in New York. Previously, she received her Licentiate in Psychology at the Catholic University of Venezuela. She holds a certification in international trauma studies from NYU, with a postdoctoral specialization in Family Therapy from the Ackerman Institute for the Family in New York.

Dr. Shiro-Gelrud has been working extensively with immigrant populations from different parts of the world and has developed a model for working with issues which includes psychosocial and political perspectives of the migration experience. Dr. Shiro-Gelrud is experienced in working with children and families with chronic illnesses such as HIV/AIDS and diabetes in the context of clinics and respite summer camps, placing them in a more systemic and contextual framework.

Earlier in her career, Dr. Shiro-Gelrud developed an interest in refugee populations and trauma, and has done extensive research with Cambodian refugees, Latin American refugees, and others, focusing on dissociative disorders, coping skills, and resilience and post-traumatic growth (PTG) in the aftermath of trauma. She worked at the clinic for Survivors of Torture at Bellevue Hospital, at the Cambodian refugee clinic at Montefiore Medical Center, as coordinator of the Human Rights Clinical Support Network (HRCSN) at Refuge, Inc., a family and community resiliency program in New York City. She has been offering workshops on trauma-based family therapy, for professionals dealing with patients in the aftermath of trauma and in the wake of September 11, 2001.

Dr. Shiro-Gelrud is fluent in English, Spanish, and Hebrew and is a member of various organizations.

SARAH THOMPSON received her BA in psychology from the University of Saskatchewan and is currently pursuing her PhD in psychology. She worked with Dr. Mehl-Madrona as an undergraduate honors student in the area of aboriginal intergenerational trauma.

LOREN L. TOUSSAINT, PhD, is an Associate Professor in the Department of Psychology at Luther College in Decorah, Iowa, where he teaches courses on statistics, methodology, stress and coping, health psychology, and forgiveness. His research interests are in forgiveness, religion and spirituality, stress and coping, and health and well-being.

GINGER VILLAREAL ARMAS graduated with honors from Manhattanville College and obtained a BA in Art History. During a semester abroad in Oxford, England, she participated in her first meditation retreat with Zen master Thich Nhat Hanh. Two years later, she had the opportunity to study at Plum Village, his Buddhist community in France. Inspired by the social activism of the monastics she met there, Armas decided to pursue a career in psychology. When she returned to Manhattan in 2001, she applied to New York University's MA program for General Psychology. In 2003, she completed the Holistic Health Counselor Training Program at the Institute for Integrative Nutrition (www.integrativenutrition.com).

In addition, Armas has worked as a Hotline Counselor and HIV Test Counselor at GMHC (Gay Men's Health Crisis, www.gmhc.org) and also as the Intake Coordinator for the American Institute for Cognitive Therapy (www.cognitivetherapynyc.com) in New York City. She has research experience under the mentorship of Dr. Ani Kalayjian. She has volunteered as an Advocate for Mount Sinai Hospital's Sexual Assault and Violence Intervention (SAVI) program. This spring, Armas will graduate from New York University, where she was a Graduate Assistant for Counseling and Behavioral Health Services (CBH). She recently began a PhD program in Clinical Psychology at Nova Southeastern University, under the mentorship of Dr. Lenore E.A. Walker. She hopes to specialize in the treatment of survivors of human trafficking and to help end modern-day slavery in her lifetime.

HILARY WEAVER, DSW (Lakota) is a Professor in the School of Social Work, University at Buffalo (State University of New York). Her teaching, research, and service focus on cultural issues in the helping process with a particular focus on indigenous populations. She currently serves as President of the American Indian Alaska Native Social Work Educators Association and President of the Board of Directors of Native American Community Services of Erie and Niagara Counties. Dr. Weaver has presented her work regionally, nationally, and internationally, including presenting at the Permanent Forum on Indigenous Issues at the United Nations in 2005, 2006, 2007, and 2008. She has numerous publications, including the recent text, *Explorations in Cultural Competence: Journeys to the Four Directions* (2005). Dr. Weaver has received funding from the National Cancer Institute to develop and test a culturally-grounded wellness curriculum for urban Native American youth, the *Healthy Living in Two Worlds* program.

ANDREA ZIELKE-NADKARNI, PhD, Professor for Nursing Education and Nursing Science at the University of Applied Sciences, Muenster, Germany, is a RN, nurse teacher, has PhD in Education (1992), and is a habilitation (German title for professorship) of nursing science (2002). She has experience as an expert reader of training text books for nurses for publishing house, teacher in geriatric nursing course; various projects, for example 1985–1988 promoting Turkish women training as doctors' assistants; 1995–1997 scientific advisor to project NOW (New Opportunities for Women) promoted by the European Union. Her university teaching background includes the University of Bristol, Great Britain; in Germany the University of Witten/Herdecke, Applied Universities of Braunschweig/Wolfenbuettel and of Muenster (since 1998) teaching nursing science and nursing education. Special research areas: care needs of sociocultural minorities and women's health issues (numerous publications in this field).